The Knowing-Doing Gap

How Smart Companies Turn Knowledge into Action

The Knowing-Doing Gap

How Smart Companies Turn Knowledge into Action

Jeffrey Pfeffer
Robert I. Sutton

Harvard Business School Press
Boston, Massachusetts

06   11

Requests for permission to use or reproduce material from this book should be directed to permissions@hbsp.harvard.edu, or mailed to Permissions, Harvard Business School Publishing, 60 Harvard Way, Boston, Massachusetts 02163.

Library of Congress Cataloging-in-Publication Data

Pfeffer, Jeffrey.
    The knowing-doing gap : how smart companies turn knowledge
  into action / Jeffrey Pfeffer, Robert I. Sutton
        p.   cm.
    Includes bibliographical references and index.
    ISBN 1-57851-124-0 (alk. paper)
        1. Knowledge management.   2. Organizational effectiveness.
I. Sutton, Robert I.   II. Title. III. Title: How smart companies turn
knowledge into action.
HD30.2.P486   1999
658.4'038—dc21   99-28307
                                                                CIP

The paper used in this publication meets the requirements of the American National Standard for Permanence of Paper for Publications and Documents in Libraries and Archives Z39.48–1992.

From Jeffrey Pfeffer

On January 19, 1985, I met Kathleen Fowler. My life has not been the same since. She inspires, encourages, teaches, and most of all, loves me in ways that I seldom even fully comprehend or appreciate. Without Kathleen, nothing is possible, and with her, anything is. January 19, 1985, is certainly the luckiest day of my life.

From Robert I. Sutton

As with almost everything good that has happened to me, this book never would have been written without Marina Park, my beautiful and patient love. I thank Marina for it all, especially for her constant and forgiving love, for being wiser than anyone I have ever met, and for our sweet and rambunctious offspring, Tyler, Claire, and Eve.

Contents

Preface   ix

|1| Knowing "What" to Do Is Not Enough   1

|2| When Talk Substitutes for Action   29

|3| When Memory Is a Substitute for Thinking   69

|4| When Fear Prevents Acting on Knowledge   109

|5| When Measurement Obstructs Good Judgment   139

|6| When Internal Competition Turns Friends into Enemies   177

|7| Firms That Surmount the Knowing-Doing Gap   213

|8| Turning Knowledge into Action   243

Appendix: The Knowing-Doing Survey   265

Notes   271

Index   295

About the Authors   313

Preface

WE WROTE THIS BOOK because we wanted to under-stand why so many managers know so much about organizational performance, say so many smart things about how to achieve performance, and work so hard, yet are trapped in firms that do so many things they know will undermine performance. This book was inspired by several intertwined events. After the publication of two books on how to manage people for enhanced organizational performance, Jeffrey Pfeffer was intrigued and puzzled to find that, over and over again, on this topic and many others, people obviously knew what to do, but didn't do it. Pfeffer also noticed that many of his colleagues at Stanford Business School almost invariably didn't do anything remotely related to what they taught when they found themselves in leadership roles. Finally, he noticed that there were more and more books and articles, more and more training programs and seminars, and more and more knowledge that, although valid, often had little or no impact on what managers actually did.

So, it was clear that knowing what to do was not enough. It was clear that being smart was not enough to turn knowledge into practice. It was evident that reading, listening to, thinking, and writing smart things was not enough. Pfeffer was taken with this problem because, while it is obvious | ix and pervasive, and there is no doubt it is important, there is precious little understanding about what causes it or how firms overcome it. He suspected the problems were largely in organizational practices, not individual psychology, but he needed much more evidence. So he decided to launch an intensive long-term research effort to discover what prevented organizations that are led by smart people from doing things that they know they ought to do.

This was, and is, an unstructured and messy question. There are relevant bodies of literature and ideas, but it was clear that the only way to explore what we came to call the knowing-doing gap was to use both qualitative and quantitative field methods for studying organizations. Pfeffer needed an ally who knew how to use these kinds of methods and who was equally intrigued by this problem. So, Pfeffer enlisted the help of Robert Sutton, a friend and Stanford colleague for many years. And off we went, to learn how some organizations failed to turn knowledge into action, how some succeeded, and why.

Our conviction that this is one of the most important and vexing barriers to organizational performance has been fueled throughout this project by the strong, and quite emotional, reactions we always get to this topic. When talking about other topics to the engineers, managers, and executives we teach or when working with the organizations we try to help, we often make brief allusions to the knowing-doing problem. Again and again, after just a one-sentence description of the problem, people tell us (often interrupting us in the middle of our second sentence on the topic) that they already know what effective organizations should do and, if they don't have such knowledge, it is usually easy for them to find a book or, in the case of executives or firms, to hire new employees or consultants to find out what they need to know. What they don't know how to do, what they get wildly frustrated about, what makes them whine, holler, curse, moan, and even cry, is to understand why their firms so often fail to turn this knowledge into action. This frustration has also meant they are curious, at times even desperate, to learn how other firms avoid or overcome barriers to turning performance knowledge into organizational actions. The depth of this frustration and the deep interest we encountered everywhere about how to surmount knowing–doing gaps inspired us to press ahead throughout the four-year program of research that led to this book.

We were also so devoted to this project ("obsessed" is probably more accurate) because our collaboration was among the most delightful and engaging working relationships we ever had. The mix of intellectual excitement and rollicking, ranting fun we shared during the last four years was a rare privilege. We both have extensive experience writing with collaborators, with over 100 coauthored books and articles between us. We know that the intellectual spark and joy we have shared during this project only happen a few times in a researcher's lifetime. There were so many wonderful moments. Or at least *we* thought they were wonderful. The people around us probably found them silly and annoying. Hollering, arguing, and jumping up and down in our regular brainstorming sessions. Ranting at each other during long airplane flights that seemed short because we had so many ideas to argue about. And, perhaps the best memory of all, an evening in September of 1997 in the Palace Hotel executive floor lounge in New York City, when a demanding Jeffrey Pfeffer kept pushing a grouchy and resistant Robert Sutton to develop ideas for the book. Sutton complained mightily that he was tired, he just wanted to eat, drink, and talk about something else. But an hour or so later, we had an outline that matches the chapter headings in this book almost perfectly.

We don't want to leave the impression that this project flowed easily and entailed no setbacks. On the contrary, we had lots of failures along the way. We devoted a full year to a failed collaboration with a consulting firm (that, by the way, is in the knowledge management business) that tried mightily, but proved unable, to implement a study of the gap between knowledge and action. We tried other ideas that also didn't work out. But once something was clearly not working, we abandoned the path quickly, stopping just long enough to figure out what we should learn before trying something new. We never stopped to worry about how much time we had wasted and never spent one minute talking about which one of us was to blame for the last dead end. Rather, we were inspired by the successful firms we studied, in which setbacks and mistakes were viewed as an inevitable, even desirable, part of being action oriented. We heeded their advice that the only true failure was to stop trying new things and to stop learning from the last effort to turn knowledge into action.

Acknowledgments

There are so many people who have helped us learn. Our students in various courses at the Stanford Business School and Engineering School not only did enlightening case studies, but were also real learning partners in an exploration into the messy but important question of why knowing–doing gaps existed. Each of them has our heartfelt gratitude. We also want to thank every person at every company who participated in the various quantitative and qualitative studies that we and our students did during the course of this project. Special thanks go to Peter B. Ashley, Dennis Bakke, Gwen Books, Charlie Bresler, Patricia Dunn, Larry Ford, Betty Fried, Ben Gibert, James Goodnight, Fred Grauer, Gary High, Jeff Jefferson, David Kelley, Tom Kelley, Annette Kyle, Diane Lumley, Charles Lynch, Dave Morthland, David Russo, Roger Sant, Steve Scammell, Elmar Toime, Burgess Winter, and George Zimmer for being so generous with their time and for helping us gather useful data and insights in so many different ways. We would also like to thank our research assistants. We are grateful for the major roles that Laura Castaneda and Tanya Menon played in the field research we did for this book. We also thank Frank Flynn and Roy Vella for their research assistance.

We thank Marjorie Williams, our skilled and wise editor, and her many colleagues who have been so helpful at the Harvard Business School Press. When we say that Marjorie is our favorite editor, we aren't just talking. We have backed this statement with action. Between the two of us, this is the fifth book that we have finished under her guidance, and both of us have another HBS Press book on the way. Marjorie's mode of operation reminds us of the most effective leaders we studied while writing this book. She never stops moving forward, never stops talking about how good things already are, how much better they can be, and exactly what should be tried next to achieve excellence. We don't always agree with Marjorie, but we always appreciate her because, more so than any editor we have ever met, she cares about the quality of the work and about maintaining long-term relationships. If people elsewhere followed Marjorie's lead and always acted as if quality and long-term relationships with suppliers were their top priorities, the gap between knowledge and action would disappear in many organizations.

We thank the institutions, and especially the supportive people within them, that provided us with the time and resources to write this book. The Stanford Business School, and particularly David Brady, the associate dean over the organizational behavior group, provided financial support of many forms, including time, the most important resource. The Boston Consulting Group provided funding for some research assistance and incidental expenses, money that was vitally important for successfully completing this project. Jeffrey Pfeffer wrote this book partly during the year he was a Fellow at the Center for Advanced Study in the Behavioral Sciences. Neil Smelser and Bob Scott are role models of how to run an academic institution and how to build a culture that encourages learning, collaboration, and personal development. Thanks don't seem adequate for the opportunity they have provided. Support for Jeffrey Pfeffer's year at the Center came from National Science Foundation Grant SBR-9022192.

Robert Sutton would like to thank colleagues, students, and staff in the Stanford Engineering School for supporting him in so many ways while developing this book. The Center for Work, Technology, and Organizations (WTO) provided financial support, and his dear friend and colleague Steve Barley (co-director of WTO with Sutton) provided emotional support on nearly a daily basis, had strange and wonderful ideas about nearly everything, and did hundreds of tasks that freed Sutton to write the book. Diane Bailey and Pamela Hinds, his wonderful new faculty colleagues at WTO, provided Sutton with support, ideas, and constant amusement. Sutton is also grateful for the research support provided by the Stanford Technology Ventures Program (STVP), an effort led by the astounding Tom Byers, one of the most caring and action-oriented human beings on the planet. STVP is supported by the Kauffman Center for Entrepreneurial Leadership and the Price Institute for Entrepreneurial Studies. Sutton would also like to thank Stanford Engineering colleagues Kathleen Eisenhardt, James Jucker, and Elisabeth Pate-Cornell for their encouragement. John Hennessy, the leader of the Stanford Engineering School, was an inspiration throughout; he just might be the finest dean anywhere. Finally, Sutton is indebted to Paula Wright, who did at least a thousand of the tasks that made this book possible.

Much of our field research was completed when Robert Sutton served as a faculty member at the Haas Business School during the 1997–98 academic year. The Haas School supported his research time, and U.C. Berkeley's Institute for Industrial Relations supported a research assistant during that year. He thanks Jennifer Chatman, Richard Meese, and Barry Staw for their ideas, their help, and most of all, their understanding.

The ideas in this book were shaped by conversations with many other colleagues. Our dear friend Charles O'Reilly gave us many ideas about the hazards and virtues of strong organizational cultures and how to change such strong belief systems. Talking to Bob Cialdini, although not nearly often enough, kept us grounded in good social psychological theory. Arie Kruglanski provided research on the need for cognitive closure.

We owe special thanks to the people who gave us detailed comments on earlier drafts of this book. Beth Benjamin did a fabulous job, under terrific time pressure, of reading a draft of the manuscript and providing insight, examples, wisdom, and encouragement. J. Richard Hackman offered both support and concrete suggestions for improving our work. We hope we learned all we could from his generous advice. Francine Gordon, once again, was kind enough to provide not only moral support and facilitate financial support of the project, but also to furnish ideas and helpful suggestions on the manuscript. Colleagues like these are more precious than any mere words can express.

The Knowing-Doing Gap

How Smart Companies Turn Knowledge into Action

|1| Knowing "What" to Do Is Not Enough

W HY DO SO MUCH EDUCATION and training, management consulting, and business research and so many books and articles produce so little change in what managers and organizations actually do?

In 1996, more than 1,700 business books were published in the United States,[1] and more are published each year. Many of these books are filled with the same analyses and prescriptions, albeit using different language and graphics, as could be found in similar books published the year before. In fact, many of the ideas proclaimed as new each year can be found in similar books printed decades earlier.[2] Yet these books find a ready market because the ideas, although often widely known and proven to be useful and valid, remain unimplemented. So, authors try, in part through repackaging and updating, to somehow get managers to not only *know* but to *do* something with what they know. And managers continue to buy the books filled with ideas they already know because they intuitively understand that knowing isn't enough. They hope that by somehow buying and reading one more book they will finally be able to translate this performance knowledge into organizational action.

Each year, more than $60 billion is spent on training in and by organizations, particularly management training.

Much of this training, on subjects such as Total Quality Management (TQM), customer service and building customer loyalty, leadership, and organizational change is based on knowledge and principles that are fundamentally timeless—unchanged and unchanging. Nevertheless, the training often is repeated. Regardless of the quality of the content, the delivery, or the frequency of repetition, management education is often ineffective in changing organizational practices.

Professor Mark Zbaracki of the University of Chicago studied Total Quality Management training in five organizations in which senior executives believed that TQM methods could enhance the quality of their products and services and that the training had changed how people performed their jobs.[3] Zbaracki found, however, that the quantitative TQM methods were not used *at all* in four of the organizations and only on a limited basis in the fifth. This result is not unique to TQM—we observed it repeatedly during our research.

Each year, billions of dollars are spent on management consultants by organizations seeking advice—one estimate for 1996 was $43 billion.[4] But that advice is seldom implemented. One consultant, making a presentation to obtain work from a large U.S. bank, showed an overhead slide that had the recommendations from four previous consulting studies conducted in just the prior six years for that bank. All four studies had come to the same conclusions, which is not surprising given that smart people from four different firms looked at essentially the same data. The presenter, selling implementation and change rather than analytical services, asked the assembled executives, "Why do you want to pay for the same answer a fifth time?" He and his firm got the job. As another example of knowing but not doing in the world of management consulting, two consultants from one of the leading firms worked on a project for a large electrical utility in Latin America that was facing deregulation. They were chagrined to discover that management already had a four–year–old, 500–page document with extensive plans and recommendations produced by a different consulting firm in a previous engagement. They reported:

> The old document was very good. It had benchmarking cost studies from best–practice utilities all around the world, summaries of the most successful training systems in other industrial companies, and pretty detailed implementation calendars. . . . As our analysis was based on the same . . . information that was given to the last consultants four years before . . . our recommendations were basically the same. The problem was not analysis. It was implementation. Although we could identify some new areas for improvement, the core was almost a copy of the old document. . . . The client already had the basic information we were giving them.[5]

Each year the hundreds of business schools in the United States graduate more than 80,000 MBAs and conduct numerous research studies on business topics. Business education and research are growing in scope and prominence in countries around the world. Yet the translation of this research and management education into practice proceeds slowly and fitfully. There is little evidence that being staffed with people who have an advanced education in business is consistently related to outstanding organizational performance. Many top–performing firms—Southwest Airlines, Wal–Mart, The Men's Wearhouse, ServiceMaster, PSS/World Medical, SAS Institute, AES, Whole Foods Market, and Starbucks—don't recruit at the leading business schools and don't emphasize business degree credentials in their staffing practices. Numerous researchers have found that "little of what is taught in college or even business schools really prepares would–be managers for the realities of managing."[6] One study reported that 73 percent of the surveyed MBA program graduates said "that their

MBA skills were used 'only marginally or not at all' in their first managerial assignments."[7]

Did you ever wonder why so much education and training, management consultation, organizational research, and so many books and articles produce so few changes in actual management practice? Did you ever wonder why the little change that does occur often happens with such great difficulty? Why it is that, at the end of so many books and seminars, leaders report being enlightened and wiser, but not much happens in their organizations?

We wondered, too, and so we embarked on a quest to explore one of the great mysteries in organizational management: why knowledge of what needs to be done frequently fails to result in action or behavior consistent with that knowledge. We came to call this the *knowing-doing problem*—the challenge of turning knowledge about how to enhance organizational performance into actions consistent with that knowledge. This book presents what we learned about the factors that contribute to the knowing-doing gap and why and how some organizations are more successful than others in implementing their knowledge.

We have spent the last four years on a crusade to learn about what causes the knowing–doing gap and how to cure it, and how some organizations avoid the gaps in the first place. We started by scouring the popular and academic literature to find stories, case studies, and large-scale studies of multiple firms that could provide insights into the knowing–doing problem. We found evidence that organizations in every industry suffer from this malady. But we found few satisfactory answers about either the causes or remedies for this vexing problem. Therefore we performed about a dozen of our own qualitative and quantitative studies of knowing–doing problems in organizations, including financial service firms, product design firms, traditional "metal-bending" manufacturing corporations, mining firms, electric power firms, and retail and restaurant chains. We also taught classes at Stanford, in both the business and engineering schools, where our management students did about 100 of their own case studies of knowing–doing problems and how these problems had been, or might have been, repaired.

We examined a wide range of organizational practices to learn about the knowing–doing gap. However, we have focused more on a set of practices that, although seldom implemented, are known by most managers, are widely talked about in organizations, and have been consistently shown to increase organizational performance: so–called high–commitment or high–performance management practices. These practices have been described, and their positive effects on performance analyzed, in numerous books and articles.[8] We will touch on this evidence as needed to make our points about the knowing–doing gap, but will not present detailed descriptions of each of these practices or an extensive review of the evidence showing their positive effects on performance. Our interest is in understanding the barriers to turning knowledge into action and how some firms overcome such barriers. The knowing–doing problems we have observed are general and seem to cross topic domains, including the application of marketing knowledge and best practices in customer service and retention and the implementation of superior manufacturing practices.

We found no simple answers to the knowing–doing dilemma. Given the importance of the knowing–doing problem, if such simple answers existed, they would already have been widely implemented. And the rare firms that are able to consistently translate knowledge into action would not enjoy the substantial competitive advantages that they do. We will provide you with insights and diagnoses of some important sources of knowing–doing problems and with examples of companies that suffer severely from such problems, companies that don't, and some that have been able to overcome knowing–doing gaps. But one of the most important insights from our research is that knowledge that is actually implemented is much more likely to be acquired from learning by doing than from learning by reading, listening, or even thinking. There is a limit to what we can do for you in this book, regardless of the insights we have acquired. One of our main recommendations is to engage more frequently in thoughtful action. Spend less time just contemplating and talking about organizational problems. Taking action will generate experience from which you can learn.

When we described the knowing–doing problem to others, we frequently got the same response. People would say that the knowing–doing problem comes from inherent problems of individuals—a lack of knowledge or skills or "personality" problems—and that its existence is a reflection of individual deficiencies. It isn't. If you work in a place where you or your colleagues don't turn your knowledge into action, it probably isn't just your fault. There is no doubt that some people are better able to act on their knowledge, that some people are mentally healthier and better adjusted than others, and that individual psychology must surely play some role in the knowing–doing problems we uncovered. But our research suggests that this is not a large part of the story. Some organizations are consistently able to turn knowledge into action, and do so even as they grow and absorb new people and even other organizations. Other organizations, composed of intelligent, thoughtful, hard–working, nice people, fail to translate their knowledge about organizational performance into action. It is almost as if there were some kind of brain vacuum in those firms that sucks the wisdom and insight out of their people. These differences across firms come more from their management systems and practices than from differences in the quality of their people. Great companies get remarkable performance from ordinary people. Not–so–great companies take talented people and manage to lose the benefits of their talent, insight, and motivation. That is why we focus on management practices that either create or reduce the knowing–doing gap.

Implementation or Ignorance: Does a Knowing-Doing Gap Really Exist?

How do we know that knowledge isn't always implemented and that this is a problem affecting organizational performance? And perhaps even more important, how can organizations discover to what degree they are not actually doing what they think they should? These are important, but relatively straightforward, issues.

Evidence of Knowing-Doing Gaps

There are a number of studies within single industries demonstrating that there are superior ways of managing people and organizing their work. Yet although these superior management practices are reasonably well known, diffusion proceeds slowly and fitfully, and backsliding is common. A study of apparel manufacturing demonstrated that modular production, with an emphasis on team-based production, produced far superior economic performance along a number of dimensions compared with the traditional bundle system of manufacturing using individual piecework and limited training.[9] Trade publications, industry associations, and the relevant unions had favored modular production since the early 1980s. Nonetheless, in 1992 about 80 percent of all garments were still sewn using the bundle method, and some plants that had adopted modular production abandoned it and returned to the bundle system.

Similarly, evidence for the advantages of flexible or lean production in automobile assembly is compelling.[10] This knowledge is widely diffused within the industry and has been for some time. Nevertheless, a five-year follow-up study of the diffusion of flexible manufacturing systems found that there was only modest implementation of flexible arrangements and that "some plants undertook only minor changes in their use of high-involvement work practices . . . and still others showed modest decreases."[11] And a large–scale study of semiconductor fabrication revealed substantial differences in performance, as measured by cycle time, line yield, and defect density, based on the management practices used. Yet the study found substantial variation in these practices, even in an industry that was characterized by geographic concentration, particularly of corporate headquarters, and substantial movement of personnel between firms. In these and other studies the evidence seems compelling that, although there are better ways of managing and organizing, these superior practices are not necessarily quickly or readily adopted.[12]

Some other examples illustrate the frequently large gap between knowing that something is important and actually doing it. For instance, the Association of Executive Search Consultants conducted a survey in which "three–quarters of the responding CEOs said companies should have 'fast track' programs, [but] fewer than half have one at their own companies." As noted in a *Fortune* article commenting on this study, "Maybe chief executives don't say what they mean, and maybe they have trouble implementing what they say."[13] Our research indicates that it is the latter problem—implementing what leaders say and know—that is more pervasive.

Evidence from various industry studies, and from studies of firms in multiple industries, shows that knowledge of how to enhance performance is not readily or easily transferred *across* firms. Moreover, there is evidence that knowledge of how to enhance performance doesn't transfer readily even *within* firms. There are persistent and substantial differences in performance within facilities in the same company. One study of 42 food plants in a single company doing essentially the same manufacturing tasks with similar technologies found differences in performance of 300 percent between the best—and worst—performing plants. The best plant earned 80 percent more than the mean, and the worst plant earned 40 percent less than the mean for all the plants.[14] A study of oil refineries reported little consistency in performance in multirefinery organizations. There was no evidence of a "company effect" on performance, indicating that there was not much consistency in management practices or philosophy across different facilities within the same company.[15]

An intensive study of an effort to make a Hewlett-Packard (HP) manufacturing unit more effective reported: "By interviewing thirteen such stakeholders from other departments, including procurement, process generation, engineering, and finance, design team members discovered that communication between departments was poor, thus limiting the degree to which they learned from each other. . . . Opportunities to share innovative process technologies or other sources of competitive advantage were being overlooked."[16] The problems associated with transferring knowledge within HP have led Lew Platt, the CEO, to lament, "I wish we knew what we know at HP."[17] Another study of the transfer of best practices, or knowledge, within firms, noted:

> You would think that . . . better practices would spread like wildfire in the entire organization. They don't. As William Buehler, senior vice president at Xerox, said, "You can see a high-performance factory or office, but it just doesn't spread." . . . One Baldrige winner [said], "We can have two plants right across the street from one another, and it's the damnedest thing to get them to transfer best practices."[18]

Measuring the Knowing-Doing Gap

We wanted to see if we could quantitatively measure the knowing-doing gap and if there were statistically significant differences between what managers thought should done and what was actually being implemented. Perhaps the observed differences in practices even within a single organization were a function of differences in beliefs about what ought to be done rather than because that knowledge wasn't being implemented. So, based on the literature on high-commitment management practices and on organizational innovation, we developed a set of 25 statements that represented these management practices. The appendix presents the full list of these statements. We describe the survey in more detail there because it is a useful tool that firms can employ to learn about themselves. We then administered a survey based on this list in a telephone interview with the managers and assistant managers in a randomly drawn representative sample of 120 units of a large, multiunit restaurant chain.

The managers were asked to what extent they agreed that the practices in the survey enhanced a restaurant's financial performance, using a six-point scale from strongly disagree to strongly agree. These questions assess managerial knowledge as we define it—that is, what leaders believe is important in affecting performance in their units. Then, both the managers and the assistant managers were asked to what extent the behavior in question was descriptive of what occurred in their restaurants—a measure of what was actually done—using the same six-point scale. In most cases, there was excellent agreement about what did, in fact, occur in the restaurant. There were, however, big differences between what the restaurant managers believed produced success and what they reported practicing in their units. For 17 of the 25 management practices, there was a statistically significant difference between what the managers thought was important for restaurant success and what they and the assistant managers reported using in the restaurant. In each instance, the direction of the difference indicated that they weren't doing what they knew to be important (see Table 1-1). The data show that, for the most part, restaurant managers recognize the importance of sharing information with their people, providing feedback, and involving them in learning about how to improve operations. These actions are easier to

Table 1-1

Differences between Knowing and Doing in
120 Units of a Restaurant Chain

Statement	We Know We Should Do This	We *Are* Doing This
Getting good ideas from other units in the chain	4.9	4.0
Instituting an active suggestion program	4.8	3.9
Using a detailed assessment process for hiring new employees	5.0	4.2
Posting all jobs internally	4.2	3.5
Talking openly about learning from mistakes	4.9	4.3
Providing employees with frequent feedback	5.7	5.2
Sharing information about your restaurant's financial performance with everyone	4.3	3.8

Note: Responses are rated on a six-point scale on which 1 equals "strongly disagree" and 6 equals "strongly agree." All differences were statistically significant at less than the .001 level of probability.

the extent that managers hire carefully, so the restaurants have the right people to begin with. Yet, there was much less implementation of these practices even though their importance was widely understood.

Time after time people understand the issues, understand what needs to happen to affect performance, but don't do the things they know they should. We did a similar study of another restaurant chain that found nearly identical results. In that study, we also observed that leaders frequently rationalized their actions—or more accurately their inaction—by creating elaborate explanations for why they chose not to do the things they knew were important to their business success. The senior executives, managers, and workers that we interviewed in this second chain invariably had convincing explanations for particular knowing–doing gaps and why they persisted. The firm paid low wages and operated in a very competitive labor market. This made hiring, particularly for service skills, difficult. Store managers also had so many reports to fill out that even had they wanted to, they didn't have enough time to devote to hiring. But when the stores hired the wrong people, turnover was higher. With higher turnover, the managers were under even more pressure to fill positions quickly and became even less selective. This led to further service and employee quality problems, more turnover, and a vicious cycle.

Does the Knowing-Doing Gap Matter?

The answer to the question of whether the knowing–doing gap actually matters for organizational performance is not as obvious as it might at first seem. It is possible that differences in organizational performance come from differences in what firms *know*—the quality and depth of their insights about business strategy, technologies, products, customers, and operations—rather than from their ability to translate that knowledge into action. There are, however, numerous reasons to doubt this is the case. We do not deny that there are important differences in knowledge across firms, such as differences in the sophistication of their understanding of management and operations. But we argue that such differences are only part of the reason for differences in firm performance, and that a much larger source of variation in performance stems from the ability to turn knowledge into action.

Why do we argue that the gap between knowing and doing is more important than the gap between ignorance and knowing? First, because there are too many activities and organizations involved in acquiring and disseminating knowledge to plausibly maintain that there are many important performance "secrets." Consider the plethora of books, articles, consultants, and training programs we have already described. All of these have as one of their objectives the transmission of information. There are organizations that specialize in collecting knowledge about management practices, storing it, and then transferring the information to those who need such information about enhancing performance. These organizations, sometimes called *knowledge brokers*, make a business of transferring performance knowledge. At least two major consulting firms, Andersen Consulting and McKinsey & Company, have units that specialize in transferring knowledge about best practices learned from work with past clients to current clients who did not know, or at least did not use, such information.[19]

Although the market for information about "best practices" may not be as efficient as financial or capital markets are reputed to be, it is nonetheless implausible to presume that better ways of doing things can remain secret for long. There are few managers who can resist the temptation to tell their counterparts at other firms or the business press about what they are doing to achieve organizational success. Managers of successful firms are also frequently interviewed and hired by competing firms in the same industry and by firms in other industries that hope to learn and implement the practices of these firms.

Southwest Airlines is a firm that uses fairly simple business practices that are widely known, but it continues to have the best financial performance in the airline industry. Numerous books, case studies, and television shows have described Southwest's management approach,[20] but the firm's competitors have either not tried to imitate what it does or, when they have, like the United Shuttle did, they have not been nearly as successful as Southwest.

Second, research demonstrates that the success of most interventions designed to improve organizational perform-ance depends largely on implementing what is already known, rather than from adopting new or previously unknown ways of doing things. Consider one representa-tive study. A field experiment was conducted with an elec-trical wholesale company with headquarters in Melbourne, Australia. The experiment compared sales changes in branches that used benchmarking with branches that set high performance goals. In the more–effective benchmark-ing treatment, "at the beginning of each month . . . each branch was sent a 'League Ladder' showing the percentage improvement [in sales] and ranking of all the branches in that group for the past month. In addition, they were sent a list of 'Best Practice' hints compiled . . . from information provided by managers of the best–performing branches."[21] Over a three–month period, these branches improved their sales performance by almost 6 percent.

The "Best Practice" hints were actually "well–known prac-tices, with the extra dimension that they were reinforced and carried out reliably in the better performing branches. . . . Most managers agreed with the hints, but claimed they were already aware of and employing most of them. . . . Given the nature of the 'Best Practice' hints, we can rule out discovery and communication of highly original and effec-tive practices as the reason for improvement in the bench-marking group."[22] Using regular schedules to plan weekly activities, conducting meetings of branch staff to review and discuss branch staff performance, training sales repre-sentatives in understanding and interpreting sales trend reports, and using practices that ensure fast and reliable customer service are far from rocket science. They are, in fact, common sense.[23] It is interesting how uncommon common sense is in its implementation.

Or consider Honda's efforts to enhance the performance of its suppliers, which resulted in productivity increases averaging 50 percent at the 53 suppliers participating in Honda's BP (Best Practice, Best Process, Best Performance) program.[24] A study of Honda's process noted that "the underlying scientific knowledge for the reengineering of production lines was primarily concrete and simple rather than abstract and complex."[25] The changes were consistent with the idea of *kaizen*, or continuous improvement, most of them being small, simple, and in many cases, quite commonsensical given the particular manufacturing process. The genius of the Honda system was in its implementation, not in particularly novel or complicated technical ideas for enhancing productivity.

If there is widespread diffusion of information on "best" (or at least "better") practices, and if the evidence suggests that many successful interventions rely more on implementation of simple knowledge than on creating new insights or discovering obscure or secret practices used by other firms, then our position that the gap between knowing and doing is important for firm performance follows logically. This conclusion means that although knowledge creation, benchmarking, and knowledge management may be important, transforming knowledge into organizational action is at least as important to organizational success.

How Knowledge Management Contributes to the Knowing-Doing Problem

One might think that with the current interest in "knowledge management" and intellectual capital, there wouldn't be a knowing–doing problem. After all, there is general acceptance that "knowledge has become increasingly important as a contributor to a country's and individual firm's success in industrial competition."[26] Tomas Stewart's conclusion is typical: "The new economy is about the growing value of knowledge as an input and output, making it the most important ingredient of what people buy and sell."[27] But the view of knowledge taken by many consultants, organizations, and management writers is of something to be acquired, measured, and distributed—something reasonably tangible, such as patents. There are two problems with this conception of knowledge or know–how. First, the conception of knowledge as something explicit and quantifiable draws a problematic distinction between knowledge as a tangible good and the use of that good in ongoing practice. The emphasis that has resulted has been to build the stock of knowledge, acquiring or developing intellectual property (note the use of the term *property*) under the presumption that knowledge, once possessed, will be used appropriately and efficiently. As we have seen, this presumption is often not valid.

There is some attention in both the management literature and in management practice to knowledge in use, but this perspective is comparatively rare. Commenting on the papers at a conference on knowledge management, Don Cohen noted, "In the U.S., most knowledge practice focuses on collecting, distributing, re–using, and measuring existing codified knowledge and information. Practitioners often look to information technology to capture and distribute this explicit knowledge; firms measure success by near–term economic returns on knowledge investment."[28] An Ernst & Young survey of 431 firms conducted in 1997 is quite revealing about why most firms' efforts in knowledge management are not likely to do much good and may even be counterproductive regarding turning knowledge into organizational action. According to data from that survey (Figure 1–1), most firms' efforts consist of investing in knowledge repositories such as intranets and data warehouses, building networks so that people can find each other, and implementing technologies to facilitate collaboration. These are

Figure 1-1

Knowledge Management Projects

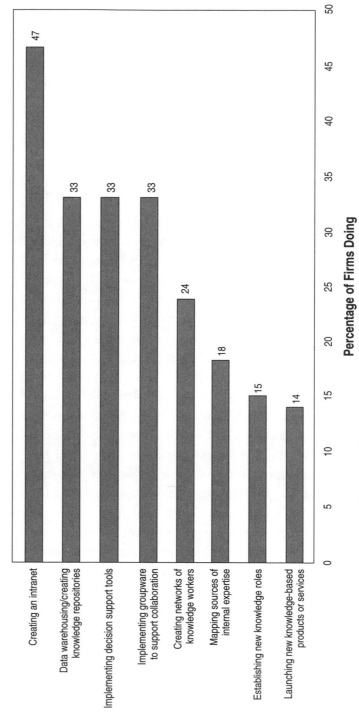

Percentage of Firms Doing

Creating an intranet — 47

Data warehousing/creating knowledge repositories — 33

Implementing decision support tools — 33

Implementing groupware to support collaboration — 33

Creating networks of knowledge workers — 24

Mapping sources of internal expertise — 18

Establishing new knowledge roles — 15

Launching new knowledge-based products or services — 14

Source: Data from Rudy Ruggles, "The State of the Notion: Knowledge Management in Practice," *California Management Review* 40 (summer 1998): 83.

all activities that treat knowledge pretty much like steel or any other resource, to be gathered, shared, and distributed. What firms haven't done very much is build knowledge into products and services, or develop new products and services based on knowledge. Furthermore, there is no item on this list of knowledge management projects that reflects implementing knowledge on an ongoing basis.

One of the main reasons that knowledge management efforts are often divorced from day-to-day activities is that the managers, consulting firms, and information technologists who design and build the systems for collecting, storing, and retrieving knowledge have limited, often inaccurate, views of how people actually use knowledge in their jobs. Sociologists call this "working knowledge."[29] Knowledge management systems rarely reflect the fact that essential knowledge, including technical knowledge, is often transferred between people by stories, gossip, and by watching one another work. This is a process in which social interaction is often crucial. A recent study of 1,000 employees in business, government, and nonprofit organizations reported that "most workplace learning goes on unbudgeted, unplanned, and uncaptured by the organization. . . . Up to 70 percent of workplace learning is informal."[30] This study by the Center for Workforce Development found that informal learning occurs in dozens of daily activities, including participating in meetings, interacting with customers, supervising or being supervised, mentoring others, communicating informally with peers, and training others on the job.

Yet, most knowledge management efforts emphasize technology and the storage and transfer of codified information such as facts, statistics, canned presentations, and written reports. A June 1997 Conference Board conference on creating and leveraging intellectual capital reported: "Most corporate initiatives to manage intellectual capital are focused on specific projects, the most common of which deploy technology to share and leverage knowledge and best practices."[31] There is an unfortunate emphasis on technology, particularly information technology, in these efforts. For instance, one recent article on making knowledge management a reality asserted that "it's clear that an intranet is one of the most powerful tools for achieving results within this [knowledge management] arena."[32] Another article asserted that "knowledge management starts with technology."[33] We believe that this is precisely wrong. As the Conference Board report noted, "Dumping technology on a problem is rarely an effective solution."[34] When knowledge is transferred by stories and gossip instead of solely through formal data systems, it comes along with information about the process that was used to develop that knowledge. When just reading reports or seeing presentations, people don't learn about the subtle nuances of work methods—the failures, the tasks that were fun, the tasks that were boring, the people who were helpful, and the people who undermined the work.

Formal systems can't store knowledge that isn't easily described or codified but is nonetheless essential for doing the work, called *tacit knowledge*. So, while firms keep investing millions of dollars to set up knowledge management groups, most of the knowledge that is actually used and useful is transferred by the stories people tell to each other, by the trials and errors that occur as people develop knowledge and skill, by inexperienced people watching those more experienced, and by experienced people providing close and constant coaching to newcomers.

The Ernst & Young survey described earlier also asked executives to rate their organizations on how well they were doing in the various dimensions of knowledge management. These results are reproduced in Figure 1-2. Managers seem to believe they are doing a good job in generating new knowledge and even doing pretty well in obtaining knowledge from the environment. What they aren't doing very well at all, by their own assessments, is transferring knowledge *within* the organization. And perhaps most important, Ernst & Young didn't even ask if the knowledge

Figure 1-2

Self-Assessment of How Well Organizations Are Doing in Their Knowledge Management Activities

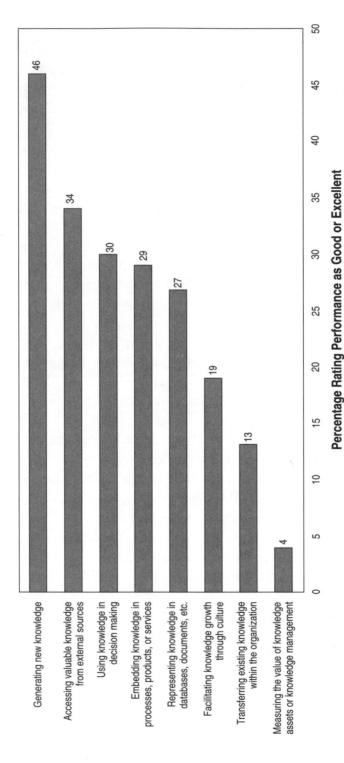

Source: Data from Rudy Ruggles, "The State of the Notion: Knowledge Management in Practice," *California Management Review* 40 (summer 1998): 82.

in these firms was being used by the firms—not just in decision making, which was covered in the survey, but in day-to-day operations and management practices.

Knowledge management systems seem to work best when the people who generate the knowledge are also those who store it, explain it to others, and coach them as they try to implement the knowledge. For example, Hewlett-Packard's Strategic Planning, Analysis, and Modeling group has had success transferring knowledge about supply chain management that has been implemented in many HP divisions. One of the reasons the group has been successful is that the same people who do this internal consulting are also responsible for storing and disseminating knowledge about it within the company. Corey Billington, the head of this group, describes his job as "part librarian, part consultant, and part coach."[35] He is responsible for knowing the technical solutions and the stories surrounding the 150 or so consulting jobs his group has done within HP so that he and others in his group can suggest ideas to help new internal clients and can actually coach the clients as they implement the ideas.

The second problem with much of the existing literature and practice in knowledge management is that it conceptualizes knowledge as something tangible and explicit that is quite distinct from philosophy or values. As Don Cohen, a writer specializing on knowledge issues, put it, "The noun 'knowledge' implies that knowledge is a *thing* that can be located and manipulated as an independent object or stock. It seems possible to 'capture' knowledge, to 'distribute', 'measure', and 'manage' it. The gerund 'knowing' suggests instead a process, the action of knowers and inseparable from them."[36] A leading Japanese scholar in the area of knowledge in organizations made a simple but important point: "Knowledge is embedded in . . . these shared spaces, where it is then acquired through one's own experience or reflections on the experiences of others. . . . Knowledge is intangible."[37]

The fact that knowledge is acquired through experience and is often intangible and tacit produces a third problem in turning knowledge into action. One important reason we uncovered for the knowing–doing gap is that companies overestimate the importance of the tangible, specific, pro-grammatic aspects of what competitors, for instance, do, and underestimate the importance of the underlying philosophy that guides what they do and why they do it. Although specific practices are obviously important, such practices evolve and make sense only as part of some system that is often organized according to some philosophy or meta–theory of performance. As such, there is a knowing–doing gap in part because firms have misconstrued what they should be knowing or seeking to know in the first place.

Why Typical Knowledge Management Practices Make Knowing-Doing Gaps Worse

- Knowledge management efforts mostly emphasize technology and the transfer of codified information.

- Knowledge management tends to treat knowledge as a tangible thing, as a stock or a quantity, and therefore separates knowledge as some *thing* from the use of that thing.

- Formal systems can't easily store or transfer tacit knowledge.

- The people responsible for transferring and imple-menting knowledge management frequently don't understand the actual work being documented.

- Knowledge management tends to focus on specific practices and ignore the importance of philosophy.

Why has it been so difficult for other automobile manufacturers to copy the Toyota Production System (TPS), even
though the details have been described in books and Toyota actually gives tours of its manufacturing facilities?
Because "the TPS techniques that visitors see on their
tours—the *kanban* cards, *andon* cords, and quality circles—
represent the surface of TPS but not its soul."[38] The Toyota
Production System is about philosophy and perspective,
about such things as people, processes, quality, and continuous improvement. It is not just a set of techniques or
practices:

> On the surface, TPS appears simple. . . . Mike DaPrile,
> who runs Toyota's assembly facilities in Kentucky,
> describes it as having three levels: techniques, sys-
> tems, and philosophy. Says he: Many plants have
> put in an *andon* cord that you pull to stop the assem-
> bly line if there is a problem. A 5-year-old can pull
> the cord. But it takes a lot of effort to drive the right
> philosophies down to the plant floor.[39]

A similar perspective is evident in the study examining
how Honda creates lean suppliers. Honda chooses its sup-
plier-partners in large part based on the attitudes of the
companies' management. "In the words of Rick Mayo, the
Honda engineer directing these activities, 'We are a philos-
ophy-driven company . . . Honda felt it was easier to teach
the technical knowledge associated with a different product
or process technology than to find a technically-capable
supplier possessing the combination of risk-taking attitude,
motivation to improve, responsiveness to future needs, and
overall competence that is valued so highly."[40]

Nor is this emphasis on philosophy just the view of some
Japanese automobile companies. The importance of values
and philosophy is a theme that was repeated by Howard
Behar, president of Starbucks International, the coffee company; David Russo, vice president of human resources for

SAS Institute, a software firm recently ranked by *Fortune* as the third-best company to work for in the United States; and George Zimmer, founder and chairman of The Men's Wearhouse, a rapidly growing, extremely profitable off-price retailer of tailored and casual men's clothing. All three of these organizations have been financially successful, and all are renowned for their people management practices. In all three instances, the message was the same: What is important is not so much what we do—the specific people management techniques and practices—but *why* we do it—the underlying philosophy and view of people and the business that provides a foundation for the practices. Attempting to copy just *what* is done—the explicit practices and policies—without holding the underlying philosophy is at once a more difficult task and an approach that is less likely to be successful. Because of the importance of values and philosophy in the management processes of many successful companies, the emphasis on the tangible, explicit aspects of knowledge that characterizes most knowledge management projects is unlikely to provide much value and may be, at worst, a diversion from where and how companies should be focusing their attention.

The First Principle: If You Know by Doing, There Is No Gap between What You Know and What You Do

People are always fascinated by successful companies. Many business books have a large dose of "what successful companies do" in them, and such information certainly can be helpful. But learning by reading, learning by going to training programs, and learning from university-based degree programs will get you and your organization only so far. You and your colleagues can certainly acquire concepts and frameworks and at least the illusion of knowledge, if not the real thing. But you will not necessarily be any closer to being able to actually implement that knowledge or turn the frameworks into action. There is only a loose and imperfect relationship between knowing what to do and the ability to act on that knowledge. The irony is that this statement is true even for this book, as it is for all books on management. If reading and understanding a book meant that you and your firm could readily implement the knowledge contained therein, there would not be the tremendous advantage accruing to those firms that are actually able to turn knowledge into action. Competitive advantage comes from being able to do something others can't do. Anyone can read a book or attend a seminar. The trick is in turning the knowledge acquired into organizational action.

Our intent in this book is to emphasize those concepts and ideas that turn knowledge into action, but taking action and having an action orientation are still necessary for anything to happen. This means a complementary principle is to learn by doing as well as by reading and thinking. If you and your colleagues learn from your own actions and behavior, then there won't be much of a knowing–doing gap because you will be "knowing" on the basis of your doing, and implementing that knowledge will be substantially easier.

This insight was first suggested to us by various Asian managers and those familiar with Asian, including Japanese, management practices. The contrast between them and their U.S. counterparts in the reactions to the questions we were asking was striking. When we described the "knowing–doing" research project to American managers, they could immediately relate to both its relevance and its importance. They were cognizant of many examples in which they and their organizations failed to implement, in practice, their conceptual knowledge of how to manage. But when we described the project to Japanese and other Asian managers, they seemed perplexed. Operating in systems in which knowledge was largely developed on the job, by doing, and in which managers were more often tightly embedded in the actual work processes, they found it hard to understand how someone could "know" and not "do." This seemed like a provocative insight—maybe there was some benefit in learning by doing that was missed in the formal classroom-, case-, and theory–based presentations and discussions so typical of much contemporary management education, though it was not missed in internship and co–op learning programs, which are often much more effective in developing job–relevant skills.

And then, through some students, we became acquainted with Kingston Technology, a company that seemed to exemplify learning by doing. Kingston, for those who don't know, was ranked as number 2 in the 1998 *Fortune* magazine listing of the 100 best places to work in America. Founded in 1987, the company is the largest maker of computer memory boards—DRAMs—in the world, with 1997 sales of $1.3 billion and a 55 percent market share in the United States. The firm has grown at a compounded rate of 92 percent since its founding. It operates in a very difficult, cyclical, competitive business that has faced rapidly falling prices and challenging market conditions.

David Sun and his partner, John Tu, have built a company in which the implementation of knowledge is fairly easy and automatic. That is because Sun believes, "If you do it, then you will know." This means that "if managers ask for input and feedback from employees, over time, they will learn what management practices to implement, alter, or discard. Sun believes that his management practices are effective because his employees, in large part, were responsible for their design and/or fine–tuning. As Sun says, 'just do what they tell you they want.'"[41]

Honda, which has successfully imported lean production techniques to its plants in the United States, also believes in knowledge development and transfer through direct, rather than vicarious, experience. In its efforts to enhance quality, it uses a process that is short on meetings and presentations and long on direct observation:

> Honda emphasizes having people actually see qual-
> ity defects directly. . . . Production workers will often
> go to another part of the plant to see a car with a
> defect. . . . Honda has a saying for this . . . "actual
> part, actual situation." The philosophy is that when
> a person sees a quality problem, s/he is more likely
> to analyze it systematically, to communicate the
> problem more accurately to others . . . , and to be
> motivated to find a preventive remedy.[42]

The U.S. Army and other military organizations provide another good example of learning and knowing by doing. When the army is not in combat, it is constantly training for combat. Much of this training is done by having soldiers perform the very actions that will be necessary during wartime. Soldiers engage in staged battles, drills, and other realistic simulations designed to have them observe, perform, and repeat the actions they will need to carry out in real combat. The army's National Training Center "is credited with almost single-handedly transforming the post-Vietnam army. . . . Several of America's most forward-thinking companies—including Motorola and General Electric—study it as a source of ideas about leadership and learning."[43] Acquiring knowledge through practice, performance, and even failure is indispensable for organizations of all sizes and types.

Thus, at one level, the answer to the knowing-doing problem is deceptively simple: Embed more of the process of acquiring new knowledge in the actual doing of the task and less in formal training programs that are frequently ineffective. As one comprehensive study of the development of executives concluded, "One learns to be a leader by serving as a leader."[44] But this practice is rarely followed. It is revealing that, at least in the United States, the philosophy of "if you do it, then you will know" is applied most consistently in occupations in which people might die if the work is done badly. Although there is obviously classroom training for surgeons, the U.S. military, and some for airplane pilots, in all of these occupations, training quickly turns to learning by doing. In surgery, there is an old, nearly true saying describing how a resident learns a new procedure: "Hear one, see one, do one."[45] People in these occupations learn primarily by doing because, regardless of how well they can answer questions about how to do their craft, we only want them to use their knowledge on us when they have shown they can actually do the task.

As we will see in the next chapter, many organizations and managers would rather talk, conceptualize, and rationalize about problems and issues than confront them directly. In business and business education and training, the principle seems to be "hear one, see one, say one." And, ironically, in many companies people are more likely to get ahead by talking smart than by doing smart and productive things. So our next chapter considers how talk substitutes for action and, in the process, impedes many companies from turning what they know about enhancing performance into action.

|2| When Talk Substitutes for Action

ONE OF THE MAIN BARRIERS to turning knowledge into action is the tendency to treat *talking* about something as equivalent to actually *doing* something about it. Talking about what should be done, writing plans about what the organization should do, and collecting and analyzing data to help decide what actions to take can guide and motivate action. Indeed, rhetoric is frequently an essential first step toward taking action. But just talking about what to do isn't enough. Nor is planning for the future enough to produce that future. Something has to get done, and someone has to do it. Yet, in case after case, managers act as if talking about what they or others in the organization ought to do is as good as actually getting it done.

For example, David Kelley, CEO of the award-winning product design firm IDEO Product Development, told us how surprised he was to find that, in firm after firm he visited, executives acted as if merely hearing and talking about methods for doing innovative work eliminated the need to actually use these methods. Kelley's reaction to seeing so much talk and so little action was to give a speech to executives in which he asserted that an obvious, but often ignored, "secret" to becoming an innovative company is realizing that "*talking* about multidisciplinary teams is not enough."[1]

Of course, talk is indispensable for inspiring action. Talking and interacting are what organizations are about. How else can interdependent activities be coordinated, people motivated, knowledge and ideas generated and exchanged? So, the question is, How and when do talk and related acts, such as planning and analysis, fail to instigate action? When do these activities become substitutes for doing anything? Our observations of organizations in diverse industries have generated insights about these questions, particularly as we compared firms that were effective in turning knowledge into action with those that were mired in talking instead of acting.

The problem of using talk as a substitute for action occurs in many organizations. This chapter shows different ways that talk substitutes for action, explains why talk that has little or no effect on action is often overvalued, and describes steps organizations can and do take to avoid this trap.

How Talk Is a Substitute for Action: Variations on the Theme

Making Decisions as a Substitute for Action: The Shift to a Project-Based Organization That Never Happened

In some organizations that we studied, there seemed to be an unspoken, but powerful, belief that once a decision had been made to do something, no additional work was needed to make sure it was implemented. Decision making seemed most likely to be used in lieu of action, or at least didn't seem to lead to action, when there where few mechanisms to ensure that agreed-upon actions would occur, when people liked each other and so disagreements were masked by public agreement, and when there was little sense of urgency because short-term earnings were acceptable. All of these factors were present in one manufacturing firm that wanted to speed up the product design and development process. The company hired an executive who had a history of leading fast and successful product development efforts. This executive led a two–day workshop intended to teach people about the culture and work methods that are needed to support rapid product development. The workshop resulted in a list of "ten actionable steps." The very first recommendation on that list was to become a project–based organization.

The decision made a lot of business sense. By giving projects budgets and deadlines, there would be more focus on the development cycle. Because the allocation of people's time would now have costs, there would be an incentive to economize on person–hours, staff projects more carefully with the right people, and get the project completed. The lack of a product– or project–oriented structure meant that people worked on multiple projects to diversify their portfolio, to build functional expertise, and to gain reputations for saying smart things, rather than devoting themselves to any particular product. Most projects had no owners. People spent the bulk of their time going from one progress meeting to another on the various projects. They also spent hour after hour sending and reading numerous e-mail messages associated with each project. One manager complained that she couldn't get anything done because, as a member of many different project teams, she was receiving and trying to read more than a thousand e-mail messages a week. The work on most projects moved slowly because people spent so much time in meetings charting the progress (or lack thereof) on the various products and sending and reading e-mail about the projects.

The decision to move to a more project–based structure emerged from a careful benchmarking process. There were explicit comparisons of the firm's management practices with other firms in ways that showed specific changes in work methods and reward systems that could be adopted. As a consequence of this analysis, the leaders of the firm became quite knowledgeable and articulate in explaining why a more project-oriented focus would enhance their product development process.

The senior management team, including the chief executive, apparently made a decision to move to a more project-based organization structure. We say "apparently" because there was some question as to whether the decision, although made, was truly accepted. The culture of the company and the history of the executives working together dictated that little disagreement on fundamental decisions would be openly expressed. Instead, there might be public acceptance but then nothing done to implement the decision. As the vice president of research and development described it:

> The CEO decided that it ought to be done. . . . The head of engineering agreed that it ought to be done. . . . He didn't agree to do it, but he agreed it ought to be done. It was communicated to the rank and file so they were all expecting it to happen, at least on some level. And nothing's happened.

More than a year later, nothing had changed. There had been no change in the formal structure, no change in the method of assigning people to projects, no change in the budgeting and resource allocation process, no change in the performance evaluation and review process to highlight project-relevant performance, and, most important, almost no change in the pace or quality of the product development process. Projects still did not have managers with real budgets and profit and loss responsibility. How could this absence of implementation have occurred, given the consensus that the change was both necessary and useful?

There are many answers to this question, some of which we will explore in subsequent chapters. But, it seems clear from interviewing the participants that the belief was that since the group had talked extensively about the issue, had all publicly agreed on what needed to be done, and had even talked about the pros and cons of specific product design practices, the problem was solved. It was as if talking made things real, that conversation, in and of itself, made things happen. There were no mechanisms in place to actually track implementation and, as short-term business results remained quite good, there was little sense of urgency to fix the problem. So, the executives never bothered to actually *do* or change anything to ensure that the decision they made was actually implemented. The leaders had forgotten an important truism in organizations: A decision, by itself, changes nothing.

Making Presentations as a Substitute for Action: BHP Executives Manage from a Darkened Room

In the large manufacturing firm just described, there seemed to be an unstated—and irrational—belief that once the decision was made, no additional work would be needed to implement it. An even more extreme form of substituting talk for action occurs when managers act as if talk, writing, and analysis are the main tasks that they, or anyone else in the firm, ever need to do. This problem seems to be particularly acute in large organizations, especially where many senior executives are financially oriented and out of touch with how work is done in their firms. Managers in such firms seem to spend much of their time preparing, delivering, and listening to flashy and well-rehearsed presentations that are designed to impress one another. Executives devote a great deal of time to presentations, but they often spend little or no time "on the ground," trying to directly learn about and improve work processes.

For example, Burgess Winter, an Irishman who had spent his career in the copper mining industry, accomplished a remarkable transformation in a short time at Magma Copper after becoming CEO in 1988. In a three-year period, by building cooperative relations with the unions and undertaking a transformation in workplace management practices, the operating cost per pound of copper declined 24 percent, production from the company's mines grew 30 percent, and the company enjoyed an overall increase in productivity on the order of 50 percent.[2] Magma was purchased by Broken Hill Proprietary (BHP), a large Australian firm, in 1996—for a price representing an increase in shareholder value of about 700 percent over an eight-year period. Winter was then given the responsibility of managing all of BHP's copper operations throughout the world, not just Magma. Within a year, however, Winter left the company. After the purchase by BHP, Magma's performance began deteriorating almost immediately, and within 18 months, BHP took a $1 billion write-off against the impairment of the asset. What had happened?

BHP was a large and bureaucratic organization that emphasized financial and business planning and forecasting meetings, financial reports, and centralized control from corporate headquarters. These management practices sometimes created problems in BHP divisions. For instance, one high-performing unit could only give 2.75 percent average raises one year because the overall corporation had done poorly and that was the centrally determined raise amount. People in the division were angry and disheartened that their excellent work and performance could not be recognized because of factors over which they had no control. Several divisions claimed that the corporate center had restricted their business development capability and complained about the time and energy lost in meetings, report preparation, and especially in developing and delivering presentations. In the case of the copper operations, Burgess Winter described to us how he spent his time after the acquisition and why he had found such difficulty and frustration in doing his new job at BHP:

> I spent almost two weeks of every month flying back and forth to Melbourne [the company headquarters in Australia] and while there, sitting in a darkened room—watching overhead after overhead being

projected on the screen. There were plans, reports, presentations of strategy, presentations of financials from throughout the organization, and so forth. But the purpose of the sessions wasn't really to learn from other parts of the organization. Instead, the agenda was to impress your colleagues with the quality of the presentation you were giving. I kept trying to remind my associates that we weren't in the business of making overheads, but in the business of mining and smelting ores, making steel, refining oil, and so forth. If we had been in the business of making presentations, we would be doing a lot better than we were. Everything was controlled from headquarters, and headquarters felt that these reports and meetings kept them on top of what was going on. The problem was there were so many hours spent in meetings and presentations that there wasn't time to actually be in the field, figuring out what was going on and actually improving operations.

Preparing Documents as a Substitute for Action: The Leadership through Quality Program at Xerox

BHP is not alone. There are many other firms where planning activities, holding meetings to discuss problems and their solutions, and preparing written reports are mistaken for actually accomplishing something. Such firms produce actions: meetings, conversations, and the generation of reports. They just don't produce actions that have much effect on implementing what the firm knows, or turning knowledge into action. An example is Xerox Corporation's implementation of a Total Quality Management approach in its Leadership Through Quality program, which got bogged down in producing and discussing written documents. According to a case study of this effort,[3] the program was first discussed in the summer of 1982 and then launched in early 1983. The program's goal was to help Xerox overcome problems in manufacturing–cost competitiveness, time to market, product quality, and customer service. This program was backed enthusiastically by the CEO at the time, David Kearns, who saw it as a fundamental part of Xerox's competitive strategy. Apparently Xerox took being a document company quite seriously, because the Leadership Through Quality program produced mostly books, manuals, meetings, and accompanying materials:

> By August 1983, the team had produced a second Blue Book, a corporate implementation plan. . . . The 25 executives who had met in February reconvened . . . to work through the Blue Book. . . . This meeting resulted in the issuance of the completed strategic plan, now called the Green Book. . . . The bulk of the 92–page document concentrated on guidelines for implementation.[4]

One member of the Quality Implementation Team had, from the start, worried about substituting meetings and documents for action:

> We would have a great idea and build a program around it. There would be special forms and 3–ring binders of instructions and reports and special meetings. Soon there was so much busy work, it overshadowed the original intent. Things became so bureaucratic that they died of their own weight.[5]

In hindsight, this concern about substituting meetings and documents for real action was justified. In 1987, four years after the Leadership Through Quality initiative began, implementation remained spotty. Approximately 70,000 Xerox people had completed six days of quality training, 420,000 person–days of training. Yet assessment interviews revealed that only 25 percent of Xerox people felt that the company used the Leadership Through Quality processes to a great or very great extent, only 15 percent felt that recognition and rewards were based on quality, and only 13 percent reported using cost of quality in their decision making.[6] Although some business measures of performance had improved in the interim, the summary assessment noted, "Despite all the effort, quality is not the basic business principle today at Xerox."[7] How could so many meetings, task forces, and documents produce so little difference? Our answer is that the small effect was *because of*, not *in spite of*, the program and how it evolved. In Xerox, like the traditional manufacturing firm and BHP discussed earlier, talk, meetings, documents, decisions, and analytical processes came to substitute for action, rather than guiding and facilitating action.

There is an interesting postscript to the Xerox case that illustrates how to overcome the tendency to substitute talk for action: Impose a real deadline with real measures:

> Congress created the Malcolm Baldrige National Quality Award . . . to encourage U.S. companies to strive for improved quality in all aspects of their operations. . . . Kearns and Allaire were intrigued by the award. . . . In December 1988 Xerox launched a concerted year-long bid to compete for the Baldrige, in the process undertaking a gruelling internal analysis. . . . According to Kearns . . . the real value of the exercise lay in forcing Xerox to focus harder than ever on its quality goals. . . . The following year . . . the company's Business Products and Systems division was one of only two recipients of the 1989 Baldrige Award.[8]

Using Mission Statements as a Substitute for Action: A Securities Firm Espouses, but Does Not Enact, Core Values

Mission statements are among the most blatant and common means that organizations use to substitute talk for action. Don't get us wrong. We believe that mission statements, vision statements, and corporate values can contribute to long-term success. Much evidence suggests that having a core underlying philosophy that is widely communicated, under-stood, and shared is important for organizational manage-ment.[9] The problem is that there are too many organizations where *having* a mission or values statement written down somewhere is confused with *implementing* those values. These firms act as if going through the process of developing a statement, perhaps publishing it on little cards that everyone carries or on plaques or posters on the walls, is enough to help the company perform better. It has a mission, it has a vision, it has values. So, now it can go on about its business.

There is no reason to expect that just compiling and dis-playing a philosophy and core values will change how peo-ple act. Yet executives act as if these statements had magical powers to satisfy customers, increase quality, and make employees happier and more productive. Because so many managers act as if such magic will occur, Eileen Shapiro suggested that one definition of a mission statement is "In some companies, a talisman, hung in public places, to ward off evil spirits."[10]

The following example shows how a mission statement helped convince leaders in one securities firm that they did not need to address a problem, even though they recog-nized the problem and the firm had done analyses to see how it could be ameliorated. The firm had a mission state-ment that, if followed, meant the problem could not hap-pen, so no steps were taken to turn knowledge about reducing the problem into action.

Investment banks and securities firms all have financial analyst programs. These programs typically recruit top undergraduates from the best schools to work for the firm for a few years before the analysts return to school to earn an MBA degree. Many investment firms are concerned about the "rate of return" on their analyst programs. Ana-lysts who have a bad experience with a firm rarely return after business school. The firm loses talent it has spent time and money developing. Worse yet from the firm's point of view, analysts who had bad experiences tell their fellow

MBAs, making the firm's recruiting efforts more difficult and costly. Conversely, if analysts have a great experience in the firm, they are more likely to return and to tell their classmates good things about the firm, which will make it easier to recruit top MBAs. Executives in every securities firm and investment bank understand the simple dynamics described above and know, at least intuitively, that the costs of turnover and a negative reputation are substantial, particularly when the market for talent is hot and potential recruits have many options.

One key problem in analyst retention is how badly the analysts are treated. But top managers in these firms seldom see this problem partly because their firms have laudatory mission and vision statements and they come to believe that those statements reflect how things actually operate. One prominent securities firm has a set of values that top management promulgates consistently and publishes at every opportunity. These are (1) respect for the individual, (2) teamwork, and (3) integrity. Executives seem to believe that these values ensure that the firm will treat its analysts well and fairly. The values are written down, they are believed, and they are viewed as important. But they are not lived, at least in the analyst program. One analysis of the firm's program states: "Yet, the words seem to have replaced action. As later interviews . . . show, . . . analysts feel like principles one and two are not carried out." At this firm, recruiting is "seen as a second tier responsibility." People who are seen as having real economic value do transactions, not recruiting. This certainly does not send a message of respect for the analysts the firm tries to recruit. This problem is compounded by the work the analysts are asked to do: "Analysts want responsibility, but get secretarial work. . . . Management's underlying belief about analysts is that they can not be trusted and will most likely make major mistakes . . . [the firm] hires people who are over qualified for the position." Throughout, the culture sends the message that "analysts are not part of the team but instead a short-term contractor with limited potential."[11] This behavior conveys a lack of respect for individuals and their talents. Analysts are not treated as individuals at all, but are stereotyped as low status, low skill, and mistake prone simply because they are labeled as analysts, members of a group at the bottom of the organization's caste system.

Teamwork is also not an enacted value at this firm, a failing common to most securities firms and investment banks. There is much talk about teams, and teamwork is often an articulated value, but few firms have team-based compensation, and the pay system instead encourages a star or free-agent mentality. This look-out-for-yourself point of view augurs poorly for the bankers' relationships with the analysts. They are too busy looking out for themselves in the short term, for their own transactions and deal flow, to worry about retaining someone years down the road.

This firm is just one of many we have seen in which leaders act as if having something in their mission or values statement meant that it must be true. It is as if wishing, or talking, made it so. When the executives see problems generated by real practices that clash with their firm's mission and values, they seem to believe that the problems can't be real or as described. They don't seem to be capable of accepting that behavior can be very different from the values the firm holds dear. And they think that nothing needs to change; they believe that since they are talking, they are also doing what they are talking about. This is precisely what happened in the securities firm just described. Senior leadership refused to believe the problem existed, even in the face of solid evidence, because it was inconsistent with their espoused mission and core values.

Planning as a Substitute for Action: BHP versus AES

Related to the "mission statement" problem is the "planning" problem. Just as people confuse talk with action and mission statements with reality, they frequently confuse

having a plan and doing planning with actually implementing the plan and learning something. There are file
cabinets in organizations filled with plans and strategies
that remain unimplemented. An enormous amount of
time, effort, and attention are consumed in the planning
and analysis process, resources that might be better spent
interacting with and changing the environment rather than
contemplating and talking about it. Recall the example of
BHP earlier in this chapter. BHP was and continues to be an
organization that values planning and, as a consequence,
produces wonderful documents and presentations. Time
and attention devoted to planning and to planning meetings is time and attention potentially taken away from
addressing business problems and from being in the field
learning and addressing the organization's issues.

There seems to be little connection between how much
effort an organization devotes to planning or even how
well it does planning and how well it performs. BHP is
great in planning but poor in operations and financial performance. In contrast, the AES Corporation, which builds
power plants intended to last 40 years, has no central planning or strategy function. By reacting with "disciplined
opportunism" to opportunities as they present themselves,
the firm has grown at a prodigious rate in what is often
considered to be a relatively stable industry. The company
has more than 400 people out drumming up new business,
more than any of its rivals, "half of them at the plant level,
a measure of the extreme decentralization and incentive-
building nature of the company's structure."[12] Relatively
junior people, in both hierarchical rank and age and experience, have the opportunity to pursue new business
opportunities, and do so. For instance, a large transaction in
Australia was conducted by a team headed by someone
who, after completing the deal, left AES to return to business school—a young man in his twenties. This is the opportunism. The discipline comes because people are expected
to get advice from their colleagues, there is active traffic

on the e-mail network that everyone can see as deals are discussed, the company has a high hurdle rate for expected returns, and it virtually never chases deals just for the sake of closing them. Instead of central planning, the company has placed its faith in having people all over the world gathering information and making decisions—a form of distributed intelligence that has thus far worked very well.

Existing research on the effectiveness of formal planning efforts is clear: Planning is essentially unrelated to organizational performance. Summarizing extensive quantitative and case study research, Henry Mintzberg wrote:

> A number of biased researchers set out to prove that planning paid, and collectively, they proved no such thing. All kinds of anecdotes have highlighted a litany of problems with planning, and the facts about leading-edge efforts to apply planning . . . proved even more discouraging.[13]

Just as mission statements and talk can substitute for action rather than informing such action, planning can be a ritualistic exercise disconnected from operations and from transforming knowledge into action. Of course, planning can facilitate developing knowledge and generating action. But it does not invariably do so and often does the opposite.

Why Does Talk Matter So Much? Evaluations Based on Sounding Smart and Saying a Lot

Why is so much emphasis sometimes placed on what people say, and so little emphasis placed on what they do or enable others to do? On the face of it, this doesn't seem to make much sense. After all, aren't managers (and perhaps management consultants) who enable things to get done likely to gain more financial rewards and greater stature than their counterparts who are all talk and no action? We found a number of reasons why people who are all talk often reap more rewards than they deserve. These reasons have implications for identifying where the problem of substituting talk for action will be most insidious.

Smart Talk Happens Now, Smart Actions Happen Later

It is a natural human tendency to form impressions of others. The literature suggests that first impressions are particularly potent and often difficult to alter, and some research even suggests that we begin to form impressions of others in the first moments we meet them. For instance, research on how firms select new employees shows that interviewers often decide whether or not they want to hire a candidate during the first few minutes of the job interview.[14] This natural human tendency to assess and evaluate others is amplified in organizations in which managers must make recurring judgments as part of their jobs: not just who to hire, but also who to promote, who to assign a specific task or project, whose advice to seek, and so forth.

Evaluations, not just annual performance evaluations, and impressions are an omnipresent part of organizational life. So the question becomes, On what basis are these judgments and evaluations formed? There are at least two possibilities that are reasonably independent of one another: (1) We can form our impressions of others based on how well they perform, how well they get things accomplished, and what they contribute to the organization through their actions; or (2) we can form our impressions of others based on how smart they seem. In many instances, this latter information—how smart someone seems—is the only data immediately at hand. Appearing smart is mostly accomplished by sounding smart; being confident, articulate, eloquent, and filled with interesting information and ideas; and having a good vocabulary.

A problem arises when smart talk is confused with good performance. A colleague who has served on a business school advisory group—senior executives who meet occasionally to give advice to the school—described how he learned the difference between smart talk and great performance. When he joined the advisory board, he met two bank CEOs who were also serving. One looked like a banker and sounded brilliant. He could talk articulately about financial issues all over the world, about financial institution strategies, about the changing competitive landscape. He was, if nothing else, a smart talker. The other banker seemed much less smooth. He didn't dress as sharply and wasn't as glib and articulate. Our colleague confided that when he first met this other person, he wondered how he had ever attained his CEO position. Over time, however, it became clear how and why the less "smart" person achieved his job: His bank has been, over the past decade, one of the consistently best performers, both in terms of financial results and customer satisfaction. The bank led by the smart talker has been a notorious underperformer, having trouble growing its revenues, and increasing its profits only through a vigorous cost-cutting program. Our colleague learned, from firsthand experience, the difference between sounding smart and smart performance. The two aren't always negatively related, but talking smart and being smart are far from perfectly correlated.

Talk, sounding smart or not, is all we often evaluate. It is all we see at first. You might not know how well a person can manage, but you can quickly assess how smart he or she sounds. Second, particularly in large, complex systems or in organizations in which people move around a lot, you can't know what a person has accomplished because it is not very visible. Overall organizational performance comes from the actions of many interdependent people, so discerning any one person's contribution is problematic and fraught with error. People also move from job to job so much that it is difficult to know, unambiguously, what any given person has accomplished. What you can know immediately and with less ambiguity is how smart a person sounds.

Negative People Seem Smarter

Unfortunately for getting anything done in organizations, one of the best ways of sounding smart is to be critical of others' ideas. The devastating intellectual put–down is sometimes part and parcel of the academic game. It is largely harmless in universities since little of consequence happens as a result. Much to our surprise, however, put–downs are often part of the corporate game as well. At a large financial institution we studied, people scored points by criticizing others' ideas in meetings. This behavior was particularly likely to occur in front of senior management, as junior executives sought status by appearing to be smart through critiquing the ideas of their peers, something that diminished the status of their victims and increased their own status.

The idea that being critical of others makes a person appear smarter isn't just based on what we have observed in organizations. Professor Teresa Amabile of the Harvard Business School published an experiment titled "Brilliant but Cruel" that showed that people who gave negative book reviews were perceived by others as less likeable but more intelligent, competent, and expert than people who wrote positive reviews of the same books. She summarized her findings by noting, "Only pessimism sounds profound. Optimism sounds superficial."[15] But, at the end of the day, something still needs to get done. If all that has happened is that those with the courage to actually propose something have been devastated in the process, the organization will be filled with clever put–down artists and with inactivity. This situation arises because the people are so clever, and so determined to appear clever, that they will succeed at critiquing everything to death.

It is always possible to find a reason to say no to some idea or proposal. People in many organizations are remarkably skilled at making excuses about why something can't be done, why something won't work, and, therefore, why the present, albeit imperfect, condition is better than trying something new and actually implementing new knowledge or ideas. Be very wary of judging people just on the basis of how smart they sound, and particularly on their ability to find problems or fault with ideas. These are dangerous people. They are smart enough to stop things from happening, but not action oriented enough to find ways of overcoming the problems they have identified.

People Who Talk a Lot Have More Stature

Another reason that talk is so valued in organizations is that people who say more are more likely to be judged by others as influential, high status, and as leaders. We once asked a new division manager why she was selected for the job over several other functional managers and how things had changed since she had been promoted. She joked, "They gave me the job because I couldn't keep my mouth shut and wouldn't let anyone else say anything and now that I am the boss, they expect me to talk even more than before." This manager's informal theory is supported by group dynamics research on how talking time and interrupting others affects how group members perceive each other. As we might expect from our discussion of smart talk, studies of leadership in unstructured, leaderless groups show that people who are viewed as making more intelligent and valuable comments are more likely to emerge as leaders. But these studies also support what has been called the "babble" or "blabber-mouth" theory of leadership. Independent of the quality of the comments, people who talk longer and who make more comments are, compared with less talkative group members, more likely to emerge as leaders in new groups, to be identified as leaders by observers of the group, to be viewed as influential by both group members and outsiders, and to have greater influence over group decisions.[16]

Anthropological research in numerous preindustrial societies, as well as observations in modern organizations, suggests that talking more than others is a means that people use to win what has been called the "conversational marketplace."[17] In addition, the fact that others allow a person to interrupt them and to take more time is a sign that the individual has achieved high status in a group. George Maclay and Humphrey Knipe put it this way in *The Pecking Order in Human Society*:

> Whenever an informal dominance order establishes itself, we can usually work out the rank of the individuals involved by measuring the length of time that they are allowed to talk. As a rule, the most influential person will be allowed the most talking time. . . . On a busy occasion, those at the bottom of the hierarchy are likely to find that they can barely get a word in edgewise. An individual who talks more than others feel he deserves will gradually be ignored.[18]

For better or worse, people who want to get ahead in organizations or to achieve influence often learn that talking a lot helps them reach such goals, perhaps even more reliably than taking action or inspiring others to act. Once people achieve high status, they are expected to talk more than ever. Dominating the group's air time is one way to let everyone know that they are still in charge. As we show next, business schools and management consulting firms reinforce the view that prestige is achieved by winning in the conversational marketplace, not by being best at turning smart ideas into organizational action.

How Business Schools and Management Consulting Firms Magnify the Problem

The tendency for organizations to place too much value on people who seem smart and who talk a lot, and too little value on people who do smart things and get a lot of things done, is exacerbated by the way that MBAs and executives are taught and by the methods used in most management consulting firms. Many executives in contemporary organizations have been to business school. And even senior managers who don't have MBA degrees often have attended executive education programs that are taught by business school faculty. Moreover, business schools currently have a great deal of prestige and allure.

Now consider the essence of the management education process—the business school experience—as practiced at leading institutions in the United States as well as those throughout the world. The essence of this education process is *talk*—learning how to sound smart in case discussions or to write smart things (talk turned into writing) on essay examinations based on business cases. In business school classes, a substantial part of students' grades is based on how much they say and how smart they sound in class discussion. Robert Reid wrote a book about his first year in Harvard Business School's MBA program. He nicely describes the classroom process in which students learn how to talk and learn that sounding smart in class is what really matters in his chapter "The Battle for Air":

> My general concern about class participation increased throughout the week. . . . My urgency was heightened by the fact that grades (and First Year Honors! And McKinsey! . . .) depended so heavily on in-class commentary. . . . The opportunity to speak was such a precious commodity that most people

were terrified about blowing it by saying something
shallow, repetitive, or . . . stupid when they were
finally called on.[19]

The policy of grading on class participation makes ped-
agogical sense for a number of reasons. These grading practices encourage students to come to class prepared. By
being more actively involved in the class, students are
more engaged in the learning process. Grading on class
participation invariably encourages more frequent, enthusiastic, and thoughtful student comments, which creates
more energy in the classroom. These are all desirable goals.
But how is class participation evaluated? By sounding
smart, by making insightful, intelligent, facile, and relevant
comments on the issue under discussion. Not by being able
to *do* anything about the situation or to be able to actually
implement the recommendations and insights that emerge
in the conversation. It is significant that at the very beginning of their training in business, and then throughout
their continuing education experiences, people learn that
what matters is sounding clever in front of your peers and
your boss—the professor. They learn that what matters is
the ability to *talk* intelligently and convincingly about business problems.

If people learn that smart talk is what matters in school,
the lessons after school only tend to reinforce this message. The hottest job market for business school graduates
right now is management consulting, with offers typically
exceeding six figures (in U.S. dollars) common for graduates
of major business schools. Consulting firms expanded rapidly after the downsizing of middle management and corporate staffs. This downsizing, much of which resulted from
advice given by these same consulting firms, has caused
many firms to hire consultants to do the work that was
once done by those "excess" middle managers and staff. The
demand for people is so great that consulting firms are

avidly recruiting not just newly minted business school graduates, but also experienced people with the right stuff to succeed in the consulting industry.

What constitutes the right stuff for succeeding in consulting? What do consultants do? More to the point, what is their work product? Written reports and presentations filled with sharp-looking overheads! Management consulting, one of the hottest and most prestigious occupations, certainly as measured by the economic rewards for its practitioners, sells talk. This is not to discount the value that management consultants can provide. Some firms offer insights on the macroeconomy, others provide industry expertise, systematic data and analysis, or valuable, novel perspectives. But what they rarely provide is implementation. Members of these firms often complain that their reports and presentations do not lead to organizational action. There is increasing talk by these firms about implementation. But at the end of the day, what consultants provide is advice—talk—and only occasionally do they get involved in the details of doing something. So, one can be a plant manager and make, depending on the firm, the industry, and the size of the plant, between $80,000 and $100,000. Or one can be in the business of giving advice to the plant manager and make about twice as much. Not only does this pose an interesting career choice, it sends a message about the value the economy currently places on being able to actually run something compared with being able to *talk* about running something.

As we suggested earlier, this emphasis on talking smart and talking a lot, first in the classroom and later on the job, seems to reflect an unstated but widely followed belief that talk is something that happens now, and action is something that happens later. The idea is that as long as we are talking about doing the right thing now, then we are using our time wisely even if we never quite get around to doing it. Steve Mariucci, the head coach of the San Francisco 49ers football team, gave a speech in which he noted that an almost identical problem has occurred on every team he has known: Players and coaches talk about what plays they should design or practice and what new coaching techniques or exercise regimens they should implement, but they often don't get around to doing these things. Mariucci told the crowd that he tries to fight this problem by never wearing a watch, because "I always know what time it is. It is always NOW. And NOW is when you should do it."[20]

Talk is also valued because, as noted earlier, the quantity and "quality" of talk can be assessed immediately, but the quality of leadership or management capability, the ability to get things done, can be assessed only with a greater time lag. Suspending evaluation until more tangible outcomes occur is difficult for several reasons. First, doing so clashes with the natural human tendency to form impressions quickly, to categorize and stereotype people equally swiftly, and to resist information that contradicts such first impressions. Second, it does not fit within the time scale of most organizations' performance appraisal and career progression systems. If I must appraise you more rapidly than I can reliably assess how well you are actually doing in terms of job performance, one of the few things I can use in my assessment of you is how competent you make yourself sound. Similarly, if the organization moves people to new positions on a time scale that precludes them ever suffering or enjoying the consequences of their decisions and actions, it ensures that people can only be evaluated on how smart and competent they seem to be—impressions based mostly on how they sound rather than what they do.

The Mystique of Complexity

Status Seeking through Jargon

In addition to saying smart things and talking a lot, another way to impress others is by using complex language, complex ideas, complex sentence structure, and complex analysis in addressing organizational issues. Academics are infamous for trying to increase their status by using complex language to mask simple ideas. C. Wright Mills, a famous sociologist, noted that the complex language used by academics usually has nothing to do with the complexity of the subject matter. Rather, "it has to do almost entirely with certain confusions of the academic . . . about his own status. . . . Desire for status is one reason that academic men [sic] slip so easily into unintelligibility."[21]

Managers are often just as guilty as academics of using complex, incomprehensible jargon to express ideas that could be expressed in simple language. Unfortunately, using complex language and ambiguous terminology confuses people and inhibits action. One organization we studied gave employees laptop computers to provide them access to e-mail and the Internet, but described this as a "transformation to a virtual organization." This jargon confused people, who thought that the laptops were part of some massive reorganization and change in work practices. This resulted in weeks of spreading rumors (e.g., "our office is closing and we all have to work from our homes") and general confusion.

The use of complex language hampers implementation even more, however, when leaders or managers don't really understand the meaning of the language they are using and its implications for action. It is hard enough to explain what a complex idea means for action when you understand it and others don't. It is impossible when you use terms that sound impressive but you don't really understand what they mean. We discovered the severity of this problem when we started asking managers to define the jargon they were using and what it meant for how people in their organizations ought to act. During the past five years, we have asked this question of managers who used terms such as *learning organization, balanced scorecard, business process reengineering, chaos theory, paradigm,* and *virtual organization.* In many instances, the managers were unable to give any definition at all or, if they gave one, it was woefully inadequate.

Confusing Ease of Understanding
with Ease of Implementation

Complex and incomprehensible talk wastes time if managers just use it to gain status. Complicated talk does even more harm, however, when managers actually try to use it as a basis for designing structures, work, procedures, and strategies. In an effort to gain status through complexity, the leaders wind up confusing others in their organizations and hinder the ability to turn knowledge into action. Few senior executives would describe their strategy as Dennis Bakke, the CEO of the enormously successful global independent electric power producer AES, did: "We try a bunch of stuff, we see what works, and we call that our strategy." Rather, complexity is valued in many firms. After all, if few people are smart enough to comprehend what the firm is doing, the management must be *really* smart!

This preference for complicated language, strategies, and concepts is based on an idea that is at once partly right and party wrong. The logic is as follows: (1) Firms seek to develop sustainable competitive advantage, which requires, by definition, doing something that is difficult to imitate; (2) it seems logical that more-complex management systems, strategies, ideas, and analyses are more difficult to imitate than simpler versions; so, (3) sustainable competitive advantage is built by doing complex (and consequently difficult to do) things. A corollary of this logic is that simple prescriptions cannot possibly be of much value. If these simple prescriptions were useful and valuable, everyone would be doing them already because of their simplicity. Since they aren't being widely imitated, they can't be worth much. This reasoning applies with particular force to old ideas. Surely if the ideas could benefit firms, they would already be widely adopted. So the logic suggests that the only rare things worth doing must be things that are rare because of their complexity. This kind of logic makes calling something "common sense" an insult. Yet it is a compliment. In the world of management and organizations, common sense is far from common.

You're Likely to Find Talk Substituting for Action When

- No follow-up is done to ensure that what was said is actually done

- People forget that merely making a decision doesn't change anything

- Planning, meetings, and report writing become defined as "action" that is valuable in its own right, even if it has no effect on what people actually do

- People believe that because they have said it and it is in the mission statement, it must be true and it must be happening in the firm

- People are evaluated on how smart they sound rather than on what they do

- Talking a lot is mistaken for doing a lot

- Complex language, ideas, processes, and structures are thought to be better than simple ones

- There is a belief that managers are people who talk, and others do

- Internal status comes from talking a lot, interrupting, and being critical of others' ideas

---

The fundamental premise of this chain of reasoning is correct. Sustainable competitive advantage is built by doing things that are difficult to imitate. But this line of reasoning confuses ease of *understanding* with ease of *implementation*. Ideas like decentralization and delegation of decision-making responsibility, sharing performance information, recruiting for job skills as well as cultural fit, and treating people with respect and dignity are easy to understand. But actually delegating, a process that entails giving up decision-making power, is quite difficult to accomplish in practice. Sharing information with all of your people entails giving up the power and prestige that comes from knowing things that others don't. Recruiting for cultural fit instead of just job skills requires the patience to develop the ability to do so and being clear about dimensions of fit. Actually putting your people first and treating them as if they matter to the organization's success, although easy to talk about and easy to understand, is notoriously difficult to implement.

Complexity interferes with turning knowledge into action because for knowledge to be implemented, it usually must be understood by large numbers of people who often work in widely scattered locales. Compared with simple ideas, complex concepts are more difficult to communicate broadly to lots of people in dispersed locations. Moreover, for knowledge, particularly about specific management practices, to be implemented, that knowledge must have meaning that is reasonably stable and is consistent over time. Think back to some of the examples from the first chapter. For instance, Honda's principle for training its suppliers in quality, "actual part, actual place, actual situation,"[22] is deceptively simple. David Russo maintains that the SAS Institute's success in building one of the best systems in the software industry for attracting and retaining talent came from recognizing that the firm's most important assets walk out the door every night and that the company needs them back the next day. The firm treats its people as if they really matter, which means taking care of the people that are important to the employees, including their husbands and wives, children, domestic partners, and parents. It is a system that not only reflects common sense but, because of its clarity and simplicity, can also be implemented even as SAS has grown to 5,000 employees operating all over the world. Simple, clear, logical principles can be communicated more readily and can be more easily implemented in a consistent fashion than complex or vague ones.

How Some Organizations Avoid Hollow Talk and Promote Action

Now that we better understand some of the reasons that talk is used as a substitute for action, we can see how some organizations avoid this problem. We argued that management education frequently teaches and rewards people for sounding smart and that the profession of management consulting is based in important respects on talk and presentations. Other companies and people without MBAs also use talk as a substitute for action. We don't reject informal talk, formal presentations, and quantitative analysis. These are often important precursors to intelligent action. It's just that they are not substitutes for action. And, obviously, hiring MBAs or outside consultants who have lots of talent and good ideas can be useful. But there are trade-offs involved that are not always recognized. Bringing people into the organization whose primary skill is talk—as either employees or consultants—may mean that, along with the ideas and skills, the firm has imported barriers to acting on the knowledge it has purchased.

We found that many organizations that avoid using talk as a substitute for action do one or more of the following:

- Have career systems that bring people into senior leadership positions who actually have an intimate knowledge of the organization's work processes because they have performed them themselves and have grown up with or been promoted from within the organization

- Have a culture that values simplicity and does not reward unnecessary complexity—a culture in which calling something "common sense" is a compliment rather than an insult, and in which the language used is simple, clear, and direct

- Use language that is action oriented and, even more important, have follow-up processes to ensure that decisions are implemented and that talk results in action and not just more talk
- Do not accept excuses and criticisms for why things won't work or can't be done, but rather reframe the objections into problems to be overcome rather than reasons not to try

Leaders Who Know and Do the Work

Many historians assert that Thomas Edison's greatest invention was not any of the objects that he is renowned for inventing, such as the phonograph, electric light, or movie camera. Rather, they argue, Edison's greatest invention was building a business, "invention factories," that produced hundreds of diverse inventions every year. One of the main reasons Edison was able to enjoy decades of success in his laboratories in Menlo Park and West Orange, New Jersey, was that he worked closely with people in the laboratories conceiving, testing, and developing ideas. Despite the myth that Edison was a lone inventor, many of the thousands of inventions produced by these labs were actually developed by people who worked for him, not Edison himself. Historians of technology suggest that Edison's working knowledge and intimate involvement in the work of the laboratories helped him make better decisions about which ideas were worth pursuing and which were not.[23]

The SAS Institute, a $750 million privately owned software firm, has been tremendously successful—22 years of double-digit growth, listed as one of the best places to work in America by *Fortune* and other magazines, such as *Working Mother*, and recognized as an outstanding company by *Business Week*. Much of its success comes from being able to attract, retain, and use the talents of an outstanding workforce. In an intellectual capital business, such as software, this is the key to success. The importance of people in a knowledge business is not a mysterious secret—all executives understand this fact. Why has SAS been able to actually implement policies that produced a 3 percent turnover rate in 1997?

There are many reasons for the firm's success, but one is that every manager is a working manager, doing a job as well as managing others. This even extends to co-founder and CEO James Goodnight, who spends a significant percentage of his time programming and leading product development teams. When asked why he did programming and development work, he responded, "Running a big company like this is pretty boring."[24] As a result, one is as likely to find Goodnight working in an R & D building on a product development team as in his CEO office.

What does this practice by Goodnight and other senior executives accomplish? First of all, by doing programming and development work, executives like Goodnight have more credibility with those who also actually do the work. People cannot complain about a boss who does not understand their problems and issues when the boss himself does many of the same activities. Being involved in the actual work process also keeps them in touch with the core technology and work processes of the organization. By understanding the day-to-day issues in software development, customer requirements, schedules, and so forth, they constantly learn about the organization, the products, and the market by doing. The result is that leaders help everyone turn knowledge into action. And, because they are intimately familiar with the work of the organization, SAS executives are less likely to be taken in or misled by "smart talk."

We saw this theme at other organizations that were particularly successful in turning knowledge into action. They often had leaders who were intimately involved in and knowledgeable about the work process. At The Men's Wearhouse, for instance, the norm is that, when in the stores, everyone waits on customers who need assistance.

A friend was actually waited on by George Zimmer, the founder and CEO, in the Palo Alto store. Charlie Bresler, the company's executive vice president for human development, learned selling and will wait on people in the store. It is a sales–driven organization, so much so that it doesn't do as much management training and development as it thinks it should. But by being focused on a core process—sales—that everyone is familiar with and does, knowledge is acquired and turned into action almost effortlessly, because nearly everyone in the firm, including the most senior executives, is involved in this core process.

Valuing Simplicity and Avoiding Unnecessary Complexity

As we noted at the outset of this chapter, talk is inevitable in organizations and necessary for decision making and action. We observed that organizations that were better at learning and translating knowledge into action understood the virtue of simple language, simple structures, simple concepts, and the power of common sense, which is remarkably uncommon in its application. New United Motor Manufacturing (NUMMI) and Saturn both have comparatively simple structures. They have far fewer job classifications than a typical automobile plant—two or three compared with seventy or more in most U.S. plants. The plants have fewer hierarchical levels as well—three or four rather than six or seven. These simpler structures permit quicker and more complete dissemination of information, because there are fewer functional silos and fewer layers to distort communications. As such, the less complex structures and the enhanced sharing of information and knowledge they permit are part of the reason that NUMMI and Saturn are better able to turn knowledge into action.

Similarly, the turnaround at Continental Airlines, which went from having the worst on–time performance to the best in about a one-year period, occurred using simple ideas and practices. As Greg Brenneman, the president and chief operating officer, stated:

> Sometimes when I talk to people about the lessons the turnaround taught us, they say, "Well, Greg, those seem simple enough." . . . Saving Continental wasn't brain surgery. The actions to revive a moribund company usually aren't. . . . The fact is, you can't afford to think too much during a turnaround.[25]

Simple talk is valuable because it is more likely to lead to action. It is less possible to second guess or dispute simple, direct ideas. One may disagree with a simple idea or a simple philosophy, but that is transparent at the outset. Second guessing and finger pointing are largely precluded when the organization operates on the basis of simple, straightforward ideas and language.

Simple language and avoiding complexity also have another advantage. Simple philosophies, practices, and ideas are, ironically, probably unlikely to be imitated by outsiders and competitors. Since most organizations are trapped in their love of complexity, few will believe that a firm's success is based on such simple premises. Consequently, they may not even try to implement what the successful organization does. Greg Brenneman of Continental Airlines put it this way: "They have many ways of saying, 'If the solution were simple, we would have already thought of it.'"[26]

Using Language That Mobilizes Action and Following Up on Decisions

Language is omnipresent in organizations. So the question isn't whether there will be talk. Rather, the question is what kind of talk there will be and what will happen as a consequence. The test of language is whether it generates constructive action.[27] Organizations that are comparatively more successful in turning knowledge into action employ talk that mobilizes action and do things that ensure that talk results in action. Rhetoric that mobilizes action generally has some combination of the following elements: "An imaginative vision of the future, a realistic portrayal of the present, and a selective description of the past which can serve as a contrast to the future,"[28] as well as enough specificity to make the action implications of the language clear.

General Electric's Work–Out process is an excellent example of these principles. The Work–Out process, begun in 1989, was an effort by Jack Welch, GE's CEO, to transform the culture. Originally begun as an effort to eliminate waste and redesign processes to take out unnecessary work, the change effort soon focused on more fundamental issues:

> Moving the company away from its long history of fine–tuned financial analysis, time–consuming strategic deliberations, centralized controls, multi-level approvals, and bureaucracy to a culture characterized by "speed, simplicity, and self–confidence," focused on meeting customer needs and winning in the global competitive environment of the 1990s.[29]

Welch's language and description for the Work–Out process was action oriented:

> A relentless, endless company wide search for a better way to do everything we do. . . . We like to say "work-out blew up the building." Consider a building: It has walls and floors; the walls divide the functions, the floors separate the levels. Workout took out the walls and floors, leaving all the bodies in one big room.[30]

Welch intentionally used simple language and concepts to describe the Work–Out process because, as his speeches and writings make clear, he valued simplicity and the action that simple ideas produced:

> Workout was nothing more complicated than bring-ing people of all ranks and functions—managers, sec-retaries, engineers, line workers, and sometimes

customers and suppliers—together in a room to focus on a problem or an opportunity, and then acting rapidly and decisively on the best ideas developed, regardless of their source.[31] . . . Simplicity is a quality sneered at today in cultures that like their business concepts the way they like their wine, full of nuance, subtlety, complexity, hints of this and that. In the '90s, cultures like that will produce sophisticated decisions loaded with nuance and complexity that arrive at the station long after the train has gone.[32]

The Work–Out process helped people talk constructively with each other about real problems and solutions, in part by overcoming the functional specialization and hierarchical power differences that inhibited the flow of information and the taking of action. As described by two observers of the process:

Typically, functions and levels in organizations often converse through reports, presentations, and studies. These are usually presented unidirectionally, followed perhaps by some form of limited "Q and A" [questions and answers]. The discussions therefore are limited in depth and in number of participants. . . . Organizations like GE came to understand that the approaches of the past 30 years each had missing ingredients. A much more sophisticated . . . pattern of dialogue and interaction was needed for companies to be successful.[33]

But even more important, the Work–Out process itself was designed to stimulate an open organizational dialogue about problems and issues and then translate that dialogue into action. The Work–Out process had the following common elements:

- Focus on a business issue or key business process. . . . The majority of sessions took aim at improving a specific business process or issue . . .

- Multifunctional/multilevel participation. . . . Sessions included people from various functions and at different organizational levels . . .

- Small-group brainstorming . . .

- Town meeting . . . a plenary session for all participants at which . . . ideas for improvement were presented to one or more business leaders. . . . At the end of each discussion, the business leader would make an immediate decision about the idea . . .

- Action follow-up. In each business, a process was developed to implement approved Work-Out ideas, and to follow-up to make sure that the changes were actually put in place.[34]

The GE cultural change process had two elements that ensured talk would not be the only thing that occurred. First, the talk itself entailed language that impelled action because of the specificity and sense of urgency it conveyed. Over time, this action-generating aspect of language improved as General Electric people learned what kinds of talk produced actions and what didn't: "When ideas were presented that were focused and tangible, they were much more often accepted than vague and general recommendations."[35] Second, the meetings did not end with dialogue, discussion, and presentations. Decisions were made and follow-up occurred to ensure implementation was part of the process. In town meetings, the business leader was required to do something with the suggestions on the spot. The idea could be accepted or rejected immediately, or more information could be requested. But if more information was needed, the boss "had to name a team and set a deadline for making a decision."[36] "By deciding on the spot how to handle each idea, the business leader was modeling the translation of dialogue into action. . . . The purpose of the dialogue is purposeful action for the betterment of the business—and not just conversation for its own sake."[37]

Following up the meetings to ensure that decisions were actually implemented was also an important part of the Work-Out process. Action-planning meetings were sometimes held right after the town meetings to plan the specific steps required to implement the recommendations that had been developed. A specific individual was charged with being the driver of the change. Schedules were set, and there was follow-up to ensure that what had been agreed to was actually done.

Closing the loop, following up to make sure something actually happens when it is decided, isn't a very complicated idea. The notion that people learn from doing rather than from just talking about what they should do isn't very complicated either. But these are potent means for preventing talk from being the only thing that occurs. Closing the loop between talk and action, along with learning by doing, are cornerstones of the methods used by the U.S. Army's National Training Center to facilitate learning during grueling two-week war games in which brigades of 3,000 to 5,000 soldiers go head to head in simulated combat.[38] Approximately 600 instructors (one for every soldier who has leadership responsibility) follow each brigade through the 18-hour day. After each day of battle, these instructors hold "After Action Reviews," in which they work with combatants to understand what went right and what went wrong and how they can do better in the next day's battle. The instructors place especially strong emphasis on learning from failure, viewing the acceptance of failure as crucial to the process of learning by doing. These exercises have led to dramatic improvements in combat performance. Instead of providing soldiers vague or abstract talk about what to do in battle, the loop between what happened during the last battle and what was said about how to fight the next battle is closed day after day during these two-week exercises.

Organizations that turn knowledge into action by not letting talk substitute for behavior are relentlessly action oriented—in their language and in ensuring through follow-up and assigning accountability that something happens as a result of talk, planning, and decisions. These organizations act on the essential truth that if you change behavior, then no matter what people are saying, planning, or feeling, there will not be a knowing–doing gap. People will know—learn—from the doing. There is a large literature demonstrating that attitudes *follow* behavior.[39] That means that people accept new beliefs as a result of changing their behavior. And the fact that behavior is preeminent suggests that action can influence talk even more powerfully than talk influences action. The genius of Jack Welch and the GE Work–Out program was the unrelenting focus on action and results, not just on reports, meetings, presentations, and documents like we saw in the Xerox Leadership Through Quality program. Similarly, the genius of the U.S. Army's "After Action Reviews" is that the talk comes immediately after each battle, so the lessons that soldiers believe they have learned can be tested in action right away.

Reframing: From Why It Can't Be Done to Overcoming Obstacles

After SAS Institute was listed as one of the best places to work, and after its low turnover rate became widely known at a time when technical talent was scarce and the attraction and retention of people was a key to success, many companies sought to visit SAS or to have someone like David Russo come speak to their organization about how the firm had achieved what it had with its people. Russo called this the "pilgrimage." But, he commented, he noticed something. When he would talk about what SAS had done—for it was no secret—frequently the managers from the other companies would begin to give him all the reasons why they couldn't do the same things. For instance, SAS has offered on-site day care at subsidized prices since 1981. Some companies would acknowledge the importance of day care and the distractions caused to people when they had difficulty with child care arrangements, but would argue that on–site day care wasn't feasible because of the increased legal exposure entailed in caring for children at the corporation's premises. Or, they would argue that the kinds of health benefits that SAS provided all of its people were too expensive. In short, they would find excuses for why they couldn't or wouldn't do what they had, ironically, just spent some effort learning about.

Russo's response was often to note that one can always find a reason not to do something. He would tell the visitors to come back when they were actually serious about doing something about their issues. There is another response, also: Reframe the task from being one of merely finding all the problems or pitfalls for a particular course of action to one in which the task is not only to uncover problems but also to solve them. This reframing transforms talk about how something that may be useful and necessary can't be done into talk about how to do it. An example illustrates the process.

A colleague worked at SRI in the 1970s before founding his own strategy consulting firm. He described work that SRI did for Merrill Lynch in developing the concept of the cash management account (CMA), an account that linked check writing, credit cards, money market funds, and traditional brokerage services. Although these combined or linked accounts are now common, in the 1970s they were a tremendous innovation and promised Merrill Lynch a competitive advantage if it could be first into the marketplace. Donald Regan was the CEO of Merrill Lynch at the time. Our colleague described what happened after the SRI presentation on the product, strategy, and the competitive advantage to be obtained from its introduction:

> Regan went around the room getting comments from the other senior executives. They all saw problems. The operations vice president noted that it now cost the firm many dollars to process a transaction. That

was fine when the transactions were securities pur-
chases and sales, in which the commissions were
large. When the transactions were deposits in money
market accounts, check writing on such accounts, and
similar things, they would have to be able to process
them for only cents per transaction. The systems simply were not able to handle the task. The legal vice
president noted the cash management account ideas
would in effect turn the firm into a bank, making it
subject to much more stringent regulation. . . . It
would have to get charters, regulatory approvals, and
so forth, and this would be difficult, given the resistance of potential competitors. The marketing vice
president noted that banks were currently some of
Merrill Lynch's best customers. They would certainly
be offended if the firm became a competitor . . . and
might take much of their business to other securities
firms. And so it went around the table, each senior
executive stating valid and sensible concerns.[40]

Regan did not dismiss the problems. After all, they were
genuine and difficult barriers to implementation. But he also
did not say, "These are all real problems, so we won't proceed." Rather, he reframed the issue, noting that he had
decided to proceed because of the importance of the product
to the company. "So the question now becomes, how do you
solve the problems you described so articulately?"[41] With the
issue now framed as not whether or not the firm was going
to introduce the product, but how to accomplish it given
the real obstacles it faced, the same vice presidents began to
think of ways around the obstacles they had identified.

Organizations that successfully turn knowledge into
action have an urgency to do so. They don't take problems
or obstacles as reasons not to do something. Rather, they
frame issues as how to get things accomplished. In so
doing, they act on wisdom that other organizations, seeing
the pros and cons, the pitfalls and difficulties, talk themselves out of even attempting.

Talk in organizations can mobilize or substitute for action, depending on the nature of the language and how it is used. Talk, and the related activities of planning, presentations, and meetings, also helps to establish precedent and an identity for the organization. This history and the identity it creates can also inhibit actions that turn performance knowledge into organizational action. We examine how this occurs, and what some firms do to avoid this problem, in the next chapter.

|3| When Memory Is a Substitute for Thinking

ORGANIZATIONS THAT FAIL to implement performance knowledge often behave as if the present were a perfect imitation of the past. And, although executives in such organizations may deny it, the ways that people are hired, socialized, promoted, and rewarded means that when newcomers join the firm, they soon act like imitations of those who came before them. People in organizations that use memory as a substitute for thinking often do what has always been done without reflecting. Even when they realize that a new problem confronts the organization, problem solving means finding practices from the organization's past that seem right for solving the present problem. The organization's memory, embodied in precedents, customs of often unknown origin, stories about how things have always been and used to be, and standard operating procedures, becomes used as a substitute for taking wise action. We have also been amazed by how rapidly such precedents are established. Experiments by behavioral scientists show that when people do something even a single time, this past action often becomes an automatic, or mindless, guide for future action, even when the action undermines a person's performance.[1] Just like in these experiments, in many companies we studied, doing something, even if only one time and regardless of whether | 69 it was effective or not, made that way of operating automatically legitimate and acceptable.

This almost mindless reliance on how things have been done in the past means that translating knowledge into action, to the extent this involves any change, is difficult. Excessive reliance on the organization's memory means that existing practices are rarely thought about, let alone questioned or examined to see if they make sense in the context of what managers know and are trying to accomplish. Even when people know that existing ways of doing things are flawed, they are often afraid to raise objections or to suggest new ways of working. For example, Mitel Corporation, a high-technology Canadian company manufacturing private branch exchanges (PBXs), almost went broke by clinging to past ways of doing things. Stephen Quesnelle, the company's head of quality programs, stated: "Sacred cows are the barriers that everybody *knows* about but that nobody *talks* about. . . . They're the policies and procedures that have outlived their usefulness—but that no one dares touch."[2]

And even when people are courageous enough to question old ways of doing things, and provide good reasons why these practices should be discarded and replaced, they are often ignored or rebuked. For example, about 15 years ago, a young manager at an electronics firm proposed that the corporate policy of giving high-ranking executives a new company car every year be changed so that they were given a new car every 18 months or 2 years. The manager did a careful analysis, taking into account the cost savings of buying new cars less frequently versus the lower trade-in value of the older cars. He discovered that hundreds of thousands of dollars could be saved just by keeping the cars another 6 months, and even more could be saved if the cars were kept a full additional year. When he presented his analysis to his boss and mentor, his boss refused to support the idea because it meant "messing with a sacred cow." The boss advised the young manager not to mention this idea to anyone else, because he would be asking for trouble. Fifteen years later, the young manager is now much more senior and powerful. When asked about the idea recently, he said, "I still think I was right and I believe that we could still save a lot of money by looking into this program. But, I've been here long enough to realize that no one here is going to let me kill that sacred cow no matter how much money we are wasting on it."

The power of precedent to guide action, even when the organization knows it is doing the wrong thing, is also illustrated by what happened following the merger of Lockheed Corporation with Martin Marietta. The merged company, Lockheed–Martin, collapsed three separate sites into one at a cost of $700 million in order to save $3.5 billion in costs over five years. But a case study of the consolidation found that neither the civil space division nor the commercial satellite division had won a single contract after the consolidation. Why? "Company policy calls for bidding based on a five year history of similar contracts, but new costs are lower. . . . This adherence to company policy caused bids to be uncompetitive."[3] Because of the policy of relying on historical costs in preparing bids, and the company's continued adherence to this policy even when it made no sense because the firm had changed the cost structure, Lockheed–Martin could not take advantage of the cost reductions it had achieved—after incurring $700 million in expense.

So, management practices persist, even if they aren't particularly useful and even if their ineffectiveness is acknowledged by organizational leaders. In this chapter, we show why memory serves as a substitute for thinking and how a strong organizational memory can be a double-edged sword that can both produce and undermine performance. We then show how organizations can and do avoid excessive reliance on the past.

Precedent in Action

Conventional Wisdom and Pressure for Consistency

Precedent substitutes for thought in some organizations because their competitors use the same practices and because there is pressure to justify past actions as reasonable ones. These forces, combined with the fact that it is easier (at least in the short term) to rely on precedent than to learn something new, cause many organizations to avoid adopting new practices even when managers realize they are doing the wrong thing. Consider this example of an outstanding pediatric hospital located in southern California. The hospital had struggled in its fund–raising efforts for many years until a new executive organized a separate fund–raising foundation, signaling that fund–raising would receive more attention and emphasis. Excellent results, in terms of increasing donations, followed. But one problem plagued the newly revitalized fund–raising efforts. Recruiting and training efforts were inconsistent with what executives knew was needed for the foundation's long–term success. This discrepancy between knowing and doing was recognized by all the parties involved.

At the time of its inception, the foundation had hired experienced fund–raisers, typically with a history of working at other nonprofit organizations where they had proven track records. These newcomers "possessed specific job skills such as grant writing or estate planning that enabled them to have immediate impact when they joined."[4] The problem was that many of them did not fit well in this particular organization. Some lacked "the personal characteristics that would have made them successful. . . . Some . . . have not fully understood or embraced the mission of the hospital. Still others have felt uncomfortable in the start–up environment, where officers need to be flexible and play a variety of roles."[5] As a measure of the severity of the problem of cultural fit, this comparatively small organization had lost 19 people in just three years. Such a high level of turnover was expensive, disruptive, and interfered with efforts to build a strong fund-raising group.

Executives all agreed that their strategy of hiring fund-raising stars and hoping that they would ultimately fit the organization was failing. They believed that "developing people internally is the best way to produce high-quality fundraisers and build a successful foundation in the long term. . . . Managers believe in the 'build from within' strategy, yet the organization does not hire less skilled, high potential employees."[6] Even though leaders knew what to do and why they should do it, the organization did not hire people who could develop into successful fund-raisers and who would also stay in the organization because they fit its culture.

Why did the organization persist in doing what its executives knew it shouldn't? When the new executive took over, he had limited fund-raising experience. The executive and other managers unwittingly fell victim to a pair of powerful forces described by Robert Cialdini, a social psychologist.[7] The first is "social proof." When people are unsure about how they, or their organizations, should act, they automatically imitate what others do. They are especially likely to imitate people or organizations similar to them. So, confronted with uncertainty about how to develop his own practices, the executive naturally looked to what other, similar organizations were doing, and for the most part, these organizations were following conventional wisdom and hiring for skills and experience rather than for fit.

The pressure for consistency was a second psychological force that reinforced the ineffective practice. People who behave inconsistently are viewed by others as confused, indecisive, and even two-faced, so we all learn to attempt to appear consistent to others. People also behave in ways consistent with their past actions because it is more efficient. They don't have to collect new information and weigh the advantages and disadvantages of each course of action.[8] In this hospital, once the practice of hiring a certain type of person had begun, it took on the power of precedent, becoming accepted as "the way things are done here." Even with little organizational history, precedent was the main reason given for continuing this dysfunctional practice: "We had always done it this way," and besides, other organizations were doing the same thing. It didn't matter if other organizations were experiencing similar problems of fit, turnover, and integrating fund-raising into the rest of the operations. The combined power of social proof ("this is how our competitors do it") and consistency ("this is how we have always done it") provided an automatic, almost mindless justification so powerful that it overwhelmed the hospital managers' more rational and mindful awareness of why this practice was harmful and needed to be changed.

Precedent poses a dilemma for managers. It is obviously impossible to revisit every policy and practice continually. Relying on precedent, the memory of how things have been done in the past, economizes on decision time and effort and, when old ways are the right ways, enhances efficiency and performance. The alternative to relying on precedent and memory—each day revisiting every organizational decision, such as what products or services to offer, how to price them, what management practices to implement—is infeasible. We all rely on the past and on what others do as useful and essential shortcuts to make complex and uncertain situations manageable. After all, important human inventions ranging from the abacus to the computer have helped people become more efficient by reducing the amount of conscious thought required to execute routine tasks. As philosopher Alfred North Whitehead put it, "Civilization advances by extending the number of operations we can perform without thinking of them."[9]

The dilemma, of course, is that although remaking every decision all the time is both unwise and infeasible, the alternative, relying strictly on what was done in the past, can also get people and organizations into trouble if the situation changes or if the past actions have produced poor results. In the case of the fund-raisers for the pediatric hospital, relying on the past hiring practices saved the trouble of thinking about what skills were needed to be successful in this organization and surely saved money on training, because by hiring experienced people, less training was required. But relying on the past also assured continued high turnover because people came in who had great fund-raising skills but who had little identification with or loyalty to the organization and lacked fit with the rest of the staff and the culture.

A Strong Culture as a Double-Edged Sword

At its best, doing things in the same way provides continuity and helps define and establish an organization's culture and values. Culture and values, by definition, require substantial continuity over time. Doing things a certain way constitutes an organization's social identity and makes it unique. A firm's culture is embodied in its various practices, including management practices and traditions, that assume a taken-for-granted quality. Challenges to doing things "the way they are done here" can constitute an attack on the very identity and values of the firm.

For instance, Hewlett-Packard, founded in 1939, has, from the outset, operated according to the "HP Way," a set of principles and values that have provided continuity, stability, and a sense of meaning and purpose to the organization and its people. A number of observers[10] have attributed much of the company's success to its development of a strong culture and consistent adherence to a set of values that are virtually unchanged since they were first written down in 1957:

- High level of achievement and contribution
- Conducting business with uncompromising integrity

- Achieving common objectives through teamwork
- Flexibility and innovation[11]

Hewlett-Packard has even recently reaffirmed that it will operate by the HP Way everywhere it does business, eschewing an earlier initiative to try to modify its management principles and practices to fit local environments. Specifically, HP had thought about operating in a different fashion in China and in Southeast Asia. Now, however, a senior HP executive told us that not only has the company decided to maintain a consistent culture throughout the world, but furthermore, that the biggest cultural issues and differences tended to arise across functions and divisions in the company, not across countries.

In a similar fashion, other organizations with strong cultures, such as Southwest Airlines, AES, The Men's Wearhouse, SAS Institute, and Starbucks, operate according to a set of philosophies, principles, and values that are fairly constant over time and consistently implemented across different geographic settings. Precedent provides a glue that holds together these firms, some of which are quite geographically dispersed with a very heterogeneous workforce (for example, only 8 percent of AES people have English as their first language). The taken-for-granted way of doing things permits the organizations to coordinate behavior and facilitate interdependent interaction through shared values, goals, and beliefs, rather than through formal, more bureaucratic mechanisms.

But precedent also interferes with doing new things or translating new knowledge into action. At Hewlett-Packard itself, an effort to bring more of a customer focus to the Santa Clara instrument division ran into an entrenched, engineering-dominated culture. One engineer commented:

> The longer you've been here, the harder it will be to change because that's not the way we were taught to think right from college. I was technology driven. . . .

> That's why SDBS [the division's new strategy of sell,
> design, build, and support] is going to be so hard to
> implement. We've done it the old way so long.[12]

Precedent, when inappropriately applied, can interfere
with both the process of learning and of applying knowledge to enhance organizational performance. Perhaps the
most serious problem with precedent is that it is used automatically, almost without thought. Scholars who study this
kind of thinking and the actions associated with it have
described it using terms such as "habits of mind," "performance programs," "programmed behavior," "automatic processing," "top of the head phenomena," and "mindlessness."[13]
Ellen Langer, a psychologist who has done the most work in
this area, described mindlessness as situations in which
people act without paying attention to what they are doing.
"The individual becomes mindlessly trapped by categories
that were previously created when the person was in a
mindful mode."[14] When people in an organization engage
in mindless acts based on precedent, such behavior precludes them from even considering whether practices need
to be reexamined.

Rigidity as a Reaction to the Threat of Change

So far, we have shown that precedent and history can forestall an organization's ability to learn, let alone to actually
implement that knowledge in actions and decisions. The
problem is often magnified in those organizations that most
need to break from their pasts. The threat of change causes
people within these firms to cling even more tightly to old
ways of doing things, as the following example illustrates.
The Fresh Choice company operates a chain of buffet-style
salad restaurants, primarily located in California, Washington, and Texas. The company recently has suffered financial problems, with its stock price plummeting from about

$32 in 1994 to $3 in 1998 and profits declining precipitously as well. As part of a corporate turnaround effort, the firm acquired three of four units of a competing chain called Zoopa, located in the Seattle, Washington, area. In addition to acquiring some good restaurant locations at a favorable price, Fresh Choice executives wanted to incorporate some of Zoopa's "guest first," more service-oriented and operations-oriented culture into the firm. They also wanted to import some elements of the Zoopa design and marketing concept into Fresh Choice restaurants. One executive who helped negotiate the acquisition and present it to the board of directors stated that an important goal was "to pick off the best, the most important elements in Zoopa and try to incorporate them into our existing process of planning and designing."[15] Zoopa had much to teach Fresh Choice, as one Fresh Choice executive stated:

> I do believe that Zoopa was a step up as far as the concept goes. Their operation was more service-oriented than Fresh Choice, which gave us a real opportunity to learn from them. . . . The people I met up there were sharp folks and had a clear understanding of how service is to be done—and not just how it's to be executed, but how it's to be communicated to the crew. And that starts with how you recruit, how you hire, how you train, and only then, how you keep a store up to your standard of service.[16]

But our case study showed that Fresh Choice failed to learn nearly as much as it could from the Zoopa acquisition. All of the Zoopa general managers left within four months of the acquisition. Turnover in the acquired restaurants increased and sales decreased compared with the period prior to their purchase. Within a month of the completion of the acquisition, senior Fresh Choice executives stopped talking about learning from Zoopa as an important reason for doing the acquisition. Part of the problem was that Fresh Choice simply installed many of its management policies and practices in the Zoopa units. This action did not result from deliberate thinking about whether this was a good decision, but simply automatically, as part of a "that's how we do things" attitude. The executive who was head of business development and had the most interest in the building and transfer of intellectual capital was moved to other projects after the acquisition. As a one-time, special event, the purchase did not cause any revisiting of the basic operational and business routines.

Many of these routines involved reporting relationships and the amount of discretion store managers were permitted in making various decisions. Our study found that Fresh Choice required its stores to report both sales and customer counts on a daily basis; in contrast, Zoopa had required such reporting only weekly. Fresh Choice required all raises over $.25 an hour for crew members to be approved by the regional manager. Zoopa had treated the general managers more as owners, responsible for meeting financial targets but given considerable latitude in how to reach those goals. Fresh Choice centralized purchasing decisions and selected suppliers largely on the basis of price, rather than developing the long-term, collaborative supply relationships that characterized Zoopa.[17] Fresh Choice management acknowledged to us that the practices it was implementing had not been consciously chosen, but rather had simply evolved and were now being carried forward into new situations, even an acquisition of a company that was, in some respects, doing a better job. The regional manager for the Seattle area noted, "Fresh Choice has really—whether or not it was this way always but seems to be the way that it's evolved—has really become somewhat of a top down management style. Fresh Choice has always hammered down policies and procedures."[18] This automatic following of what had been done in the past hindered Fresh Choice's ability to acquire the intellectual capital that had been one of the main rationales for acquiring Zoopa in the first place.

Unfortunately, the financial problems faced by Fresh Choice probably made it even more difficult for executives in the firm to act on their intentions to learn from Zoopa. Professor Barry Staw from the U.C. Berkeley Business School has shown that, at least initially, people and organizations respond to problems by clinging even more tightly to what they know how to do best and have done in the past. At the same time, these external threats cause people to resist trying new things; even when they do try, their anxiety makes it difficult for them to learn. Staw calls this the "threat–rigidity effect," as threats and difficulties cause people and firms to do what they have done repeatedly in the past and, therefore, to engage in even more "mindless" behavior than usual.[19]

As an example of this effect, a study of the financial collapse of the Atari Corporation found that when demand for the company's products declined and competition increased in the early 1980s, the firm responded by focusing on developing outdated video game computer hardware and software and ceasing work on superior, newer products. Although Atari had a working prototype made with inexpensive parts in 1982, the company stopped developing a personal computer that, according to both engineers and executives we interviewed, was much like the wildly successful Apple Macintosh not introduced until 1984. Atari abandoned this project even though executives told one another at the time that they would probably be sorry for doing so.[20] Hunkering down and focusing on what the firm has done in the past is wise when the organization has done the right thing, done it well, and the present is much like the past. But the human tendency to react to problems, at least at first, by using old and ingrained practices and abandoning new and untried ideas makes it difficult to try new things even when people know they should do so.

Saturn: Helped and Trapped by Its History

There is perhaps no better example of how organizations are at once helped and hindered by their history and the identity created by that history, and by the desire to bring that history into the future and thereby rely on precedent, than the Saturn division of General Motors (GM). Saturn was established as a separate division in General Motors in the mid–1980s to find a way to develop and manufacture a small car profitably in the United States. The Japanese were dominating the small–car segment of the market and taking market share from the U.S. manufacturers at that time. The Saturn philosophy and way of operating was created by a committee of 99 people (originally there were 100, equally divided between union and management people, but one quit). One of the first things the committee did was to travel around studying what other successful companies in various industries did, including what management practices they implemented. The committee was, in large measure, a consequence of the vision of Donald Ephlin, a United Auto Workers official who was convinced that, despite a history of deep animosity, GM management and the union could cooperate to build a workplace that was both productive and better for the employees. The Saturn division was established in General Motors in 1985, and its plant in Spring Hill, Tennessee, made its first car in 1990. The interim period was used to recruit and train a workforce, build the manufacturing facility in Tennessee, design and engineer a car, and establish a dealer network.

Saturn developed a unique (within General Motors at that time) mission and philosophy. The mission statement, which included the importance of transferring knowledge to the rest of the company, was "Market vehicles developed and manufactured in the United States that are world leaders in quality, cost and customer enthusiasm through the integration of people, technology and business systems and to exchange knowledge, technology and experience throughout General Motors."

Almost 100 percent of Saturn's workforce was recruited from within General Motors: people who worked in other plants and other parts of the organization, often in plants that were being closed. The division bore the expense of moving these people to Tennessee. But Saturn's recruiting and selection practices ensured that people who joined the new division would have a strong cultural fit with the phi-losophy, values, and way of operating. Candidates for both blue collar and white collar jobs were typically interviewed by two management and two union people, and the recruits often couldn't discern which was which. Cultural fit was an important part of the selection process:

> Most of our early time was spent around a couple of different things. . . . The first one was the culture. What's it like to be a Saturn employee? It was a big part of the recruiting strategy. . . . We were hunting for people that opted in and opted out. . . . We were pretty sure that people with very large egos were going to have a lot of trouble . . . because most of the trappings were gone. The big offices were gone. The private parking is gone. The dining rooms are gone.[21]

Candidates were taught that they had to sacrifice some things to work at Saturn and that it would be a different kind of automobile plant:

> The whole recruiting process, in my opinion, was very, very well done. We made plant visits [to exist-ing GM plants] and said, "You know, there's this thing called Saturn. The compensation system, it's going to be different. You're going to be inside a team environment. That's not optional." . . . We took them through a series of screens. . . . And at the end of those meetings, they understood that if you come to Saturn, you're going to sign a quit form when you

> leave your plant. . . . Seniority [at GM] had no mean-
> ing in the Saturn environment. So, no matter how
> long you had worked for General Motors, it was a
> share the pain, share the gain, and everybody was
> going to work the same working hours. They knew
> there would be rotational shifts. . . . The application
> was an eight-page document that was every bit as
> detailed as a college application would be. . . . We
> did paper and pencil testing. We did group skills
> assessment. . . . They went through a two-day
> screening process, at the end of which they got a job
> offer, or they didn't.[22]

Saturn's emphasis on careful recruitment for cultural fit, and a substantial investment in training, including five and a half days of awareness and orientation training, has led to a world-class record in employee retention. Communication with people is also emphasized, and the plant shuts down when team meetings are conducted.

In large measure, Saturn came to be composed of people who were rebels and risk takers within the company, especially in the management ranks. These were people who had seen pockets of operational excellence within GM over the years. They wanted Saturn to be a place where they could implement what they had learned and where they could feel enthusiastic about where they worked. Anna Kretz, now a senior vehicle line executive in the large-car line, described the kind of person who ended up at Saturn:

> You had to like risk, because as a new employee,
> they couldn't make any assurances about your job
> security. So, you had to be willing to go into a new
> unit that potentially in three months would disap-
> pear. They couldn't tell you how they were going to
> pay you. . . . So from a personal standpoint, you had
> to say, "All right, we'll work on it. It's not important.
> And if it doesn't work, I'll find another job." . . . And
> because you had that attitude, you also had a desire
> to make a change. So, you put those two together

> and you get a lot of rebels, because you were now
> surrounded by a group of people who knew that's
> what they wanted to do.[23]

By many measures, Saturn has been remarkably successful, in large part because of the distinctive culture and
traditions that were created by the processes we just
described. Saturn was started by people who were willing
to take risks and who, over time, came to share a philosophy and perspective that have remained remarkably constant over the years. The good news about Saturn is that it
really is very different from other parts of the automobile
industry, particularly GM. It has enjoyed, until the recent
decline in the small-car market, good sales success, an
excellent reputation for quality as assessed by various
measures, and a wonderful feeling and spirit. It has had
good relations with the union, low turnover, and a constructive, action-oriented, and proud culture.

The bad news is that Saturn is also trapped by its unique
past and distinct social identity and faces tremendous
obstacles as a result. It is important to recognize that Saturn
is not an independent car company, it is a division of General Motors. Part of the original Saturn mission was to
transfer what they learned to the rest of the corporation, a
responsibility that was supposed to be shared by people
within Saturn and in other parts of GM. As a division in a
larger company, Saturn cannot determine, on its own, its
product offerings or technology strategy. And, it is expected
to fit into and be part of an increasingly integrated North
American operations production strategy that is pursuing
economies of scale by developing specialized factories to
make parts for multiple car models. Efforts to integrate Saturn's people and practices into the rest of GM, a part of
the process of benefiting from their learning, have been
hampered by the division's history of independence.

Many people we interviewed reported that General
Motors has learned little from Saturn. For instance, Anna

Kretz, now back in a more traditional and integrated part of GM, commented:

> I remember when I left Saturn, probably within the first six months, someone called me, and said, "Well, what have you been able to implement in your new job that you learned at Saturn?" And I'll never forget that question because the answer was, "Nothing." . . . There needs to be enough people sufficient to cause momentum. . . . There are some fundamental beliefs you have to share with a group of people. And if you don't have those fundamental beliefs, then the rest of the stuff—the little things—have nothing to hang onto, so they don't become as meaningful to implement on an individual basis.[24]

The problem, however, is not just differences in philosophy or operating principles, although these are important. And the problem is not just that GM does not want to learn from Saturn, or does not know how to do so. The problem is that many people at Saturn, because of its own history, are not especially interested in being part of GM. Our interviews at Saturn indicated that managers, union leaders, and employees who had a long history at Saturn often viewed themselves as being part of a company that was different and better than the rest of GM. This lack of identification with GM was dramatically illustrated by a long-time Saturn employee who brought us to GM headquarters in Detroit to meet with some other people. The receptionist asked him if he worked for General Motors. His first answer was, "No, I work for Saturn." He corrected himself a few moments later, but his first response showed how he thought of his social identity.

Because of the differences in culture and history, and now the issue of distrust because people in Saturn do not think GM has kept its commitments to develop the division, the possibilities of mutual learning and of implementing knowledge have diminished. Recently, Saturn people voted to authorize a strike against the company because GM is planning to build another car in the Saturn division at a different plant in Delaware. Mike Bennett, the highest-ranking United Automobile Workers official in the Spring Hill, Tennessee, plant, expressed the feeling of many Saturn people, including some in management:

> Product and process decisions are now being made not by Saturn. They're being made by GM now . . . North American Operations, to the global agenda. . . . It limits us in terms of what we could be building. We only got this one small car. But the commitment was made to us, "If you succeed, we'll give you the rest of the capital to finish the product line." And we succeeded, and they didn't give us the capital. They put it up there [in Delaware].[25]

Although Saturn uses many effective practices, it has not implemented many elements of lean or flexible manufacturing. People at GM headquarters in Detroit said that was because Saturn felt it was special and did not want to do anything that might break with its past way of doing things. Tom Lasorda, charged with implementing lean manufacturing principles throughout North American operations and enhancing manufacturing efficiencies, a big issue at General Motors, commented:

> The experience I've had with them has been more, I'll say, on the sidelines because they've been a very independent organization. . . . The issue with Saturn is they have the best team concept and people engagement process around. It's outstanding. . . . The issue that I would have with them is how efficient really are they? If you walk through the factory, there's room to get people more engaged in taking waste out of the system. The reality of the business is setting in. How do they respond to that?[26]

The lesson of Saturn is that the same distinctive history and culture that have made Saturn a success have also contributed to its problems with becoming as flexible and efficient as it might possibly be, even while maintaining its philosophy of employee involvement in the process, and with transferring its skills in team-based management to the rest of General Motors. We admire all that the people at Saturn have accomplished and have visited few other manufacturing organizations where people are so dedicated to their work or to one another. But our visit to the plant and our conversations suggested that they would resist almost anything they saw as a fundamental change, for instance, in manufacturing processes, because it is "not the Saturn way." It is obviously possible, albeit difficult, to build strong cultures founded on principles and philosophy that also can innovate and change. But doing so requires much thought and attention. Otherwise, firms are readily trapped by their history, even if, or particularly if, that history has many positive elements in it, as Saturn's does.

Other Human Frailties That Cause Organizations to Get Stuck in the Past

Why do firms rely on precedent instead of fresh thinking and analysis? We have already suggested a number of forces that contribute to a veneration of history at the expense of trying to implement relevant knowledge about enhancing organizational performance. Commitment to past decisions signals consistency and persistence. These are often considered to be desirable traits. And commitment to past decisions ensures that those past decisions are not easily questioned. Commitment to the past also reaffirms the company's social identity. By carrying the past into the future, managers reaffirm the value of that history and, by implication, the worth and the cultural values that are embedded in that history. In addition, the threat of change may actually cause organizations to cling even more tightly to old ways of doing things. There are also two other factors we have not yet discussed, aspects of the way that all human beings process, store, and react to information, that are also important for understanding why organizational memory substitutes for active thinking. The first is the universal human need for cognitive closure; the second is that people often have strong, but implicit and unexamined, assumptions about the forces that drive behavior in organizations.

The Need for Cognitive Closure

According to social psychologists, the "need for cognitive closure refers to an individual's desire for a firm answer to a question and an aversion toward ambiguity."[27] One consequence of the need for closure that has been identified in experiments is the "permanence tendency": the inclination of most human beings to seek closure, to freeze on past knowledge and avoid evidence that disconfirms what they believe. People are especially likely to freeze on past knowledge when (1) they feel pressure from deadlines, the need to make a decision, or other time pressures; (2) they are fatigued, thus lacking energy to process new information; (3) they are in any other condition that makes it difficult to process information, like feeling physical discomfort or fear; and (4) "when closure is valued by significant others."[28]

The factors that affect the motivation for cognitive closure—fear, deadlines and decision pressure, stress and fatigue, and valuing certainty by important others—highlight organizational factors, including the behavior of leaders, that we have already seen and will see in subsequent chapters as contributing to the knowing–doing gap. In that sense, our field–based research produced insights that parallel in important respects the findings of a large literature in experimental social psychology.

Unexamined and Misguided Assumptions about Human Behavior

A second factor that produces mindless and almost uncon-scious behavior is being rooted in a set of theoretical assumptions about organizations and people that are implicit and, as a consequence, not directly examined or questioned. For instance, consider the following example about the use of incentive pay in schools. In January 1998, New York City schools embraced a program by one of the city's largest business groups to pay $30 million to super-intendents, principals, and teachers if students' test scores improved. The article announcing the program noted that, although this approach had not yet been tried in New York City, it had been implemented elsewhere, with poor results:

> But in Kentucky, which has had a bonus program for three years, disputes have broken out . . . and schools have inflated grades. The problems there and with a similar program in Texas raised questions yesterday about whether lessons learned from prof-its and stock prices can be so easily transferred to test scores and graduation rates.[29]

An article the previous fall had noted that Kentucky's use of incentive pay had "spawned lawsuits, infighting between teachers and staff, anger among parents, widespread grade inflation—and numerous instances of cheating by teachers to boost student scores."[30]

What is interesting is that the use of incentive pay in schools was not new, and neither were the problems. An article in the *Wall Street Journal* more than 15 years prior to these incidents detailed problems with implementing incentive pay plans for teachers. For instance, in Penn Manor, a school district outside of Pittsburgh, Pennsylvania, that had implemented incentive pay in the early 1980s, "most of the losers and many of the winners aren't happy about the selection process. Penn Manor administrators and school board members still aren't sure whether the payments do more harm than good."[31]

What is clear from these articles is that almost nothing had been adapted on the basis of previous experience, either about what to do or how to do it, even though that experience was well known. New York City apparently learned little from Kentucky, and Kentucky learned little from the earlier experiences, either about the fundamental behavioral premises of these programs or even about details of implementation. Here is the knowing–doing problem with a vengeance. When we use this example in our teaching, we have our students describe, in some detail, all of the various assumptions about the motivation of teachers and students and the implicit theory of student and school performance inherent in these plans. Some of the assumptions are patently false, others merely questionable. Then we ask what assumptions would have to be true to make these incentive programs, as they are currently designed and implemented, make sense. The assumptions that emerge from this part of the exercise are actually quite consistent with a simplistic, economistic theory of human behavior: Performance is the result of a series of individual decisions by students and teachers, among others; these decisions are largely motivated by extrinsic rewards, including money and recognition; student and teacher performance is largely a function of motivation as opposed to endowments or abilities, including the resources available to the school system; and similar types of behavioral assumptions.

What is important is that the theory of behavior that forms the foundation for this particular intervention is almost completely implicit and founded more on ideology than on either thought or social science. As soon as the implicit assumptions that form the foundation of these practices are brought to the surface, insights about what to do to better design the programs to make them more effective are immediately obvious. Since this is not a book about schools or learning, we won't pursue this example further. But the implications are clear. People and the organizations in which they work are often trapped by implicit theories of behavior that guide their decisions and actions. Because the theories are not surfaced or conscious, they can't be refuted with data or logic. In fact, people may not even be conscious of how the theories are directing their behavior. But they are influencing actions. So, precedent becomes important in affecting management practices because precedent embodies some unstated, untested assumptions about individual and organizational behavior that get automatically carried into new situations.

You're Likely to Find Organizations Trapped by Their History When

- The company has such a strong identity that anything new is viewed as being "inconsistent with who we are"
- There are pressures to be consistent with past decisions, to avoid admitting mistakes, and to show perseverance
- People have strong needs for cognitive closure and avoiding any ambiguity
- Decisions are made based on implicit, untested, and inaccurate models of behavior and performance
- People carry expectations from the past about what is and isn't possible, and what can and can't be done, into the future

---

The example above also illustrates one of the most powerful interventions we have uncovered to free people from the unconscious power of implicit theory: making people think carefully about the assumptions implicit in the practices and interventions they are advocating. We have tried this exercise with numerous organizational and public policy practices and decisions, and we have found it to be very effective. By bringing to the surface assumptions that are otherwise unconscious, interventions and decisions become much more mindful and incorporate what people know. We have learned that freeing ourselves and our organizations from the tyranny of mindless precedent requires that we surface the frequently implicit, theoretical foundations of that precedent, including the behavioral assumptions on which past decisions rest. Once we do so, it is possible to design different and better practices that reflect our conscious, mindful knowledge.

How Organizations Avoid Using Memory as a Substitute for Thinking

Not all organizations are trapped in the past, doomed to repeat the same errors simply because they were done before, or constrained by their history from learning new things or applying what they know. There are three main ways that organizations avoid relying on the past as a mindless guide to action. First, people can start a new organization or new subunit, one that is designed to have a distinctive character and to be free of the constraints and history of the parent corporation. The practices used by new organizations might be invented by their founders or, like Saturn, be an original blend of practices from an array of other organizations. Second, organizations hampered by excessive reliance on the past can, sometimes through dramatic means, make people mindful of problems with doing things in old ways, make it difficult to use the old ways, and create and implement new ways of doing things. Third, and most rarely seen, organizations can be built and managed so that their people constantly question precedent and resist developing automatic reliance on old ways of doing things. We show how each of these approaches to avoiding using history as a substitute for thinking has been implemented.

Building a New Organization

Starting a new organization or a new organizational division or subunit is expensive and requires great time and effort. But it is probably the most reliable way, and one that is frequently used, to ensure that, at least for a while, people will use active thinking rather than precedent as a basis for action. If there is no history or existing procedures, guides for action and decisions must be made de novo. The active thinking done in new organizations is one reason why high-technology industries are frequently dominated by new companies. For example, the ROLM corporation was a successful Silicon Valley start-up that pioneered computer-controlled phone systems. It was known as being a fun, informal, and humane place to work before it was purchased by International Business Machines (IBM) in 1984.[32] Co-founder Bob Maxfield (the "M" in ROLM) once told us how he and the other co-founders mostly learned by trial and error because they didn't know how a business was "supposed to be run" and didn't know "what the technology was supposed to do." He said they made lots of mistakes, but they also invented new ways of managing people and made technical discoveries they would never have made "if we had known better."

One of the reasons that Saturn could innovate was that it was a new division, mindfully designed to do something different and better. The Saturn factory was built far from GM headquarters, so that it was more difficult for people at GM who did not share the Saturn vision to impose ingrained ways of doing things on the new division. This pattern of creating physical, structural, and psychological barriers that make it difficult for people to act on the basis of history and difficult for outsiders to create pressure for following precedent, is a hallmark of new organizations that are not bound by history. Many of the organizations that have been best able to implement high–involvement or high–performance work arrangements similar to those used at Saturn are in green–field locations. As new start-ups away from other plants, they have an opportunity to innovate and surmount history, to implement their knowledge about how to build high–performance work arrangements without facing as many questions or constraints as older organizations. Implementing this knowledge in established organizations that are trapped by their history is much more difficult.[33]

Dick Hackborn, the executive who successfully led Hewlett–Packard's printer business into the consumer market, believed that it was important that his group be located in Boise, Idaho, away from HP headquarters in Palo Alto, California. Although HP gives business managers great autonomy, Hackborn believed that HP's traditional focus on high–margin, low–volume products that engineers frequently designed for one another meant there were numerous ingrained precedents in the company that would make it hard for him to develop and sell low–margin printers in the fiercely competitive consumer market. Hackborn is credited with bringing about radical changes in how much of HP does business, but he had to fight many internal battles to do so. His group's distance from headquarters made their actions harder for others in the company to see or to change. One HP executive, who we talked to several years before Hackborn retired in 1994, described him as "that guy who hides out in Boise, changing the whole way the company does business, and making us rich."[34]

Starting a new organization does not, however, always ensure that a break from the past will occur. When this new unit arises in a larger organization, there is the risk that people may bring existing ways of doing things with them.

That is why, as the Saturn example illustrates, recruiting the right people into the new subunit is essential if the new division is going to operate differently. And even completely new firms may simply embody a mindless reliance on what has been done in the past in other successful firms. A successful Silicon Valley venture capitalist recently told us that he worries that he and his other partners seem to automatically fund people and technologies that are similar to one another and to those funded by other venture capitalists. He described this as a "monkey see, monkey do situation." He went on to say that after his firm funds a start-up, they put pressure on the management to use structures and practices that are much like every other firm they have funded, even though "we don't really know if we are making them do the right thing. We are just making them do what we always make them do." So, although starting a new unit or new organization can help, it is no guarantee of the ability to break with precedent.

Breaking from the Past in an Existing Organization

It is not always either possible or desirable to start a new organization or even a new division to break from the past. And, as the Saturn example shows, new organizations soon start their own precedents. Every time the world changes so that the present is not an imitation of the past, people in organizations that once used even the best of practices need to engage in careful thought about which practices to keep, which to invent, and which to borrow from other organizations. As we documented earlier in this chapter, overcoming these ingrained behaviors can be difficult. But it isn't impossible.

There are many well-documented cases of organizations that have been freed from their reliance on actions that are no longer, or perhaps never were, effective. Mitel, facing substantial competitive and financial challenges in the private branch exchange marketplace, attacked precedent with a series of workshops designed to rid the firm of the "sacred cows" we talked about at the outset of this chapter:

> R & D employees spent three days identifying rules, rituals, and attitudes that stood in the way of doing great things fast. . . . The 450-person R & D department gathered in five separate groups and produced a list of sacred cows that filled 71 pages. . . . So many signatures were needed to approve a business trip that R & D people rarely visited customers to discuss their needs; and engineers responsible for spending hundreds of thousands of dollars had to sign a bunch of forms before they could even take home a laptop [computer]. . . . The sessions weren't just about finding cows. They were about killing them as well. Every participant had to identify two "personal cows" and to devise a plan for attacking them the following Monday morning.[35]

These workshops on getting rid of past practices that weren't useful "ended with a celebratory beef barbecue—complete with beef, of course."[36]

The transformation that occurred in the late 1980s at Magma Copper (prior to its merger with BHP in 1996) is one of the best examples we know of an organization that freed itself from a dysfunctional past. Magma was spun off as a public company from Newmont in 1987. It had a high debt burden, inefficient mines with low-grade ore bodies, and a culture characterized by acrimony between management and its unionized workforce. The firm achieved a remarkable turnaround. Between 1988 and 1995, the stock price went up by 400 percent, productivity increased by 86 percent, and the amount of ore mined by Magma increased by 70 percent.[37]

Burgess Winter, the CEO at the time, and Marsh Campbell, the head of human resources, had much precedent to overcome. People had become accustomed to an autocratic management style. Supervisors had grown accustomed to giving orders and being responsible for what happened in the mines. Employees were accustomed to resisting orders and essentially leaving their brains at the plant gate. People had become acclimated to high levels of destructive conflict. Shortly after assuming the CEO position and moving to Tucson, Winter engaged in protracted, conflict-ridden negotiations with the unions. During that period, someone fired a shot at Winter's home one night.

The people at Magma also took for granted that, because of the low-grade ore and depth of the reserves, Magma was doomed to be a high-cost producer that was always on the brink of financial disaster. Given the technology of copper mining, people believed that nothing could be done about the costs. People had worked and tried hard in the past; why should there be anything about the future that would be different?

We see this attitude all the time. Organizations carry management practices from the past into the future. Similarly, the people in them, from top to bottom, carry expectations about what is possible—in performance, profits, innovation, and culture—from the past into the future. Shedding these worst aspects of history is a skill that all organizations would do well to cultivate. Some specific actions of leaders are critical in getting beyond precedent and history. What Burgess Winter and his colleagues at Magma did was at once deceptively simple and difficult to do. Winter demanded that the people at Magma leave the past behind and collectively forge a new future:

> The usual place to stand is in the existing set of constraints, issues, and opportunities that confront the organization. . . . Using this approach, managers typically conduct a financial and organizational analysis, identify what opportunities and threats exist, what strengths and weaknesses the organization has, and then formulate a strategy that is intended to exploit the opportunities and minimize or eliminate the threats. . . . The boat is patched but it is still the

same boat and most likely will only continue on the old course at about the same velocity or a little faster. . . .

Our recommended approach is to stand in a future that is not directly derived from present conditions and circumstances. . . . Although the future is informed by the past, it is as "past-free" as possible. . . . When I say the future is "past-free," I mean that the future should not be an extrapolation, extension, or modification of the past.[38]

Letting go of the past at Magma, while retaining the same ore bodies, the same unions, and the same people, meant changing relationships and changing what the organization thought was possible:

We have stopped complaining about the quality of our ore bodies and each other and instead have focused on what can be done to make our core operations productive and profitable. We gave up our attachments to conversations regarding transgressions and events of the past, and committed ourselves to the fulfillment of a future which we invented together.[39]

Winter was determined to offer people training and many opportunities to change. But if and when they didn't, he showed that he was serious about leaving the past behind. At the Pinto Valley mine, Winter fired four managers, including the general manager of the mine, on a single day when, after one year, the managers were still either resisting or sabotaging the changes. The Magma case illustrates the need to be resolute and determined to get beyond the past, as well as an interesting approach of having people come together to jointly invent a new future.

An equally dramatic and effective effort to break free from the past was led by Annette Kyle while she was manager of Bayport Terminal in Seabrook, Texas, for the then Chemical group of Hoechst Celanese Corporation.[40] Throughput of the terminal had more than doubled since it began operation in 1974 to three billion pounds of chemicals per year loaded onto trucks, barges, and ships by the time Kyle took over in 1994. She soon discovered most of the practices were the same as they had always been, even though the volumes handled and the complexity of the site had changed dramatically over 20 years. Facilities were very tight, as nearly 230 ships per year were loaded or unloaded at the terminal's one dock, nearly a thousand trucks were loaded at the terminal's one truck rack, several hundred barges were loaded or unloaded at two docks, and nearly 1,500 rail cars were unloaded. Very little planning was done and, as a result, the operation was inefficient. For example, a standard practice in the marine industry is that when a ship arrives to be loaded or unloaded and needs to wait because the customer is running late, the customer pays a waiting fee called demurrage charges, which are often $10,000 per hour. In 1994, the terminal was paying about $2.5 million a year in such charges. Kyle was also troubled to find many other inefficiencies. For example, it took people at the terminal an average of three hours to load a truck, even though the industry average was less than one hour.

The terminal had a traditional structure in which four supervisors watched and closely managed work done by "operators" who did the loading and unloading. Kyle and other members of the management team recognized that the supervisors and a few of the operators were extremely comfortable with the ways of the past 20 years and resisted changes suggested by the staff. Hoechst Celanese terminology of "root guards" was appropriate, as these people held on to the deeply rooted culture of the past and guarded against change, even when these old ways hampered the speed and quality of the work. Most of the managers preceding Kyle had limited contact with the supervisors and the operators. It was a job managers held for a few years before they were transferred to another job at Celanese.

Most managers came to work in a suit and played little role in the day-to-day operations. Kyle used a different approach. She wore flame-retardant coveralls just like the operators and spent a lot of time watching and helping them work in order to understand the work conditions, the work flow issues, and to suggest ways to make the work more efficient. She brought in new tools, instituted training, and tried to implement dozens of small changes in the procedures used at the terminal.

But by late 1995, Kyle and her management staff had decided that incremental changes were not working. The group was inspired to make rapid and dramatic changes at Bayport after attending a seminar by management guru Tom Peters on "The Pursuit of Wow." Kyle and her staff were energized by Peters' assertions that sudden and massive changes could and should be made in organizations. But they also found that Peters' speech and his book on "Wow"[41] gave them few, if any, specific ideas they could use to actually implement radical changes in their organization. So, Kyle and her staff generated their own ideas for transforming Bayport.

The Bayport management team spent about two months planning a sweeping revolution at the Bayport terminal. On the morning of January 3, 1996, the terminal was closed for the first time in its history and, even though this was a 24-hour operation with four shifts, all employees who worked at the site were required to attend a meeting. The changes that she announced and immediately implemented included the following:

1. The shift supervisor position was eliminated. The people who had previously held these jobs were called "marine planners," with the new job of planning the flow of materials for ships and barges.

2. Operators were now self-managing and worked without immediate supervisors. Kyle designated distinct work areas, and each operator worked several days at

each area, rotating among the areas on a set schedule. The operators were given substantial responsibility and authority to plan the flow of their work.

3. Kyle instituted a measurement system for each major area. Schedules, and current information about how well they were being met, were displayed on a large board that everyone in the terminal could check at any time.

4. To reinforce the message that managers should not hide in their offices, and that there should be no "corner office mentality," Kyle's corner office and the offices of the shift supervisors were demolished while the meeting was occurring. Kyle auctioned her big green desk for $60 on the spot because "I shouldn't be sitting behind a big desk. I should be contributing to our team goals however possible."

5. Kyle had "no whining" patches (little round patches with a red line through the word "whining") sewn on every uniform.

To emphasize that the past was dead, Kyle obtained a coffin, a pine box, in which she put various items symbolizing the past, like the "Ships Happen" sign from the shift supervisor's old corner office, which reflected the old philosophy that the arrival of a ship was something that was not planned for in advance.

For the next several months, Kyle and her team were on hand during every shift to ensure that the new methods were being used and to resolve problems that arose on the spot. The positive effects of the revolution were evident almost immediately. For example, demurrage fees dropped from over $1,000,000 in the first half of 1995 to less than $10,000 in the first half of 1996. More than 90 percent of the trucks were loaded within an hour of their arrival. There were dozens of other indicators showing that efficiency had increased. Although the supervisors and operators were shocked at first, they soon developed positive reactions to the new ways of working. Interviews and employee attitude surveys by independent researchers indicated that people were satisfied with and motivated by the change.

The change at Celanese illustrates three principles we see in other organizations, such as Magma and Mitel, that have been able to get beyond history in their efforts to turn knowledge into action. First, there is a sharp interruption in what people are doing, thinking, and feeling. Something occurs to get their attention and to convey that reliance on precedent is doing harm. Second, something occurs that makes it difficult or impossible to go back to the old ways of doing things. This break has to happen, because otherwise the stress of a sharp interruption can cause people to cling even more tightly to what they have done in the past. Third, clear, feasible new ways of acting are developed, communicated, and implemented. People receive the information, emotional and tangible support, and training and other resources required to use the new and more effective practices.

Another theme that runs through the cases of firms that overcome precedent is leaders who take the time to understand the work that people do and take actions to reduce status differences between themselves and others in the organization. Burgess Winter helped leave the past behind at Magma Copper by creating a more egalitarian culture. He would go to the union hall after work and have a beer or two with Magma people. Similarly, after Annette Kyle spent a year on the docks with the operators and supervisors, helping and watching them work, she had the credibility and personal relationships to get them to leave the past behind.

A final theme that we see in those firms that were able to overcome precedent is creating a feeling of shared fate. So, at Magma Copper, Burgess Winter created a "140 person cross-section of the entire company of 5,000 people, which we called the Voice of Magma, to join in a conversation that would set forth what could be possible for

Magma as an organization. Out of this eleven day dialogue came the Magma Charter, which is a declaration of who we are as an organization."[42]

Building an Organization That Resists Mindless Action

Overcoming precedent and history is one thing. Preventing the buildup of unproductive rituals, rules, and practices in the first place is even better, and even more difficult to do. AES, the global independent power producer, has consciously pursued a set of management practices designed to ensure that precedent never becomes overly important in the firm and that people are continuously encouraged to learn and try new things. One policy that encourages developing and applying knowledge is radical decentralization. The company has only five levels even today, even though it operates nearly 100 power plants in 17 countries and has close to 40,000 people working for it either directly or for joint ventures in which it is involved. Decentralization of decision making encourages people to learn because they know they will have the opportunity and, indeed, the responsibility to use their knowledge in their daily activities. The decentralization also facilitates the actual use of knowledge because it is the people on the front lines who get to make the decisions.

The company's 1993 stock offering prospectus describes the decentralization:

> Most of the Company's plants operate without shift supervisors. The project subsidiaries are responsible for all major facility–specific business functions, including financing and capital expenditures. . . . Every AES person has been encouraged to participate in strategic planning and new plant design for the Company.[43]

A passage from the 1997 annual report details the consequences of this policy for the firm:

> One of the delightful side effects of a fun workplace where individuals closest to the action make business decisions is rapid learning. In the AES "university" individuals are encouraged to seek advice. . . . Their responsibility is to get themselves educated before making a decision. . . . One result is illustrated by the first people who joined then–Plant Manager Dave McMillen at the start up of the AES Thames plant in 1988. Of the 23 people who stayed longer than a few months, two are AES Vice-Presidents–Group Managers, seven are Presidents of individual AES businesses, and eight are plant leaders.[44]

Perhaps the company's most important management practice is to frequently give people the opportunity to take on totally new activities, even tasks for which they have little or no formal preparation. This practice is encouraged by the firm having virtually no central staff—no human resources people even in the divisions, no central strategic planning or environmental department, only a minuscule legal group, and a central finance function that sees its role as being as much about teaching and facilitating the capital–raising activities of others as about doing the job itself. "Hard as it is to imagine, CFO [Barry] Sharp has raised less than $300 million of the approximately $3.5 billion of funding for AES's 10 power plants. The multidisciplinary project team working on each new plant is charged with that task, even if the team has little finance experience."[45] At the AES plant in Thames, Connecticut, a task force of frontline people invest the plant's debt reserves.

As Dennis Bakke, AES's CEO, has said, the better and more competent central staff functions are, the worse it is for the organization. A particularly skilled and competent central staff encourages people to turn over issues such as public relations, strategy formulation and implementation, quality, safety, and so forth to the central office departments responsible for those activities. If the staff people weren't too competent, people in the field would not trust them and would want to be involved themselves. So, ironically, the better the central staff, the more the rest of the organization comes to depend on those people. And the more centralized knowledge and skill becomes, the less responsibility people closest to where the work is done take for that work.

Specialization, of course, also provides benefits, including the fact that people don't have to continually learn how to do things they haven't done before. AES has carefully considered the costs of eschewing precedent and having people learn new things, which certainly does take more time, against the cost of being trapped by the past and not learning as much. Given the firm's business strategy and approach, which emphasize the competitive advantages of speed and having people willing and able to do whatever it takes to get the job done, AES has opted for a culture in which precedent receives little status and in which people are encouraged to continually learn and think of new ways of doing things. Paul Burdick, an AES person, commented on some of the advantages of a firm in which job descriptions don't exist and in which cross-training and moving to new activities is encouraged:

> My task, when I first came, was to "go sign up a billion dollars worth of coal." I hadn't done that before ... but I knew enough to ask.... So, you spend three weeks making phone calls. In a sense, you're not getting your job done, but you're learning what it takes to get the job done....
>
> And the value, I think, is that you give people the ability to innovate a little bit more if you leave them that latitude. I mean, the minute you systematize something, you suck the life out of it. You impose a set of rules or procedures for doing something, and nobody asks questions any more—questions such as, "Why is it done this way?" ... The human spirit needs some variety to maintain its vitality.[46]

Finally, AES, which has had far less precedent to overcome than most companies, also continually tries to do things to signal its break with convention in ways consistent with its values. For instance:

> One of our outrageous goals related to maximizing fun and dignity in the workplace is to eliminate hourly compensation. In most major businesses so-called "important" people get paid salaries, are eligible for bonuses and stock options, and have the freedom to control more fully their worklife that goes with such compensation schemes. Other people get paid for how many hours they physically spend in the workplace plus overtime. . . . We want to give people worldwide the option to choose between these two approaches. . . . In two years, the number of AES people compensated hourly has decreased from 90% to 50%. We think "allowing every person to be a business person" requires a salaried approach to compensation.[47]

Those organizations that use precedent wisely and aren't trapped by their memories of how things used to be, or the "good old days," share the trait of being conscious of the costs and benefits of precedent and memory. Their leaders understand the wisdom we saw in David Kelley of the product design firm IDEO, who introduced a new structure to the firm this way: "This is the best we can think of right now. But the only thing I am sure of is that it [the structure] is temporary and it is wrong. We just have to keep experimenting so it keeps getting better all the time." This willingness to thoughtfully decide when the experience of the past is more a burden than a blessing requires substantial effort and constant vigilance, but it has tremendous payoff. The payoff, as Professors Paul Nystrom and William Starbuck remind us, comes because the willingness to forgo mindless reliance on precedent helps organizations avoid the problem of inertia and the trap of success:

> Organizations learn. Then they encase their learn-
> ing in programs and standard operating procedures
> that members execute routinely. These programs
> and procedures generate inertia . . . As their suc-
> cesses accumulate, organizations . . . grow compla-
> cent and learn too little.[48]

It is easier to encourage questioning behavior, to have people take on new assignments they have never done before, and to create dramatic breaks with the past, including starting new units, in an atmosphere of trust and safety. Conversely, fear is an enemy of the ability to question the past or break free from precedent. That is why we have devoted the next chapter to the topic of fear as it contributes to the knowing–doing gap. Getting beyond precedent requires having courage, and driving fear out of the organization helps to encourage courageous behavior.

|4| When Fear Prevents Acting on Knowledge

I N ORGANIZATION AFTER ORGANIZATION that failed to translate knowledge into action, we saw a pervasive atmosphere of fear and distrust. We came to appreciate the wisdom of quality guru W. E. Deming's prescription for success: Drive out fear.[1] Unfortunately, there is some skepticism that fear and its first cousin, distrust, remain pervasive problems in today's supposedly enlightened workplaces. There are also still many people, including stock analysts and business reporters, who admire "tough," "hard-nosed," or even mean-spirited bosses. We have never met anyone who actually wants to work for one of these people. But the stories that *Fortune* magazine occasionally runs on the "toughest bosses" suggest there are still people who believe that when bosses are feared or even distrusted because of their mercurial and unpredictable nature, then they are doing a good job.

This chapter has two purposes. First, we show that fear and distrust of management remain problems even today in many workplaces. There is far more talk than action about using enlightened and humane management techniques. Second, we will show how fear and distrust undermine organizational performance and, more specifically, the ability to turn knowledge into action. Fear helps create knowing-doing gaps because acting on one's knowledge requires that a person believe he or she will not be punished for doing so—that taking risks based on new information and insight will be rewarded, not punished. When people fear for their jobs, their futures, or even for their self-esteem, it is unlikely that they will feel secure enough to do anything but what they have done in the past. Fear will cause them to repeat past mistakes and re-create past problems, even when they know better ways of doing the work.

Fear as a Deliberate Management Technique

Business best-sellers such as *Mean Business*, Albert Dunlap's tale of the virtues of downsizing as he practiced it at Scott Paper and Sunbeam, and *Only the Paranoid Survive*, Andrew Grove of Intel's description of his management philosophy and the Intel culture, demonstrate that there are still leaders and firms that view fear, distrust, and meanness as desirable management techniques. The fact that these books are so successful in the marketplace for ideas suggests that many others agree with them.

"Chainsaw Al" Dunlap was, for a time, seen by Wall Street as a management genius. On the day he was appointed CEO of Sunbeam, the stock rose 49 percent.[2] In the first quarter after he was appointed, Sunbeam's stock appreciated 63 percent.[3] The business press loved him for his outspoken ways and his apparent devotion to shareholder interests. The business educational establishment, where future business leaders are trained and socialized, also loved him. He gave talks at many major business schools, including Chicago, Northwestern, Harvard, Wharton, Florida, and Florida State.[4] Dunlap was named as a business strategist to watch by the *Journal of Business Strategy*.

Dunlap's management approach was designed to inspire fear in the workforce. The *Wall Street Journal* reported that "Mr. Dunlap was notorious for bellowing at subordinates who brought him news he didn't want to hear."[5] At his talk at the University of Chicago, "he drew big laughs from an audience of 400–plus Graduate School of Business students when he described the pleasure he took in firing a 'morale officer' at one troubled company he headed, and 10 of Sunbeam's 11 management-committee members."[6] Dunlap himself talks openly about the efficacy of fear and intimidation in the workplace. He summarized his turnaround strategy as follows:

> How does an outsider wrest control of a resistant organization? . . . I don't start with the old foundation. . . . I tear the whole thing down and start over. I rarely see any good in what came before. If it was any good, they wouldn't need me. . . . At Scott, I released 70 percent of the management team.[7]

Dunlap also seems proud of how he humiliated an executive at Scott Paper:

> In my first week at Scott Paper, I called a meeting of all the senior managers. . . . I wanted to see front-line management. I made everybody stand up and say what they were going to do for the company.
>
> One guy stood up and started talking about what he had already done for the company.
>
> "I don't care what you have *done*," I said, making an example of him. "I want to know what you are going to do for me, now and in the future!"
>
> He looked at me, dumbfounded.
>
> "I'm not prepared to talk about that," he said.
>
> "Then sit down," I said.[8]

Dunlap is now widely discredited because of the accounting and performance problems at Sunbeam that drove its stock price down by more than 80 percent. "Mr. Dunlap's two-year tenure left the company [Sunbeam] in tatters, with a Security and Exchange Commission investigation, a slew of shareholder lawsuits and 1997 financial results that nobody can agree on."[9]

As we discussed in Chapter 3 with examples such as Burgess Winter at Magma Copper and Annette Kyle at the Bayport Terminal, dramatic changes are often needed in organizations that mindlessly rely on old and ineffective ways of doing things. But executives such as Chainsaw Al use an equally mindless approach, assuming that everything from the past is bad and instilling so much fear in others that people are afraid to suggest or try new things. When the business press and stock market analysts like Paine Webber's Andrew Shore were still praising Dunlap's ability and his accomplishments at Sunbeam,[10] management writer Tom Peters, who often advocated tearing down bureaucracy, was calling him a "retrograde old SOB" who was destroying people's lives and the company:

> Let me make it perfectly clear, I am not praising the Al Dunlaps of this world, who tear things down, take a big chunk of the resulting profits, and move on to the next victim. Al Dunlap is a first–class jerk, and I wish you would quote me on that and throw in a few four–letter words. What I am advocating is the idea of destroying something in order to create something better.[11]

Although Dunlap has been discredited, Andrew Grove, the chairman of the board and former CEO of Intel, remains a management icon, venerated by the business press and business schools. So, it is instructive to see what he says about the role of fear and pressure in the workplace:

> The quality guru, W. Edwards Deming, advocated stamping out fear. . . . I have trouble with the simplemindedness of this dictum. The most important role of managers is to create an environment in which people are passionately dedicated to winning in the marketplace. *Fear plays a major role in creating and maintaining such passion.*[12]

Being tough and "motivating" people through a fear of failure seem to be part and parcel of the Intel management approach. The company has treated so many people, particularly some who are older, so harshly that a group, FACE-Intel, has arisen with its own web site, created by current as well as former employees of the firm, to document Intel's management transgressions.[13] Intel has the site blocked from all of its corporate PCs, and employees fear termination if they are caught viewing the site.

There is evidence that, confronted with a shortage of employees, some organizations are now "making nice" with their people. These efforts represent an attempt to undo a legacy in which people were taught they were disposable and should look out for themselves. We question how sincere or long-lasting such changes in approach will prove to be. Once the labor shortage eases, we suspect that many firms will return to their old, mean-spirited ways. It is, unfortunately, still the case in many organizations that taking care of their people, putting them first, is considered soft-headed and not very businesslike.

The Pervasiveness of Fear-Based Management

But how pervasive are fear and distrust in the workplace, really? A few examples don't demonstrate that this is a pervasive problem. Are these just isolated instances? Apparently not. Our view that the problem is deep and widespread is also supported by several large-scale studies. The first is a nationally representative 1994 survey of more than 2,400 employed adults conducted by Princeton Survey Research Associates. A number of findings from this study show that fear and distrust are important workplace issues confronting U.S. organizations:

- In today's environment of corporate downsizing, many workers may consider themselves privileged just to have a job. Only a minority (38%) are very confident of their ability to quickly find new employment.[14]

- The survey finds a sizeable gap between the amount of loyalty workers feel toward their employer and the degree to which workers feel they can trust their employer to keep its promises to employees. . . . Fewer than four in ten (38%) place a lot of trust in the company to keep its promises.[15]

- One in six workers (16%) claim to have withheld a suggestion about improving work efficiency out of fear that it would cost someone their job.[16]

- American workers demonstrate little knowledge of labor laws and regulations regarding workplace rights. Most workers assume they have more legal protection than actually exists, but say they want still more protection in some areas. In an environment of corporate downsizing and restructuring, worker demand is highest for more laws to protect them from being fired at will, replaced by part-time employees and having their jobs eliminated through layoffs or plant closings.[17]

Other recent surveys from the United States and the United Kingdom present a similar picture. A survey of 1970 Bucknell University graduates reported that 91 percent felt that firms have become less loyal to their employees, 60 percent believed that the working atmosphere has become angrier, and "three-quarters of the respondents had either been laid off or knew of a relative or friend who had been so."[18] A poll by the *Observer* in the United Kingdom found similar results: "Nearly half those in the survey had lost a job, were working longer hours, had taken a new job at lower pay or were on short-term contracts. Only a third believed finding a new job at the same salary would be easy."[19]

Additional data from surveys in two organizations during 1997 further illustrate the pervasiveness of fear and distrust. Two points are important to know about these data.
First, both surveys were conducted by the organizations (or
outside firms that they employed) for their own use in assessing employee attitudes. Although we had access to the survey
results, we did not conduct them ourselves to prove anything
about the workplace climate. Even more important, neither
organization is considered particularly notorious for rampant
fear and distrust. One firm is a large industrial company with
loyal and long-term employees and senior managers who
have a reputation—and a self-image—of being attentive to
employee motivation and attitudes. The company has
invested heavily in training and management development,
attempting to become a high-performance workplace. The
second organization is a large quasi-governmental international financial institution with a staff association (that conducted the survey) and with employment regulations that are
civil service-like in the protections they provide to staff
members. This second organization does use a number of
contract employees and has faced strong pressures for
change. But compared with private-sector firms in many
industries in the United States, one would think that the
workforce, which is largely professional and highly educated,
with many holding advanced degrees in economics and similar disciplines, would be relatively secure.

Figure 4-1 presents the survey results for the private corporation, comparing the proportion of favorable responses
in this particular company on a number of relevant items
with norms for a set of high-performing organizations provided by the firm that conducted the survey. The data are
striking. Only slightly more than half of the people provided a favorable response to the question of whether "the
company operates with integrity in its internal dealings."
Fewer than half of the people responded favorably to questions about being treated with respect and challenging traditional ways of doing things. Only slightly more than a

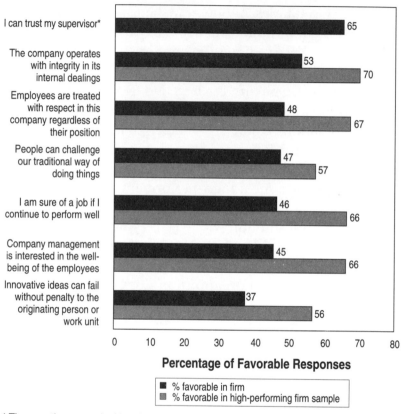

Figure 4-1

Percentage of Favorable Responses to Questions Measuring Trust and Security in a Large U.S. Firm

	% favorable in firm	% favorable in high-performing firm sample
I can trust my supervisor*	65	
The company operates with integrity in its internal dealings	53	70
Employees are treated with respect in this company regardless of their position	48	67
People can challenge our traditional way of doing things	47	57
I am sure of a job if I continue to perform well	46	66
Company management is interested in the well-being of the employees	45	66
Innovative ideas can fail without penalty to the originating person or work unit	37	56

Percentage of Favorable Responses

■ % favorable in firm
■ % favorable in high-performing firm sample

* The question was asked in only this company.

third agreed that "innovative ideas can fail without penalty to the originating person or work unit." Even the national norms in high–performing firms, although higher than the scores for this particular firm, demonstrated substantial distrust and fear. The particular pattern of results from this company seems to show a remarkable level of insecurity and distrust, even in a large, successful, generally well-regarded, and certainly comparatively humane firm.

The data from the large, quasi-public or governmental international financial institution were equally telling (see Table 4-1). Less than a quarter of the highly educated staff in this prestigious organization felt there was mutual trust and confidence between senior management and the staff. Few thought that senior management cared about the staff; many of the employees felt pressure, including pressure to cut corners and compromise quality; and, again, only about half of the people felt comfortable taking informed risks in doing their work.

Table 4-1

Percentage of Favorable Responses to Survey Questions from a Large, Quasi-governmental International Financial Institution

Item	Percentage of Favorable Responses
I feel encouraged to find new and better ways of doing things	57
I feel free to take informed risks in doing my work	50
I experience pressure from my managers to cut corners and compromise quality	47
Best practices are widely shared among colleagues	37
The institution supports honesty and truthfulness in the workplace	30
What priority do you think the institution's management gives to the satisfaction and well-being of its staff?	25
How much mutual trust and confidence do you feel there is in the relationship between senior management and staff?	21
How much pressure do you feel in your job?	18

It is unlikely that there can be much sharing and blend-
ing of what different people know or even much individual
learning in firms with such widespread distrust and mutual
suspicion, and in which there is so little emphasis on learning from one another or from trial and error. These organizations were not selected because they were extreme cases.
In fact, they are likely to be better than most. Yet the picture
that emerges from these studies is that there is far more fear
and distrust in the workplace than is beneficial or than
many observers would expect.

How Fear and Distrust Create Knowing-Doing Gaps

It may seem obvious that fear and distrust not only pervade
too many workplaces, but also that these nasty feelings are
counterproductive. Again, however, we frequently encounter
managers who are skeptical of this argument. After all, they
say, if some paranoia, some pressure, some fear, is a good
thing, maybe more is even better. Downsizing and placing
people's jobs at risks should "keep them on their toes" and
forestall shirking on the job. The implicit theory of motivation seems to be that without some pressure, people will
just take it easy and not do very much. Because it's a competitive world out there, people can't afford to be complacent.
There are even prominent economic models of incentives in
organizations that propose that the fear of being fired
ensures diligent and continued effort,[20] although they provide no actual evidence to support this claim.

Fear-based approaches to management presume that
unless people are under pressure and fearful for their
futures, they won't work diligently simply because they
want their organization to perform well, because they want
to help others in their work group, or because their work is
intrinsically fun and interesting. Many management systems

also presume that people cannot be trusted and that monitoring for compliance to organizational requirements, and punishment for violating those requirements, is important for keeping organizations under control. These approaches to managing and motivation are pervasive enough to have assumed a taken–for–granted, unquestioned quality, although the evidence for their validity is remarkably meager and there is far more evidence that monitoring and punishment undermine performance.[21] A fear– or sanction–based approach to management also has some aura of social approval. The business press often has an attraction to mean and tough, even fearsome, managers. Let's consider some evidence about how fear and distrust in the workplace affect organizational performance.

An instructive example comes from a careful study of Analog Devices. This study, which followed the company over time, showed how fear, produced by layoffs, undermined a once successful Total Quality Management (TQM) program. In 1987, the company, a manufacturer of integrated circuits, instituted a TQM program that, within three years, produced remarkable results:

> Defects in product shipped plummeted from 500 to 50 PPM [parts per million], on–time delivery . . . rose from 70 percent to 96 percent, average yield soared from 26 percent to 51 percent, and cycle time fell from 15 to 8 weeks.[22]

Because the program did not have as rapid or as pronounced effects on product development time, and because of some mistakes in pricing, margins fell and the extra productivity could not be immediately translated into higher sales. As a consequence, in 1990 the company reduced employment by about 12 percent. The effects were, unfortunately, predictable:

> These layoffs were Analog's first. Despite extensive outplacement assistance . . . morale suffered. . . . A divisional TQM manager noted, "a lot of [employees

in a particular plant] were working their tails off for TQM . . . and their reward was their [operation] was moved to the Philippines in search of lower cost labor. So [TQM] was another path to a layoff." . . . "After the layoff, TQM stalled. People didn't want to improve so much their job would be eliminated."[23]

A plant that, in 1989, had been number one in Hewlett–Packard's list of ten *best* suppliers had, by 1991 following the layoffs, become number two on HP's list of ten *worst* suppliers.[24]

A study of a workplace change effort at Hewlett–Packard's Roseville surface mount manufacturing facility, which assembles printed circuit boards, demonstrated similar adverse effects of fear, produced through employment insecurity, on the ability to implement changes that draw on employees' knowledge and insights. Hewlett–Packard had undertaken the redesign of this division to address pressing problems of competitiveness. Some changes had occurred. For instance, the production line had been reconfigured and training classes had been established. Overall, however, an effort that began with enthusiasm and insight had bogged down. An analysis by Deone Zell for her book about managing change at HP found that "none of the planned changes designed to support self-managing teams, such as changes to the center's performance, selection, evaluation, or ranking systems, had occurred."[25] The reason was fear:

> The impending downsizing curtailed any remaining effort to implement self-managing teams because employees became more concerned about their jobs than about redesigning the center. One production operator explained, "uppermost in most people's minds is not redesign or what they learned. . . . It's finding a job. People want to know if they're going to be here tomorrow. . . ." Dennis Early, the center's production manager, [said], "We learned it doesn't work very well to ask a team to redesign itself into a much smaller configuration."[26]

This happened in a company, Hewlett-Packard, that values people, where people address each other by their first names, and where layoffs are avoided if at all possible. When workforce reductions have been necessary, the company has usually been able to avoid layoffs by transfers to other HP units, retraining employees in new skills, offering enhanced incentives for early retirement, and cutting travel and other discretionary expenses. Even in this unusually enlightened corporate setting, however, the threat of job loss hindered organizational improvement efforts.

Fear of job loss has also been identified as one of the main reasons for the widespread failure of so-called business process reengineering efforts. The original proponents of reengineering claimed that their methods for making work processes more efficient need not entail downsizing. But, the management consulting company most associated with reengineering, CSC Index, itself reported that in 73 percent of all companies they surveyed, reengineering was being used to eliminate jobs.[27] While U.S. firms paid consultants more than $7 billion in 1994 for reengineering help, evidence indicated that reengineering efforts had failure rates as high as 70 percent, and one source estimated that 85 percent of reengineering projects failed.[28] "Part of reengineering's failure was its association with layoffs,"[29] and the fear and resistance that such an association engendered. Employees who feared they would be laid off as a consequence of streamlined work processes had good reason to undermine efforts to make work more efficient and equally good reasons for refusing to offer suggestions that might cost them their jobs.

Fear also inhibits the ability to turn knowledge into action because people are so afraid of their bosses that they do everything they can to avoid being the one delivering bad news about the company, even if they are not to blame. Psychologists have identified something they call the MUM effect, which means that people try to distance themselves from bad news. People don't want to deliver bad news to others because they fear they will be blamed by association, a worry that numerous psychological experiments demonstrate is well founded. Unless managers actively encourage the surfacing of bad news, the MUM effect means that the people around them will avoid bringing negative information to light, even if such information is essential for turning knowledge into action. The effect also means that people will avoid making suggestions for improvement if doing so first means implying that something is wrong.[30]

The executive assistant for one CEO told us she does all she can to avoid delivering news to her boss that will upset him because her job is less pleasant and more difficult to do when the boss is in a bad mood. To keep the CEO in a good mood, she avoids scheduling appointments with people who will deliver bad news to him about how things are going in the company. This tendency for gatekeepers to screen out negative information means that leaders often develop remarkably inaccurate images of their organizations, believing that no action is needed even though there is knowledge throughout much of the organization about the need for change and what needs to be done. For instance, NASA administrators developed inaccurate images about the failure of the space shuttle. The Nobel Prize–winning physicist Richard Feynman served on the Rogers Commission investigating the explosion of the Challenger space shuttle. Feynman asked a group of engineers to estimate the probability that the shuttle's main engine would fail. Their estimates ranged from 1 in 200 to 1 in 300. When Feynman asked their boss to make the same estimate, he proposed a failure rate of 1 in 100,000. Feynman asserted that this was just one of the many illustrations that managerial isolation from reality was rampant throughout NASA.[31]

This is not an unusual observation. We encountered numerous firms in which top management had an excessively rosy view of things such as quality, client satisfaction, employee attitudes, and even objective data such as employee turnover and sales because the people around them were afraid to tell them bad news or to provoke wrath by disagreeing with inaccurate beliefs. The ambivalence that leaders feel about subordinates who bring them news they don't want to hear is evident in a half-joking comment by Samuel Goldwyn, the Hollywood studio head: "I don't want yes-men around me. I want everyone to tell me the truth—even though it costs him his job."[32]

People who fear their bosses do more than hide bad news to avoid guilt by association. They have considerable incentive to lie about how things are going. Fear, created by managers who demand results no matter what, leads to falsification of information and the inability to learn, let alone apply that knowledge to improving the organization's operations. Even Andrew Grove of Intel recognized this dysfunctional consequence of workplace fear and paranoia:

> Fear that might keep you from voicing your real thoughts is poison. Almost nothing could be more detrimental to the well-being of the company. . . . Once an environment of fear takes over, it will lead to paralysis throughout the organization and cut off the flow of bad news from the periphery.[33]

As we conducted interviews at a large financial institution, we encountered over and over again tales of fear in the workplace that had hindered the firm's ability to develop knowledge and translate that knowledge into action.

> For years we used bank cards in the U.S. as being a Mecca of quality. . . . Little did we know that at the top of this organization was the cancer, the biggest cancer I was talking about. Demanding control. If you have a mistake with your numbers today, or some failure in your indicators, you will find that error and fix it and know about it tomorrow morning at eight o'clock. Or you are dead.

> Talk about fear in an organization. . . . See that hill, he'd say. You take that hill and I don't care how many of the enemy or our own people get killed. I want that hill, and I want it by eight o'clock and don't come back telling me it's not taken. The people were scared to do anything. And people began to cheat and manage the numbers in order to meet the goals. They were doing surveys—customer surveys on phone calls, phone centers, simple one pagers. On the phone call itself, questions such as how was it, were you satisfied with the call, the person? They had a goal of 95% for the top two boxes of satisfaction. That was the goal, and if you didn't make it, you would lose things, such as parts of your body. So this is what they did. The people just filled in the boxes to meet the numbers, regardless of the answers. And the people rationalized what they were doing.

> The business manager lost valuable feedback because the surveys of actual responses just went into the waste paper basket because they didn't count them. Horrible things went on.

The top management was so fooled into believing that this part of the firm was giving outstanding customer service that they actually applied for the Malcolm Baldrige Award. The organization didn't even receive a site visit, because it was clear to the examiners even at a distance that there was no employee involvement and little evidence of the kind of leadership that drives out fear, which the quality movement values.

Fear has two other pernicious effects in organizations. First, fear causes a focus on the short term, often creating problems in the longer run. For instance, in the Hewlett-Packard Roseville plant, recall how the fear of job loss inhibited a change effort designed to improve the plant's performance. This resistance occurred even though, in the long run, performance improvement was perhaps the only way to protect both the organization and their jobs. Nonetheless, and we see this often, fear drives out consideration of the longer run. Only the immediate, frightening prospects of job loss, pay cuts, demotions, and unwanted transfers loom in people's minds. Consequently, efforts to implement knowledge that might actually reduce the threat in the long term founder on short-term fears of the consequences of their implementation. This is why Deming, as an advocate of total quality and the change that this represented in many firms, was so adamant about driving out fear.

Consider what finally happened to Al Dunlap at Sunbeam. He was fired when Sunbeam's financial results were questioned. In an effort to boost short-term results, the company shipped a lot of barbecue grills to retailers during the winter, offering them the opportunity to not actually pay for the grills until the season and, of course, to return any they didn't want. But the company booked revenue as the grills were shipped. Not many barbecues are sold in the winter, but in the short term, this boosted the company's financial results. Booking business that wasn't real was also a problem during the mid-1990s at Informix, a database software company, and at Oracle, another database management software company, in the early 1990s. In both instances, the companies reported as actual sales any product shipped to distributors for resale, even though sales were not completed until the software was actually sold to end users. Informix had to write off literally hundreds of millions in phantom revenue—much of the firm's profits—when the phantom sales were uncovered. The scandal at Oracle was smaller in size, but of the same form.

At Sunbeam, Dunlap first claimed that there hadn't been any financial shenanigans and then that he hadn't authorized any of this behavior. But he didn't have to explicitly tell people to do something illegal. It probably would not have mattered if he had told them to scrupulously adhere to all financial reporting regulations. Faced with the fear of what would befall them if Chainsaw Al Dunlap didn't get his results, people at Sunbeam acted to ensure their short-term survival—and if that required doing some things to cook the books, so be it. The fact that such financial game playing would likely come to light in the longer term, which makes the short-term behavior seem irrational, may never be considered by people who are desperately trying to survive in the short term. Fear makes the short term almost the only thing that people see or focus on. You can bet that companies that have engaged in various kinds of financial misrepresentations to make the numbers in the short run are those where fear reigns. People in these places are afraid to admit any problems, hoping that somehow they will get by or that tomorrow will never come.

The other problem is that this kind of fear creates a focus on the individual rather than the collective. You know the old story about the tiger chasing two people: The one who survives doesn't have to be fast, just faster. Similarly, in organizations where there is fear of being blamed for short-term problems, people will focus on individual self-preservation rather than the collective good. Executives at Sunbeam knew that Dunlap had released 70 percent of his executive team at Scott Paper. They also knew that Dunlap believed that "I rarely see any good in what came before." If they wanted to keep their jobs, they had every reason to blame other executives for problems and no incentive for helping others to succeed or for admitting mistakes in an effort to help others avoid such errors in the future.

Similarly, at the large financial institution we discussed earlier, people are held to short-term financial measures and are punished and blamed for not meeting their numbers. As a result, the managers we interviewed often seemed obsessed with taking credit for their own good performance and blaming others for poor performance, as well as belittling others in similar positions to make themselves look better. One branch manager we interviewed, for example, focused only on his individual performance throughout our conversation, emphasizing the reasons he deserved more credit than he was getting. He never once described anything he had done to help another branch manager, or described anything that another manager had done to help him. He also explained how he was under pressure from his boss to drive more fear into his branch even though he thought it was among the most profitable in the firm. But he was only rated as being average as a people manager because "[she wants me to] push them a little bit harder and get more out of them."

In organizations such as these the management philosophy is that people will work hardest if they are trying to avoid punishment. Avoiding punishment for yourself means finding ways to blame and punish others. In such a setting, there is no reason for people to work together for collective benefit, and lots of reasons for them to undermine each other's work and reputations.

How Some Organizations Drive Out Fear

A number of organizations have, in an intentional fashion, developed practices to drive out fear. By doing this, the firms have built healthy companies where knowledge is readily developed and shared. One such organization is PSS/World Medical, a company that began in the highly competitive business of selling medical supplies to physicians in Florida. PSS/World Medical has since expanded its business nationwide and, more recently, into Europe and expanded its scope to sell diagnostic imaging equipment. The company has grown at a rate of almost 60 percent per year since it was founded in 1983, becoming a $1 billion business in 15 years. One secret to its success in managing this rapid growth and geographic expansion, often accomplished through acquisition, is encouraging open and free communication throughout the firm, so that no hidden problems or issues fester. "The right to communicate with anyone, anywhere, without fear of retribution is one of the core values at PSS."[34] The company has an open–door policy and encourages people to go over their boss's heads. This extends even to the CEO, Patrick Kelly, who encourages board members to interact with others in the company so that they don't have to rely solely on him or other senior management for their information.

Another key to the firm's success, and to the success of many of the firms that turn knowledge into action, is decentralized decision making. This practice encourages people to learn things and to actually implement their knowledge. But there is always a concern about decentralized decision making—what if someone makes a mistake? (It is interesting that the unstated assumption is that the higher you are in the organization, somehow the fewer mistakes you will make.) If mistakes, which are inevitable, are punished, people will be fearful of taking independent action. At PSS, the firm goes out of its way to ensure that honest mistakes are not punished:

> Most companies get something . . . backward, too. They think that holding people accountable means punishing them for their mistakes. This was the kind of thinking Chris [an employee who had accepted returned merchandise] was expecting.
>
> Well, Chris hadn't made a mistake. But what if he had? People do. And the more decisions you expect them to make, the more often they'll screw up. In fact, if they aren't making mistakes, they probably aren't making decisions.
>
> . . . Go ahead and make a decision. If you make the wrong one, acknowledge your mistake and learn from it. Then move on. Nobody at PSS will punish you.[35]

PSS/World Medical promotes from within and has encouraged people to take on big responsibilities at a young age. Not everyone is expected to be able to meet these new challenges. But people are often willing to try a new job with greater responsibilities because they know that if they fail, they will have a "soft landing":

> *It's no crime to fail at PSS.* If you don't work out in a new job after giving it your best shot, you can have your old job back. . . . This is what we call our *soft landing.* It's the exact opposite of the up–or–out approach to careers. . . . We *want* people to stay with us. We want them to go as far in the organization as they possibly can. And we will *never* punish them for taking on a job that turns out to be beyond their abilities.[36]

SAS Institute uses a similar approach in the software industry, which is otherwise infamous for punishing failure. David Russo, SAS Institute's vice president of human resources, has said, "We punish nothing. We reward creativity. Very much like Maria Montessori [the famous educator], we believe creativity should be followed, not led."[37] The company is willing to let software developers try new things. This is how it entered the educational software and video game businesses, areas that are far afield from the company's principal focus on statistical analysis, decision support, and database management. Moreover, these new lines of business have come not through acquisitions but from internal development. Not all of the new ventures or new projects can be successful:

> Have you ever heard us talk about the holes? He [James Goodnight, one of the co–founders and the CEO] says that he's dug a lot of holes. The only smart thing is knowing when to quit digging. . . . We don't know if it's going to make a lot of money for the company, or not. But the technology out there is exciting and it might turn into something. Go for it.[38]

Then there's The Men's Wearhouse, the successful retailer of tailored men's clothing. The top managers of this firm deeply believe in driving out fear. The company will often not fire employees the first time they are caught shoplifting. And sometimes, not even the second time. If this seems strange, consider the following. George Zimmer, the chairman and founder, has said, "We're in the people business, not the suit business."[39] Retailing is a relatively low-wage industry. Charlie Bresler, the firm's executive vice president for human development, has noted that many people selling on the front lines in the retailing industry have troubled backgrounds—problems in school, career problems, personal problems, and other things that have caused them to be confined to a comparatively low-wage and, in many firms, low-skilled occupation. The Men's Wearhouse sees its task as developing these people, raising their skills, their self-esteem, and their level of success.

By giving people a second chance, the company inspires gratitude and loyalty. Most of these people haven't been given a second chance, or even much of a first chance, before. The norm of reciprocity, virtually universally held and observed, requires that the favor of the extra chance be repaid. In addition, as Charlie Bresler explains, the firm has already selected the people as best it can and invested in their training. If it simply fires them at the first sign of trouble, it will have to go back to the same labor pool and hire again. What are the odds that it will do significantly better? Bresler believes it is far more sensible to develop those people already in the firm rather than to get rid of them, go back into the same labor market, and start all over with people who may not be better and could, in fact, be worse.

Driving out fear starts at the top—just as paranoia does. Herb Kelleher of Southwest Airlines agreed to appear in American Express advertisements because he lost so many credit cards—something he admitted openly as a way of showing he, too, made mistakes. Dennis Bakke, the CEO of AES, tells everyone that in 1997 he made only one decision, as a way of illustrating that the company truly does decentralize decision making and that the CEO is not omnipotent. In AES's annual report, the company openly admits mistakes and problems to show that even in a tremendously successful year in a very successful company, not everything goes perfectly, and it is fine to admit this in public:

> Not everything we touched in 1997 turned to gold or even copper. We lost numerous bids. . . . The acquisition of Destec's international generation assets has been the most disappointing economically. At this point, it looks like returns will be lower than expected.[40]

> Our people want and deserve a safe place to work. Last year the corporate bonus was reduced based on advice from an overwhelming number of AES people that our safety record wasn't good enough. This year was better, but we still had more lost time accidents than reasonable. . . . However, even in the greatest year we have ever had by all other measures, we have again adjusted our corporate bonuses downward to acknowledge the unsatisfactory safety record.[41]

There is no learning without error. Benjamin Zander, conductor of the Boston Philharmonic, is a frequent speaker on leadership. He understands that in an orchestra, the conductor is the one person who is not physically making music, so that person really does accomplish something only through the efforts and cooperation of others. Zander has argued that we should celebrate our mistakes. He illustrates this principle by playing a simple tune in various ways. The first way, that of the beginner, hits no wrong notes but is also deadly dull. Zander notes that it is only when the performer lifts his or her sights from simply not playing a wrong note to something more that beautiful music can occur. And it is only by risking hitting wrong notes that learning results. He also trains his musicians to react to their mistakes by exclaiming "How fascinating!"

Companies that encourage people to act on their knowledge have leaders like Benjamin Zander who praise people whether they succeed or fail and who view the only true failures as the failure to take action and to try something new. Designers at IDEO Product Development, an industrial design firm that has won numerous awards for its work, like to say that to succeed in the long run, you need to "fail early and fail often." The designers don't want to fail, but they believe that the best products and the best organizational practices result from constantly trying new ideas and learning from successes and failures.

The cost of failing in product design is trivial compared with making mistakes during surgery. But research on surgeons shows that, although they are perfectionists, they recognize that everyone makes technical errors and that there are constructive ways of dealing with these failures. Charles Bosk, in an 18-month intensive study, found that surgeons are vehement in their expectations that mistakes should be admitted and discussed with other surgeons.[42] Trying to hide an error or denying one has made it are viewed as unforgivable, because such behavior makes it harder to help the patient. Bosk observed that in the hospital where he did his study, the expectation was that when surgeons made errors, they should "forgive and remember." By remembering the failures that are inevitable in life, people can learn means for avoiding well-known errors in the future.

How to Drive Fear and Inaction Out of Organizations

- Praise, pay, and promote people who deliver bad news to their bosses.

- Treat failure to act as the only true failure; punish inaction, not unsuccessful actions.

- Encourage leaders to talk about their failures, especially what they have learned from them.
- Encourage open communication.
- Give people second (and third) chances.
- Banish people—especially leaders—who humiliate others.
- Learn from, and even celebrate, mistakes, particularly trying something new.
- Don't punish people for trying new things.

Bosk's research suggests that if surgeons—or people in any other organization—punish one another for admitting mistakes, the resulting fear would make constructive outcomes, such as learning to avoid errors in the future and making necessary changes in practices, impossible. To learn from others, one must be willing to admit that one has something to learn. In an organization full of fear, that is going to be difficult if not impossible. To turn new knowledge into action, one must be willing to try something different, and such behavior risks error. There won't be much experimentation, much innovation, much learning, or much turning of knowledge into action in climates of fear and distrust. There is almost nothing more important that organizations and their leaders can do to enhance performance in the long term than to drive out fear. What a shame it is that so many do the opposite.

Driving Out Fear during Hard Times

Many of the companies that we have mentioned as driving out fear have had the luxury of strong financial performance, although each has often confronted challenges at times during its growth. It will strike many readers as being far easier for leaders to "drive out fear," to embrace failure, to reward employees for contributing to the collective good, and to generally act like fine human beings when the company is successful. The true test is when times get tough. It is not always possible to avoid layoffs, pay reductions, plant closings, and other unwanted and unpleasant changes. But the duration and amount of fear that such changes provoke can be greatly reduced—or magnified—by how the situation is managed.

Consider the difference in how two large U.S. corporations, Levi Strauss and Citibank, announced and implemented large-scale workforce reductions in late 1997. In October of that year, Citibank announced that it would dismiss 9,000 of its 90,000 employees to cut costs and improve the efficiency of its back-office operations.[43] In November, Levi Strauss announced it would close 11 manufacturing plants and lay off 6,395 people, which was 34 percent of its manufacturing workforce in the United States and Canada.[44] Both firms provided displaced employees with generous severance packages. But there were important differences in how the layoffs were done. These differences illustrate four important guidelines for implementing stressful, negative changes in ways that reduce the fear that employees feel and the amount of fear in the organization. The key to driving out fear even during difficult times is to provide people as much *prediction, understanding, control*, and *compassion* as possible.[45]

On the day that layoffs were announced, Levi Strauss made clear exactly which employees would be dismissed, exactly how much severance pay they would receive (three weeks for each year served plus six months pay after the closing announcement, even if they found another job), and what other benefits they would receive. CEO Robert Haas explained that excess capacity made the closings necessary and that no jobs would be moved overseas. By contrast, at the time of the Citibank layoff announcement, no given employee could knew if he or she would lose a job. This lack of predictability meant that thousands of people in the firm had reason to fear job loss, even though their jobs would eventually be spared. Although employees in both firms could understand the financial pressures that led to the layoffs, Levi's employees were provided more detailed and comprehensible explanations of why it was necessary to eliminate their particular jobs.

Levi's employees, laid off or not, had a good idea of what steps they would need to take to control their own destiny. Those laid off knew what benefits they would receive and when. In contrast, people at Citibank who continued working for the firm had a less clear path for retaining control. Specifically, it was unclear if people should invest time and effort into doing their jobs effectively or into looking for another job. And, there was a marked difference in expressed compassion between the two firms. Levi's management conveyed, in many different ways, that they realized that harm was being done to human beings and tried, in words, emotional tone, and actions, to mitigate that harm. In contrast, we could find not even a single acknowledgment from a Citicorp executive in any public pronouncement that human beings were being hurt. We could only find talk about reduction in "positions" and "jobs." Although both Levi Strauss and Citicorp spent a fortune on severance benefits, Levi's demonstrated how giving people as much prediction, understanding, control, and compassion as possible can reduce the number of people who feel afraid, and how deeply and how long they experience such fear.[46]

The lesson from this example, as well as from a study conducted by Jerald Greenberg on implementing pay reductions in two manufacturing plants,[47] is that it is how things are done, not just what is done, that matters. Even under adverse circumstances, firms can take actions that increase or reduce fear in their organizations. The idea that "circumstances made me do it" has little validity.

We have seen in this chapter that fear is not something from the distant past, but is present in many organizations. And we have seen that fear, whatever its other virtues and vices as a management approach, is almost certainly going to make the knowing–doing gap worse. Various examples documented how to drive fear out of the workplace, for leaders who want to do so. As we saw in Chapter 3, people's theories of organizations and individual motivation, often unconscious or implicit, matter a lot in affecting management practices. Although many people apparently believe that stress and fear are productive management approaches, there is surprisingly little evidence consistent with this view.

Driving Out Fear during Hard Times

- *Prediction:* Give people as much information as possible about what will happen to them and when it will happen.
- *Understanding:* Give people detailed information about why actions, especially actions that upset and harm them, were taken.
- *Control:* Give people as much influence as possible over what happens, when things happen, and the way things happen to them; let them make as many decisions about their own fate as possible.
- *Compassion:* Convey sympathy and concern for the disruption, emotional distress, and financial burdens that people face.

There is one other important point. If, all other things being equal, organizations that have mean–spirited, fear-inducing management practices are no more or less effective than those that treat their people with dignity and respect, then there is no excuse for not treating people well. Indeed, even if firms that treated their people well did, on average, slightly worse than those that managed through fear and intimidation, there is still a strong ethical or moral argument for treating people well. The trade-off between some sacrifice in financial performance and the enhanced welfare of the workforce would be worth it. But, the evidence is quite compelling: Managing through fear and building organizations that are filled with distrust is not only inhumane, it is bad business.

|5| When Measurement Obstructs Good Judgment

MEASURES AND THE MEASUREMENT process, especially badly designed or unnecessarily complex measurement systems, are among the biggest barriers to turning knowledge into action. In our field research, we encountered example after example of measurement processes that fueled destructive behavior inside organizations. What is even more striking, however, is that when we encountered counterproductive measurement practices, managers often recognized and complained bitterly about them and described to us why and how they should be changed. Yet the use of such unproductive measures persisted.

This chapter has three objectives. First, we document the problems that measurements create in turning knowledge into action. Second, we show reasons why organizations persist in using flawed measurement practices, even when their leaders are aware of doing so, and what this fact implies about closing the gap between knowing and doing. Third, we present examples of organizations that have used measurements that produce intelligent behavior, and from these examples infer some general principles that distinguish measurements that cause problems from those that help organizations solve problems. It is clear to us that merely knowing what measurement practices should be | 139 used does not, by itself, cause leaders to implement measures that produce intelligent, mindful, learning behavior rather than the reverse.

Measures That Create Problems

Everyone knows that measures focus attention on what is measured. Everyone also knows that because what is measured is presumed to be important, measures affect what people do, as well as what they notice and ignore. As a consequence, everyone knows that what gets measured gets done, and what is not measured tends to be ignored. The importance of measurement is news to virtually no one. Moreover, there is evidence that measures have powerful effects on behavior even when they are not coupled with rewards. People want to do well on dimensions that are important to their organizations, even if there is no immediate consequence, other than social status, that accrues as a result of scoring well on the measures.[1]

You might think, given this common knowledge, that firms would routinely use measurement systems that cause their people to pay attention to issues that top managers say, and know, are important for performance given their specific business strategy. You might think that they would focus their measurements on elements of management practice, business strategy, and firm culture that truly matter for long-term performance. And, you might think that firms would recognize the commonsense wisdom expressed in a line from Otis Redding's song "Sitting by the Dock of the Bay" on the need for fewer, focused measurements: "Can't do what ten people tell me to do, so I guess I'll remain the same." Yet, firm after firm fails to implement these well-known and commonsense principles.

To illustrate, recruiting and retaining people with the right technical skills is critical for high-technology firms.

People costs are a large proportion of total costs in these knowledge–intensive businesses. Top executives in the computer software and hardware industries regularly complain about the scarcity of talent and the shortage of skilled people. You might think that, given these business realities and the shortage of knowledge workers, there would be well–developed measures of the costs, benefits, and consequences of turnover, training, and other employment practices. But a study of workforce management practices in the Silicon Valley by A. T. Kearney found that "most employers do not understand their total cost of employment." Moreover, "most employers do not specifically track their training or recruitment costs."[2] Even though skills, training, and employment are critical to business success, most firms have virtually no measures relevant to their performance on these dimensions. Why is this neglect of measurement, or failing to measure the right things in the right ways, so pervasive? Frederick Reichheld, a Bain consultant who wrote *The Loyalty Effect*, said this about why firms neglect these measurement issues and about the problems this neglect creates:

> The most aggressive minds in an organization rarely focus on measurement systems. . . . Leaders, they feel, should concentrate on important, exciting things like vision and strategy, and let the people with the green eye shades worry about measurement. The trouble with this attitude is that measurement lies at the very heart of both vision and strategy. . . . Most executives today work with inherited measurement systems that distort their business strategies.[3]

What follows is a small set of examples illustrating common measurement problems. These cases help us understand how measurement systems and practices contribute to the creation and persistence of knowing–doing problems. We see in these examples that measurement practices caused these organizations not only to have gaps between knowledge and action, but also to act in ways that were the reverse of what their executives believed should be done.

Focus on Short-Term Financial Performance: Problems at Hewlett-Packard

There is an ongoing struggle for the soul of Hewlett–Packard. On the one hand, the firm was founded and has flourished on the basis of strong values, the HP Way, and has long been recognized for its strong culture. Many management books have cited Hewlett–Packard as an outstanding organization and argued that the HP culture was an important source of the firm's success.[4] The company is still ranked quite high in surveys of the best places to work[5] and enjoys turnover much smaller than the norm in the Silicon Valley. On the other hand, Hewlett–Packard has recently had difficulty in maintaining its growth and in meeting Wall Street's earnings expectations. In fact, the company recently announced it was splitting up into two parts. Many of its businesses, such as computers and printers, have become increasingly price competitive, and the firm has been under pressure to increase its margins. The result is that the firm is being torn between its values and beliefs and a set of short–term financial pressures, made real by a set of measurement practices that emphasize results in the present at the expense of being prepared for the future.

In the very competitive labor market for engineers in the Silicon Valley, the ability to attract and retain talent is crucial to HP. Moreover, because HP is operating in very competitive, high–technology industries with shrinking product life cycles, intellectual capital and talent are critical to the firm's continuing success. So, the firm *knows* that "morale governs motivation which is key to timely product development; strong culture fosters a healthy work environment" and that "employees need rewards for key contributions and successes."[6]

Yet, there is pervasive evidence that the firm's commitment to acting on the basis of what it knows has been sorely tested and that the company's measurement practices have induced pressures inconsistent with its culture and with doing what it needs to do for long-term success. Numerous senior managers in Hewlett-Packard have argued that the company has drifted away from some of the practices and principles that made it a great firm and a great place to work. A survey in one division assessing employee morale on a five-point scale (in which 5 is high) showed a decline of 1.2 points, or almost 25 percent, for both engineers and managers over a 12-month period. The same survey revealed that 59 percent of the engineers and 75 percent of the managers thought that advancement opportunities had decreased in the last year, 76 percent of the engineers and 50 percent of the managers thought adherence to the HP Way had decreased, and 76 percent of the engineers and 75 percent of the managers felt that rewards had decreased.[7]

The measurement process, in which achieving targeted budget results in order to meet the quarterly expectations of Wall Street is paramount, has contributed to the company's doing a number of things that are potentially inimical to its long-term business health. For instance, in the division that was the source of the data on morale, the preceding two years had seen two laboratory-wide reorganizations, a 40 percent reduction in the manufacturing workforce, imposition of stringent expense controls, and the virtual elimination of employee celebrations and rewards. People in the division claimed that HP was more concerned with the financials than with the people. But in a labor market that offered many options, less reward for accomplishment and lower morale increased turnover and decreased work performance, making the division's prospects even worse.[8]

Some of Hewlett–Packard's other current management practices, promoted by its measurement system, have also had negative effects. These practices include using a lot of outsourcing, including contracting out manufacturing and software programming, using temporary workers, and not recruiting for talent far enough in advance to ensure the company is able to attract the best people. We should be clear that these practices are, in fact, inconsistent with basic elements of the firm's culture and values. The company explicitly talks about its tradition of not using contract and temporary help. For instance, during a half–day seminar on the company, its culture, and its founders, one summer intern "learned about HP's historic avoidance of using temporary workers (outside contractors)." The same intern heard a similar account from long–time employees: The company had typically avoided hiring temporary employees in areas central to its business. There was a business case, not just cultural values, for this policy:

> They [Hewlett and Packard] firmly believed that if a company provided a great work environment, trusted its employees, and gave employees the authority to make decisions, then the company's employees would value this commitment and develop loyalty to the company resulting in higher morale and *more productivity* than could be accomplished by other companies.[9]

Recently, however, the company has outsourced more and more of its manufacturing activities and has come to rely more on temporary employees and contract programmers. At one point, in the early 1990s, the company was featured on a *60 Minutes* television program for its use of illegal aliens furnished by a so–called body shop. Hewlett–Packard has been investigated by the U.S. Immigration and Naturalization Service and the Labor Department because of its use of contract workers from India.

What's wrong with outsourcing manufacturing and using temporary help and contract labor (who typically earn much less and do not receive benefits) in order to make budget numbers? In the first place, "outsourcing important electronic components" means that "HP no longer has a manufacturing feedback mechanism in-house from which it can gain information about the quality of its hardware designing capabilities in terms of manufacturability, quality, defects and costs."[10] Outsourcing manufacturing can in the end inhibit the ability to learn about product design because of the separation of design from manufacturing across organizational boundaries. Perhaps even more important, as a case study concluded, this practice sends some important symbolic messages:

> Another cost of increasing the use of outsourcing . . . is that it sends a subtle message to division managers throughout the company that costs, revenues, and efficiency metrics are more important than preserving employment opportunities within the company. It also means that short term planning becomes more important than long term planning. . . . Deciding to outsource . . . because of short run inadequacies in comparison with outside vendors . . . necessarily implies that these inadequacies will never be . . . addressed internally. In adopting a short term business view, this type of mentality lends itself to hiring temporary workers to fill short term demand fluctuations. . . . Temporary workers become more important when division managers begin to focus more on meeting short term financial and production goals than on long term planning on how to utilize permanent employees. . . . The focus becomes more tactical and less strategic.[11]

The focus on making the budget numbers not only produces behavior that is inimical to developing long-term capabilities and contrary to the history and culture of the company, but also some behavior that is almost unethical. For instance, the case study also found:

> There is a lot of counterproductive budgetary gaming behavior that occurs to make the numbers seem better than they otherwise would. An example . . . was one manager "parking" funds with an outside vendor during one quarter to be spent on projects in a future quarter. The purpose of doing this was to even out the costs from quarter to quarter, but what it amounted to was prepaying an outside vendor three to four months ahead of time. . . . Managers will [also] use temporary workers indefinitely, rotating new people in every so often, rather than hiring a permanent employee and blowing the head count budget.[12]

The lessons from Hewlett-Packard are sobering. Even an organization with a strong culture and long tradition and history of valuing people can get into trouble when there are intense pressures to "make the numbers" and a measurement system that emphasizes primarily those numbers. These pressures arise both outside the firm, in the form of demands from the capital markets, and inside, because of a divisionalized structure in which people compete with each other to meet their budget targets. Blind adherence to making the budget leads to all kinds of games in setting the budget targets in the first place and then to doing numerous things, some of which are harmful to the firm and its development of capabilities in the long term, to obtain short-term results that meet or exceed targeted expectations. And, a measurement system that is so strictly financially focused leads to neglecting other aspects of the company and its development. Interviews with numerous managers at various levels inside the company repeatedly come back to the budgeting system as a major cause of the firm's loss of its culture, history, and traditions. Few have made convincing arguments as to what the company has gained to correspond to these losses, as many echo the sentiments of the quotations above concerning the company's loss in terms of the ability to develop and build long-term knowledge and competence. What is also striking is how widespread these views are, as well as the pervasive sense of the inevitability of the situation.

The Hewlett-Packard example also illustrates another important point: The time scale of the measurements—how often the firm assesses results—helps to establish the time horizon that tends to govern behavior in the organization. A quarterly budget focus at HP has produced an emphasis on the short term and actions designed to manage performance that take a short-term perspective. Time horizons are not inevitable but are, in fact, the result of organizational measurement practices.

Overly Complex Measurements: Citibank and a Large Financial Institution

Citibank, along with many other companies, has embraced the idea of the balanced scorecard, as the company's published material and cases written on the firm make clear. In principle, the balanced scorecard makes a great deal of sense. Rather than just measuring and evaluating managers on the financial performance of their units, which largely reflects what has happened in the past, the scorecard emphasizes getting ready for the future. Managers are assessed on dimensions such as customer satisfaction, employee attitudes and development, and new products and services—all dimensions that are important in affecting the current and future performance of the firm, not just on measures of short-term financial performance. A second advantage is that the balanced-scorecard approach recognizes that a firm's measurement system reflects the theory of the business. What ought to be measured are those elements of organizational operations that are the most crucial for performance, reflecting the firm's theory of the ultimate causes of performance. What does get measured is what the organization attends to in any event, so it becomes the theory under which the firm operates. So, the measurement system either reflects or becomes the firm's implicit theory of what affects performance. This, too, is enormously sensible, because it is common sense to measure those aspects that are the most consequential for affecting the success of the organization.[13]

Nonetheless, even though it is great in theory, a number of problems often emerge with the balanced–scorecard approach. These problems include the following:

1. The system is too complex, with too many separate measures.

2. The system is often highly subjective in its actual implementation.

3. Precise metrics often miss important elements of performance that are more difficult to quantify but that may be critical to organizational success over the long term.

Consider, first, the issue of complexity. Most organizations use at least four categories of measures and have numerous indicators within each category. As a consequence, balanced–scorecard systems frequently become enormously complicated. For instance, a Harvard Business School case study reported that California branch managers at Citibank faced the following scorecard measures in 1996:

FINANCIAL:

Revenue
Expense
Margin

STRATEGY IMPLEMENTATION:

Total households
New to bank households
Lost to bank households

Cross–sell, splits, mergers households
Retail asset balances
Market share

CUSTOMER SATISFACTION

CONTROL:

Audit
Legal/Regulatory

PEOPLE:

Performance Management
Teamwork
Training/Development
 Self
 Other
Employee Satisfaction

STANDARDS:

Leadership
Business Ethics/Integrity
Customer Interaction/Focus
Community Involvement
Contribution to Overall Business[14]

Each component of the Scorecard was scored independently into one of three rating categories: "below par," "par," or "above par." For those measures that could be measured quantitatively—financial, strategy implementation, customer satisfaction, and control—pre–defined performance thresholds determined where performance fell in this three–level scale. However, ratings related to people and standards lacked an appropriate objective indicator: in these cases, performance was determined subjectively by the branch manager's superior.

In addition, the manager's boss gave a global rating for each of the six components of the Scorecard and an overall rating for the branch manager. . . .[15]

At Citibank, to ensure that the Scorecard was meaningful, bonuses were tied to the ratings:

> ... a branch manager's bonus was tied to his or her final Performance Scorecard rating. A "below par" rating did not carry any bonus. A "par" rating generated a bonus of up to 15% of the basic salary. ... An "above par" rating could mean as much as 30% bonus.
>
> Without "par" ratings in all the components of the Scorecard, a manager could not get an "above par" rating.[16]

Note that there are more than 20 separate indicators of performance and six categories in the balanced scorecard as it was implemented at Citibank. Nor is this unusual for companies using the balanced scorecard. Mobil Oil's balanced-scorecard system, used to determine compensation, has a similar level of complexity. This is a lot of information to keep in focus. Also, being rated below par even in one category means that regardless of how well a person did in other categories, he or she cannot obtain the highest performance bonus. This is particularly a problem because ratings in many of the categories are so subjective.

In a large financial institution we studied, one successful branch manager objected to the balanced scorecard's inherent subjectivity even as it appeared to be objective:

> It's still very subjective. My boss who does my rating sits down and talks to me on [a] quarterly basis about team work, my people management skills, my ethics, things like that. For the first two quarters of this year, I've been rated "par" in people. But meanwhile, I've given up my sales manager to be a branch manager in another branch. I've given up a personal banker to be a branch manager in another branch. I just gave up another personal banker. So, I'm developing talent, and people are taking my talent, but as a people manager, I'm just par.

> [My boss] came to that judgment because I
> have one person in my branch that she thinks I
> should be probably managing a little harder . . .
> but [my boss is] not here to visit and see what
> I do and . . . doesn't really know how I manage
> these people, because maybe I don't put them on
> documentation.

Because of the complexity of the balanced-scorecard system, people can't really focus very well on a few key dimensions. Research indicates that human beings can keep only about seven things in their heads at any one time.[17] Having more than 20 indicators of performance in six categories dilutes the attention employees can pay to any single issue or even a small set of issues. With so many indicators and measures, it is easy to simply ignore the whole thing because of the impossibility of comprehending so many dimensions at once. The behavioral effect of the scorecard is further diluted because of the appearance of subjectivity. People believe the ratings are subjective, biased, and not necessarily valid, so they don't believe the ratings are fully under their control. They conclude that their performance does not necessarily translate into good ratings because of the subjective aspects of the system. Consequently, it is, again, easy to simply disregard the entire system. In response to a question about the effects of the scorecard, a person who had worked on developing the scorecard system and who was considered to be a good branch manager said:

> I don't think it's really changed people's behavior.
> In the beginning, people were excited about the
> scorecard because it seemed like an opportunity to
> make a lot more money. When that didn't happen
> it kind of went: "this is just like SBL [another man-
> agement change initiative at the bank]. I wasn't get-
> ting money then, I'm not getting money now. I'm
> still getting my 4% merit increase. Life goes on."

I think that some people are judged differently from others. When you allow someone subjectivity, what happens is that they tend to favor certain people not maybe knowing all the details. My boss manages probably 30 other people and can't spend a whole lot of time interacting with me. We'll have a meeting once a week for two or three hours. My boss doesn't visit my branch all that much. We don't have phone conversations. But yet, at the end of the quarter, [my boss] can look at my numbers which is half of my scorecard and then the other half is all . . . perceptions based on maybe 12 hours of interaction during the quarter. I don't really think that's fair—whether I benefit from it, which in most cases I do, or whether there's a lot of other people who don't benefit from it.

Finally, the balanced-scorecard examples illustrate another phenomenon we frequently observed: Hard measures drive out the soft, and precise metrics can miss important elements of performance. For instance, the branch manager quoted above was apparently reasonably successful in identifying and developing managerial talent, since people from his branch were often promoted to positions in other locations. This is an important part of being a good leader—being successful in the people development process. But he didn't get much credit for this success. It would be possible, of course, to just add another quantitative indicator to the system, for instance, the number or proportion of people from one's direct reports promoted to higher positions. But that would make the system even more complex and, in any event, misses the point. It is often difficult to specify in advance every dimension and every aspect of managerial performance. Trying to obtain precise metrics of performance can miss critical, subtle elements of performance, elements that vary across people and that cannot always be defined in advance, let alone objectively and precisely measured.

The lessons from several financial institutions' experience with the balanced scorecard are that, at the end of the day, effective measurement systems that will drive behavior need to be simple enough to focus attention on key elements and fair enough so that people believe they can affect the measures. Also, the measurement systems cannot be so powerful in directing people that important elements of behavior and performance that are not, and cannot be, fully captured in the measures receive too little or no attention because of the unrelenting emphasis just on the quantitative measures incorporated in the system. No measurement system is going to perfectly capture all of the important elements of performance or all of the behaviors that people need to do for the organization to be successful. So, measurements should be guides, helping to direct behavior, but not so powerful in their implementation that they substitute for the judgment and wisdom that is so necessary to acquire knowledge and turn it into action. This "light touch" in the implementation of measures is particularly important because such systems are invariably going to be changed much less frequently than the rate at which new circumstances arise and new knowledge of how to enhance organizational performance develops. Given this difference in cycle times, firms need measurement systems that don't restrict or inhibit the development and implementation of performance knowledge.

Although implemented in many companies with the best of intentions, the balanced scorecard often fails on these dimensions. Important elements of performance knowledge not captured in the formal measurement system get neglected, for instance, the people development process. Measures come to focus attention to such a degree that intuitive wisdom and tacit knowledge cannot be readily implemented. At that point, the good intentions don't matter. Either behavior is largely unaffected, people are demoralized, the wrong behavior is encouraged, or some combination of these unanticipated outcomes occurs.

In-Process versus Outcome Measures: General Motors

Why is it so hard to implement good manufacturing practices, such as those embodied in lean or flexible production, even though virtually every automobile executive knows that such systems produce higher-quality cars at lower cost? As we reported in Chapter 1, a study of the diffusion of flexible manufacturing systems over a five-year period found only modest implementation of lean manufacturing systems, and in some plants, these management practices had been taken out. The measurements that are made—and not made—by automobile firms contribute to these implementation problems. Managers at General Motors told us that part of the problem is that the company uses too many end-of-process measures—measures that tell them how well they have done—and not enough in-process indicators and controls that help them understand what is going right and what is going wrong. So, learning at General Motors and elsewhere is inhibited because companies are measuring the wrong things and not gathering data that permit them to really understand, manage, and control the process. In that regard, budgetary figures, costs, and even the balanced-scorecard measures are too far removed from processes in many instances to guide behavior and permit knowledge to be developed and turned into action.

Tom Lasorda, a senior executive at General Motors charged with the responsibility of improving manufacturing operations by implementing flexible production techniques, was articulate on this issue:

> We are outstanding at providing what I call end of process measures. So, what was your absenteeism? What was your first time quality number? What was your scheduled production? What was your cost per car, and all that stuff? Now walk it back from there and say, "give me your in-process measures." And from an individual level of how you relate to those, you won't find it as detailed as you will in other companies. Can

> I go to this station and find the SPC [statistical process control] charts that are controlled by the individual, and the standardized work charts that are being checked by the individual? If you had that level of detail what you will find is a far more robust organization with fewer measures, I might add, at the end of the process. *Because the company that is not in control has far more measures because they're not changing the basic management systems that are in place.*
>
> We've got to shrink the number of measures, get the organization focused on them, and then build a pyramid that says, "these are primary measures, progress measures, and in process measures," so everybody can link their job to the overall measures.[18]

The irony is that the end–of–process measures cause those subjected to them to feel a great deal of pressure, to feel tightly controlled. The problem is that they are not being measured or controlled on the things that really matter and things that they can directly affect—their specific behaviors and actions on the job. So, people at General Motors may feel more tightly controlled than those at Toyota, for instance, even though the process is actually much less under control at GM and even though there is much more control over specific work practices at Toyota. The lesson is that measuring people on outcomes and not giving them in–process measurement can help create stress and frustration, but often does not result in a more controlled or effective operations process.

Lasorda had a specific plan to overcome the measurement problem in the manufacturing part of North American operations:

> It's a set of measures that is much more refined so that everybody understands how he or she links to them. . . . Any company has an enormous number of measures. The ones you might see are the end of business measures. What did you do on profitability? Go down to each level of the organization and

say, "Can you show me your measures?" What I've typically seen is 15 to 18 measures. And then you'd say to them, "What are we doing in-process?" And there would be nothing.

So here is what I have said to the organization. We've developed what we call the Business Plan Deployment Strategy, which says what are the key business plan measures that are going to affect the viability of the enterprise. Let's focus on those and how you drive those into the organization. And how do you engage people in business issues and work on trying to improve performance against the goals. . . . All of a sudden, you start engaging people in the business where before they really didn't understand the measures and how they related to them.[19]

The General Motors example teaches us that real control does not come simply from having a plethora of outcome measures. Control and improvement come from measures that provide information about processes, measures that give people immediate and understandable information about how they need to act. In this instance, these lessons seem to have been learned and are being implemented. But the learning came with difficulty. Lasorda and others first needed to overcome the belief that the best measurement systems assess mostly end-of-process outcomes—a perspective that fails to take into account that measurements are only useful when they can actually guide behavior.

Why Poor Measurement Practices Persist

The negative consequences of the measurement systems we described above were widely known and understood by people in each of these firms, including top management. Similarly, in dozens of other cases that we need not repeat here, the story is the same: Numerous people in the organization understand and are able to explain in articulate detail that they are using a flawed set of measurement practices. So, the question becomes, If measurements create problems in developing and implementing knowledge, if some measurement practices make the knowing–doing gap worse, and if people in the firms involved know this, why do these ineffective measurement practices persist?

There are no easy answers to this question. But our conclusion from doing our own research and from reading pertinent work by others is that there are three interrelated processes that explain why these flawed measurement practices persist:

1. Many companies operate using an oversimplified or incorrect model of human behavior.

2. Because that model of behavior is widely shared, it has become institutionalized in certain types of measures and measurement systems, which have assumed a taken–for–granted quality, have become a signal of competent management (even if they are actually the opposite), and are so widely diffused that firms are reluctant not to follow them.

3. The primacy of the capital markets and shareholder concerns creates pressures for measurement practices that are relevant to shareholders' interests but may be irrelevant or even counterproductive for the ultimate success of the business.

The model of behavior implicit in the measurement systems used by most firms is that individuals are atomistic and economic, rather than social, creatures. The atomistic view is captured in having measures for each individual. This procedure presumes that (1) individual results are the consequences of *individual* decisions and actions and that (2) individual outcomes and individual behaviors are under the control and discretion of these individuals, so that results and decisions can be reasonably reliably attributed to individuals. Think back to the Citibank balanced-scorecard system and its associated bonus plan. Each individual in a managerial role receives his or her own scorecard measures. That presumes that performance, as assessed by the scorecard or, for that matter, by any other measurement system, results from individual decisions and behaviors—which is why individual incentives are tied to the measures. For this measurement and incentive scheme to be sensible, it is also implicitly assumed that it is possible to make valid judgments about performance using dimensions of the scorecard. In other words, the process assumes that performance can be assessed and assigned to individuals.

But if there is one thing that we know for certain, it is that organizations are systems in which behavior is interdependent. What you are able to accomplish, and indeed, what you choose to do and how you behave, is not solely under your individual control. Rather, your behavior and performance are influenced by the actions, attitudes, and behaviors of many others in the immediate environment. Consider the Citibank balanced-scorecard example. Is teamwork, one dimension along which people are evaluated, just under the influence of the branch manager? Or is teamwork also a consequence of many organizational management practices, including rewards and measurements, that the branch manager can't affect very much? How much effect does that person, by himself or herself, have on customer satisfaction? Customer satisfaction is the result of interactions with numerous other people and of decisions that the branch manager doesn't even fully control. One branch manager, in commenting on the Gallup survey results used to assess customer satisfaction, noted:

> They don't tell you the questions but they tell you the answers, and even when they tell you the answers, it's not very specific. They'll say, the lines were too long. Well, the lines were too long at what time? Maybe there's a reason. Today if you told me my lines were too long this afternoon I'd understand

why. It is because I had to send two people home sick. So, if a customer came in and that customer actually got polled, and it's someone who happened to come in today, the person is going to say that the lines were too long.

The fiction in most measurement systems is that individual performance measures assigned to individuals presumably reflect the effort and skill those people used in doing their jobs. But individual performance in an interdependent system will always be difficult or impossible to measure. Individual performance and behavior, even if they could be accurately assessed, are the result of many things over which the person has little or no control, as the above example nicely illustrates.

Measurement practices are heavily institutionalized, which means that they are taken for granted and used in a mindless way. There is a profession, called accounting, that has made a business of developing and institutionalizing certain measures, even if they are the wrong ones. Consider the following. How much variation do you see in companies' business strategies? A lot. How much variation do you see in organizational cultures? A lot. How much variation do you see even in company incentive systems? Again, a great deal. Now consider, how much variation do you see, not just in public financial reporting, but even in management accounting measures and practices? Not much. Does that make sense to you? Does it seem sensible that firms that vary dramatically in their strategies, their cultures, their incentive schemes, and so forth, should all have and use essentially similar managerial measurement and reporting systems? As long as accountants have control of internal measurements, not much will change. We have nothing against accountants, but are simply noting that they are pursuing a different set of goals. Specifically, we have seen few accountants or controllers who worry about the effect of measurement systems on turning knowledge into action or on the organization's ability to develop and transfer skill and competence.

And this brings us to our last, interrelated source of the problem—the primacy of capital market interests. Public accounting is first and foremost designed to ensure that investors have accurate and consistent financial information on which to base their decisions. Of course, management accounting is presumably separate and distinct from public financial reporting, and information systems and measures could, in theory, be designed to accomplish anything that managers wanted. But public companies have an audit committee, and the public accounting firms have to assure the audit committee that the company's financial controls are sound. So even internal audits and financial controls soon become focused on the public, capital market aspects of financial reporting as developed and enforced by public accounting firms. For good or for ill, this capital market influence further ensures uniformity of practices. Since there is much less uniformity of business conditions, culture, and strategy, this uniformity in measurement practices almost guarantees measurements that have little connection to the particular business problems and issues confronting a specific organization. But even in the face of institutionalized pressures and generally shared models of behavior, some firms have been better able to get their measures right. The situation isn't hopeless. Let's consider some examples.

Using Measures to Enhance the Development and Use of Knowledge

We found that a simple principle was applied in firms in which the measurement systems helped—rather than undermined—the ability to turn knowledge into action. Such firms measured things that were core to their culture and values and intimately tied to their basic business model and strategy, and used these measures to make business processes visible to all employees. For example, at Wainwright Industries, a privately owned manufacturing company that won the Baldrige Award in 1994, "measures are simple, visual indicator systems to operationalize the goals so everyone can tell at every moment whether or not their actions are producing the desired results."[20] Also, in most instances the measures used were aggregate, measuring the results at a group, subunit, or organizational level rather than attempting to do the impossible by assessing the performance and contributions of individuals working in interdependent systems.

In a sense, the underlying premise of the balanced scorecard is right—measures should embody a theory of organizational performance. At Wainwright Industries, the five key indicators are, in order of importance, (1) safety, (2) measures of employee (internal customer) satisfaction and continuous improvement, (3) customer satisfaction, (4) quality, and (5) financial performance. The relative importance of the various measures reflects leaders' beliefs about how the company and its business works. Quality is comparatively low in importance because "at Wainwright, quality is an automatic result of employee satisfaction, training and involvement." Similarly for financial performance: "Strong business performance results from employee satisfaction, training, involvement, customer satisfaction, and highest product quality."[21] There are two key differences between what these firms did and the balanced-scorecard approach: (1) The measurement systems are far simpler and understandable, and (2) they took mindful actions to build measures that suited their needs rather than mindlessly adopting measures that were well institutionalized in accounting firms. These organizations recognized the trade-off between having a measurement system that captured the full complexity of the sources of performance and having a system that focused attention on fewer, but the most critical, aspects of operations and culture.

Measures Linked to Cultural Values and Philosophy: The Men's Wearhouse

To understand the wisdom of a company's measurement system, it is first necessary to know something about its business model and culture. The Men's Wearhouse sees its salespeople as professionals—which is why it spends so much time and effort training them—whose goal is to develop an understanding of customers' wardrobe needs and to cultivate a high-service relationship so that the company becomes *the* source to fill those needs. Their sales philosophy is described in their training materials:

> The Men's Wearhouse sales philosophy is consistent with the Company's goal of creating Win-Win-Win situations for our customers, wardrobe consultants, and the Company . . .
>
> The customer wins because we have consultants. As team-oriented, professional consultants, we seek to create a quality relationship with the customer. . . . Unlike other stores with "clerks," The Men's Wearhouse is able to show and assist a gentleman with an entire wardrobe concept. This helps him to look and feel better, while saving time and money.
>
> Since you have met the customer's clothing needs well beyond those he initially identified, you have made a great sale *and* a customer for life. . . . The Men's Wearhouse wins with every customer that is delighted by the quality of service, the value of the clothing and the unique shopping experience.[22]

Charlie Bresler, one of the most senior executives at the company, in his orientation talk at Suits University, emphasizes the importance of team selling and personal relationships with other people in the company:

> My most important job is really maintaining an environment in our stores which is a positive work environment. . . . As a wardrobe consultant, you are

expected to define your success in part as only achieved when your teammates, the sales associates, the tailors, and other wardrobe consultants and management people in the store are also successful . . . and that you will, over time, define your success not only in terms of your own goals, but also the goals and aspirations of the other people in your store. And that you will come to really care about them as human beings and as people who finally realize their potential, too.[23]

The company has over 400 stores throughout the United States. Maintaining this culture and philosophy is a challenge. But the firm has developed measures that help them accomplish this task. To sit with Charlie Bresler and look at sales figures for wardrobe consultants in each store is to learn how the measurement system helps the company enforce and track its culture. One important measure he and the other leaders use is the number of transactions for each wardrobe consultant in the store. This number should be approximately the same for all of the people in a given store. If it is not, it means that someone is not sharing walk-in business equally with the other people. To hog customers is to not display the proper team spirit, and people who persist in this behavior get fired, even if their sales volumes are high. The second number is the average size of the ticket, or sale. The company actually has a higher commission for transactions over $500 because of the belief that wardrobe consultants, not clerks, are able to learn about an individual's wardrobe needs and fill more of those needs, particularly by selling accessories such as shoes, ties, and shirts. This ability to "accessorize," measured from the sales tickets, helps managers assess training needs and the success of their efforts to produce sales professionals who truly are wardrobe consultants.

To reinforce the cultural values, the firm's performance appraisal system is focused on specific behaviors—behaviors that can be coached and learned. For instance, in addition to specific sales figures and measures that indicate how much cross-selling of merchandise the person is doing, some of the other dimensions on the appraisal include "Participates in team selling; ensures proper alteration revenue collection; treats customers in a warm and caring manner; contributes to store maintenance and stock work; is familiar with merchandise carried at local competitors; greets, interviews, and tapes all customers properly; and contributes to store maintenance and stock work."[24]

The Men's Wearhouse has developed quantitative and more qualitative but still behaviorally specific indicators that closely match its intended culture, values, and business model. The quantitative measures are produced routinely by the firm's management information system and are used to identify problems and to recognize successes. By making the measures behaviorally specific, the company has come closer to actually having in-process measures that can be taught, learned, and implemented, as contrasted with the more typical outcome or end-of-process measures.

Few, Simple Measures: SAS Institute

SAS Institute, a software firm providing statistical analysis, data mining, data warehousing, and decision support software, has a business model that emphasizes relationships. "Rather than selling a product and then selling upgrades on a regular basis, SAS offers an annual licensing arrangement after a thirty-day free trial period that provides for free upgrades and customer support. . . . Over time, revenues from a given customer will be higher, *as long as the customer renews the licensing agreement* [emphasis added]."[25] It is also in an industry in which knowledge and intellectual capital are critical. Its measurement practices reflect both these business imperatives and the philosophy of the firm, as expressed by James Goodnight, one of the co-founders and currently the CEO: "What we tried to do was to treat people who joined the company as we ourselves wanted to be treated. . . . If you take care of your people, they will take care of the company."[26]

SAS Institute believes that people should work at a place because they enjoy the work and the people they work with—financial incentives are less important. Consequently, the company offers no one stock options or phantom stock. People are paid good, competitive salaries, and at the end of the year there is typically a small bonus (less than 10 percent of salary). Merit raises are given once a year. There are no short-term individual incentive pay schemes—no sales commissions for account executives, for instance. The company deemphasizes individual competition by not posting comparative sales data by name. Barrett Joyner, vice president of North American sales and marketing, had this to say about incentive schemes and their associated measures:

> We have sales targets, but mostly as a way of keeping score. . . . We're big on a long-term approach. I'm not smart enough to incent on a formula. People are constantly finding holes in incentive plans. . . . A lot of incentive plans represent ways of signalling to people what they were supposed to do and to emphasize. . . . Here, we just tell people what we want them to do and what we expect.[27]

The firm has done away with its performance appraisal forms. David Russo, the vice president of human resources, commented:

> If there were a good performance appraisal process, everybody would be using it. . . . I don't think you can really manage someone's performance. I think you can observe the results. I think you can give them the tools. I think you can set short and long-term goals. And you can sit back and see if it happens or it doesn't happen. . . . Our idea is to have performance management be based on conversation instead of documentation.[28]

Although apparently a radical idea, a number of other companies—including the GM Powertrain Group and Glenroy, Inc., a privately held manufacturer of packaging materials—have eliminated the annual performance review measurement with good success:

> Too many leaders confuse feedback with paperwork. "Filling out a form is *inspection*, not feedback," says Kelly Allan . . . "History has taught us that relying on inspections is costly, improves nothing for very long, and makes the organization less competitive."[29]

Jim Goodnight of SAS sees a simple one-page financial report each month. Managers are evaluated primarily on their ability to attract and retain people. The company monitors turnover very carefully, and in 1997 had voluntary turnover of only 3 percent—a fraction of what is typical for the software industry. The company also tries to ensure that it is a great place to work, and takes the results of surveys and studies such as *Fortune*'s list of the 100 best places to work in America (it ranked third) very seriously.

In a relationship-oriented business based primarily on intellectual talent, SAS encourages long-term relationship behavior through its measurements and through what it chooses *not* to measure and make public. In a place in which the attraction and retention of talent is key, turnover and factors related to the building of talent are what the firm measures. The emphasis, even in a geographically dispersed organization of 5,000 people, remains on interpersonal communication—an emphasis consistent with the relationship-oriented business model and philosophy. You have relationships with people, not with reports or numbers.

Using Measures to Maintain Focus on What's Important: Intuit

Intuit is a large firm that develops and sells financial planning software for both individuals and small businesses—the best-known titles are TurboTax, Quicken, and QuickBooks—

implemented initially in both the Macintosh and PC environments and now on the Internet as well.[30] The firm today has about $600 million in annual revenue and 3,000 employees. The company has a set of operating values that include the following:

- Integrity without compromise
- Do right by all our customers
- It's the people
- Seek the best
- Continually improve processes
- Speak, listen, respond
- Teams work
- Customers define quality
- Think fast, move fast
- We care and give back

In 1998, three-quarters of the employees responding to the firm's annual employee survey agreed with the statement "Intuit lives up to the corporate operating values."

The company has faced numerous challenges, including increasing product market competition, the development of Internet-based financial planning services, an attempt by Microsoft to buy the company that was stopped by antitrust concerns, and the demands of recruiting and retaining a talented workforce in the Silicon Valley. The company is publicly traded and offers stock options as a recruitment and retention strategy, and so is concerned about its stock price. It would be easy to get diverted from doing what it knows it should. How has Intuit stayed focused? Mostly through its employee survey. Employees know the survey matters, so the response rate is quite high—73 percent in 1998. And, the company uses the survey results to guide its behavior. Between 1995 and 1998, the proportion of people agreeing with the statement "We care and give back" doubled to 77 percent. Of course, the survey by itself is of little value. Many companies have surveys and don't do anything with the results. Intuit people and the firm's cultural values are what make the surveys work. At the same time, generalized cultural values and intentions to be a certain way, without measures to assess how well the firm is doing, could easily become merely good intentions that do not drive action. The values, culture, and quality of the people provide the knowledge and intentions, and the surveys help turn that knowledge and values into action.

In 1995 employee morale was not where Intuit wanted it to be, so the company refocused on its people. Intuit moves around valuable employees, even at the cost of short-term efficiency, to reinforce its commitment to career development for its people. Moving people to different units also helps to reinforce the team culture by causing individuals to identify more with the company as a whole than with just small units. When an employee complained about not getting a raise, he received one a few days later after a thorough review by management. The company reemphasized its social activities and celebrations, and did not let financial challenges divert its focus from building morale and spirit.

Intuit uses both its formal employee survey and informal feedback to quickly identify gaps between its aspirations, embodied in its core operating principles, and what it is doing. Then, leaders move quickly to address these gaps. The measurement system at Intuit provides an ongoing check on how the company is living up to its values—values that reflect what managers know to be related to the firm's ultimate financial success. The measurement, nothing more than an employee survey, but one that is taken very seriously, affords a way of focusing managerial effort on those dimensions of the culture that most need attention at a given moment. At Intuit, the measurement system helps to reinforce and build the culture and to implement practices that leaders know are vital to the firm's success.

Measures That Produce Change: Sears

One response we often hear when we talk about firms that have fewer knowing–doing gaps is, The examples you have given are companies that have done things correctly from the beginning. Can firms ever change? How? These questions make the Sears story particularly interesting, because Sears confronted difficulties that were surmounted in large part through changes in measurement practices. But before we get to this case, we need to also confront a potential misperception: The examples we have provided, such as SAS Institute, Intuit, and The Men's Wearhouse, did not implement the right measurement practices from the beginning. In each instance there was, and is, ongoing learning about what worked and what didn't. In all these cases, mistakes occurred and were used as information about changes that needed to be made, not as bad news that should be swept under the rug or used as a reason to blame or punish individuals. So, rather than being used to instill fear in these organizations, both the process of developing the measurement systems and the measurement practices themselves are used to support learning and to drive out fear. Measurement practices and measures evolved as the organizations developed a better understanding of their business model, a better–defined culture, and more clarity concerning their guiding philosophy. What distinguishes these examples from many others is not that they did things perfectly from the beginning but their willingness to focus measurement practices on the important task of turning knowledge into action. And, the leaders of these firms were willing to break with convention and place less emphasis on what everyone else was doing and measuring.

In the case of Sears, the reinvention of measurement practices resulted from a financial crisis. In 1992, Sears had revenues of $52 billion, "nearly 9% lower than 1991 revenues of $57 billion, and lower than annual revenues in each of the three preceding years. Sears generated a net loss from continuing operations of $1.8 billion and a total net loss of $3.9 billion."[31] The financial problems were, in large measure, the result of Sears' failure to put knowledge of successful retail practices into action. As for the knowledge of retailing part, Anthony Rucci, the company's head of human resources, noted:

> The basic elements of an employee–customer–profit model are not difficult to grasp. Any person with even a little experience in retailing understands intuitively that there is a chain of cause and effect running from employee behavior to customer behavior to profits, and it's not hard to see that behavior depends primarily on attitude.[32]

The problem was that as competition, from Wal–Mart, Kmart, and Target, among others, had intensified over the preceding years, Sears had made changes in response to competitive pressure and declining profits that were inconsistent with this knowledge of how retailing worked. These changes created a continuing cycle of poor performance and ineffective responses:

> In the 1960s and 1970s, you could feel success as you walked through the stores. Managers and employees were loyal, energetic. . . . Employees were mostly full time and they really knew their product. . . . Then came the competition and profitability declined. . . . Everyone down to hourly–paid supervisors . . . had been on incentives, but over time those incentives were eliminated. . . . Corporate also reduced the number of central administrative support groups. . . . The stores got less support. They also eliminated several positions in the store. As a result, there were fewer *knowledgeable* salespeople out on the floor, and store managers ended up doing less merchandising and employee coaching and more paperwork and logistics.[33]

Sears' problems, manifested in an "intense internal focus,"[34] were magnified by a measurement system that was also internally focused and focused on the past. The traditional cost accounting and financial measurement system assessed costs and profit margins that had already been achieved, but did not register the diminishing levels of both employee and customer satisfaction.[35] So, the measurement system could not assess the damage being done to the firm's long-term viability by actions being taken to increase profit margins and decrease costs in the short run, actions that included putting more part-time and less-experienced—but cheaper—people on the floor to serve customers. Most important, the measurement system did not reflect the essential retailing business model of the link between employees, customers, and profits. As a result, measurement practices hindered the implementation of what Sears knew about how to enhance its performance.

Arthur Martinez arrived in the fall of 1992 and led a remarkable transformation at Sears that drove up both operating results and its stock price. Martinez took a lot of short-term measures to enhance service, such as emphasizing training, putting the best people in the stores during evenings and weekends when the best customers were shopping, offering Sunday deliveries, and similar steps. Martinez also set in place a strategy of cultural transformation, based on a change in measurement practices, that would ensure that the changes at Sears would last. The company developed a vision called the 3Cs or the "three compellings": Sears was to be a compelling place to shop, a compelling place to work, and a compelling place to invest. These objectives were translated into specific metrics. A compelling place to shop was measured by overall customer satisfaction and customer retention. A compelling place to work was measured by attitudes about the job and the company. And a compelling place to invest was measured by revenue growth, operating margins, asset utilization, and indicators of productivity improvement.[36] Sears' measurement practices were based on the desire to develop leading, not lagging, indicators of performance. The measures were validated in econometric studies that quantified exactly how much effect improvements in various dimensions had on other indicators.

Refinement of the measurements and the model predicting performance is part of an ongoing process that continues to the present. Measures change as more knowledge becomes available. Like Intuit, Sears began to pay more attention to employee surveys, partly because the company wanted to retain and motivate good people and partly because of the demonstration of the empirical connection between employee attitudes, customer attitudes, and store performance. Executives in Sears believe that the changes in measurement practices were crucial to the firm's turnaround:

> The point is that we know vastly more than we once did, that all that information helps us run the company, and that some of it has given us a decided competitive edge. . . . Our model shows that a 5 point improvement in employee attitudes will drive a 1.3 point improvement in customer satisfaction, which in turn will drive a 0.5% improvement in revenue growth. . . . These numbers are as rigorous as any others we work with at Sears. Every year, our accounting firm audits them as closely as it audits our financials.[37]

The changes in the measures at Sears permitted the firm to recapture and implement what it once knew—the connections between management actions, employee attitudes, customer attitudes and loyalty, and profits. In a company that had for years taken measures of employee attitudes because of a commitment to the importance of its people, managers, with the help of the new measurement model, reaffirmed the importance of Sears' people to the firm's success. As one result, frontline people received much more training in understanding the business, the firm's strategy, and the competitive environment. And, employees were given more say and authority in helping the company regain its competitive footing. Just as one set of accounting measures had driven the company off course, a different set of measures, more embedded in the actual business model and operating processes of the retail business, helped the firm recover.

Measurement That Turns Knowledge into Action

Based on the examples of both good and bad practices we have seen in this chapter, we can conclude that measurement practices that help organizations develop knowledge and turn that knowledge into action typically have the following properties:

- The measurements are relatively global in their scope, focusing less on trying to assess individual performance, which is always difficult in interdependent systems, and more on focusing attention on factors critical to *organizational* success.

- The measures are often focused more on processes and means to ends, and less on end-of-process or final outcomes. This focus results in measures that facilitate learning and provide data that can better guide action and decision making.

- They are tied to and reflect the business model, culture, and philosophy of the firm. As a result, measurement practices vary from one firm to the other as the business imperatives, cultures, and philosophies vary. And, in measuring things such as adherence to values, recruitment and retention, and working cooperatively with others, the measures depart from conventional accounting-based indicators.

- The measures result from a mindful, ongoing process of learning from experience and experimentation. There is not the sense that the system is ever completed. Rather, there is the view that the measurement system can always be improved and, because the business environment is likely to change, practices that are effective now may be ineffective in the future. Measures evolve to serve a fundamental core business and operating philosophy or strategy that is more constant.

- The measurement process uses comparatively few metrics. Although these firms may collect a large amount of data, they emphasize and attend to a small set of measures that are believed to be especially crucial for supporting the company's business model, philosophy, and culture. A focus on critical issues and processes is emphasized at the expense of comprehensiveness and complexity—things that dilute attention and that mix the important with the trivial.

- At its best, measurement closes the loop, auditing and assessing what the organization is doing, thereby ensuring, as in the case of Intuit, that the firm does what it knows.

Unfortunately, just knowing these guidelines for designing better measurement practices does not ensure that they will be implemented. We have shown that there are substantial barriers to implementing these principles, regardless of their wisdom or validity, not the least of which is the accounting industry and conventional accounting and measurement practices. But there is some cause for optimism. Some of the firms in which we have seen the most effective measurement practices are publicly traded. So, a company need not be private or even owner-controlled to implement measurements that help it build and implement knowledge. At The Men's Wearhouse and SAS Institute, leaders are mindful that their philosophies and business models run contrary to the conventional wisdom in their industries, and believe that a focus solely on the short term will undermine long-term performance as well as sacrifice other values these firms hold dear. In the case of Sears, a financial crisis gave leaders an opportunity to break with the immediate past and to develop a measurement system that supported their business model. In other instances, the measurement approach arose from a particular business philosophy and culture that wouldn't tolerate either rampant short-termism or measuring things that didn't matter. In each of the instances in which effective measurement practices were used, knowing what to do, why it needed to be done, and having the persistence and courage to do it helped leaders turn knowledge about how to enhance performance into organizational action.

|6| When Internal Competition Turns Friends into Enemies

T HE DEGREE OF COMPETITION in any society or company is largely a matter of choice, not the inevitable result of some property of human nature.[1] Companies and societies vary dramatically in how much they use competition to organize what people do. Some companies and cultures have less competition and instead emphasize cooperation. Others, particularly in the United States, emphasize competition as an organizing principle. Most Americans believe that competition is good for national economic systems, producing innovation and the efficient allocation of resources. "Competition . . . is believed to inspire superior performance and to be the engine that drives the economy and accounts for the success of capitalism."[2] Competition fits the cultural emphasis on individualism in the United States, where a Puritan tradition maintains that suffering is redeeming and a Social Darwinist philosophy emphasizes the many benefits from a survival-of-the-fittest contest.

In an analogous fashion, competition inside firms is also widely thought to promote innovation, efficiency, and higher levels of organizational performance. The Lincoln Electric Company is justly famous for its successful individual piece-rate incentive system. The Harvard Business School case on Lincoln is among the most widely used in management education. James F. Lincoln and his brother, | 177

John C. Lincoln, founded and led the firm together from 1895 to 1972, and James wrote numerous management articles and books that proclaimed the virtues of competition and individual achievement. For example, he asserted:

> Competition will mean the disappearance of the lazy and incompetent, be they workers, industrialists, or distributors. Competition promotes progress. Competition determines who will be the leader. . . . It is a hard taskmaster. . . . If some way could be found so that competition could be eliminated from life, the result would be disastrous. Any nation and any people disappear if life becomes too easy. There is no danger from a hard life as all history shows.[3]

Andrew Grove, past CEO and current chairman of Intel, appears to be a modern incarnation of James Lincoln. Grove has led one of the most successful corporations of his era and is highly regarded, at least by the business press, for his management acumen. Grove is also like James Lincoln in that he has written popular management books and articles that proclaim and reinforce widely held beliefs about the virtues of competition. In 1983, he wrote in *High Output Management*:

> Eliciting peak performance means going up against something or somebody. . . . For years the performance of the Intel facilities maintenance group, which is responsible for keeping our buildings clean and neat, was mediocre, and no amount of pressure or inducement seemed to do any good. We then initiated a program in which each building's upkeep was periodically scored by a resident senior manager. . . . The score was then compared with those given the other buildings. The condition of *all of them* dramatically improved almost immediately. Nothing else was done. . . . What they did get was a racetrack, an arena of competition. . . . Conversely, of course, when the competition is removed, motivation associated with it vanishes.[4]

Grove's example illustrates the essence of competition: mutually exclusive goal attainment, a situation in which one person's (or firm's) success requires the failure of another.[5] On the "racetrack," only one person or group can win the race.

These beliefs in the benefits of competition are largely taken for granted in U.S. business culture. Few distinctions are made between competition within companies and across them, and analogies are casually drawn between the benefits of competition at the level of national economic systems and at the level of individuals and units within firms. The beliefs about competition are so ingrained that they serve as mindless, automatic, but powerful principles for organizing and managing individual behavior. As a consequence, firms do all kinds of things to encourage competition, whether that competition is focused on external competitors or internally on other, similar units within the firm. Organizations act to create a "racetrack" where only one person, group, division, or subunit can win.

Management practices that produce internal competition are so common that they seem unexceptional. Examples of such practices include (1) forced distributions of performance evaluations, so that only some fraction of people can earn the highest evaluation; (2) recognition awards given to individuals, such as employee of the month or year programs; (3) forced distributions of individual merit raise budgets, so what one person receives another cannot; (4) contests between departments or divisions, units, shifts, or even individuals within units for various monetary and nonmonetary prizes; and (5) published rankings of unit or individual performance. Each of these practices creates a zero-sum contest in which the success or rewards of one person or department *must* come at the expense of another. There can be only one top-ranked person or unit, so for someone to be first, others must be ranked farther down, including last.

There is no doubt that these zero-sum games can inspire people to work hard, and the individual winners of these internal competitions benefit from their victories. In our research, however, we uncovered case after case in which the costs of such individual victories were borne by those people, groups, and units that lost the contests. And, these internal competitions didn't just harm the "losers." The competition harmed everyone who had a stake in these organizations, because these practices undermined the overall ability of the companies to turn knowledge into action. In this chapter, we first describe some different ways that internal competition creates knowing–doing gaps. We then examine why, in spite of these problems for organizational learning and organizational action, internal competition remains so pervasive as a management approach. Finally, we illustrate how some organizations avoid the negative effects of internal competitive dynamics that turn friends into enemies.

How Internal Competitive Dynamics Create Knowing-Doing Gaps

Undermining Organizational Loyalty: Creating Turnover in Investment Banking

Investment banking is an industry that depends heavily on the knowledge and skill of its people. It is an industry in which the assets walk out the door each night, and in which a firm's success depends on the knowledge, skill, contacts, and reputations of its people. Investment banking is also an industry characterized by high turnover and, when times are good, a very competitive recruiting environment. Turnover is expensive. New employees often demand and receive guaranteed payments for a year or two, regardless of their production, and frequently obtain large signing bonuses as well. The churn in personnel hampers performance on any task that requires interaction with others, because every investment banker constantly struggles to keep pace with the constant influx of new names and faces, not to mention to learn what each newcomer knows and which skills each has and lacks. Knowledge, including technical knowledge, understanding of the firm's culture, and information about the firm's customers, departs each time another investment banker leaves.

Top executives in virtually every investment bank recognize all these facts, claim to value their people, and say they want to reduce turnover. The means required to reduce turnover are neither magical nor secret. Such information is easy to find, is already known to most of these executives, and, as performance knowledge goes, is not especially difficult to implement. But such knowledge is not turned into action. And one of the main reasons is that an individualistic and competitive culture characterizes almost all of these firms, interfering with efforts to build strong organizational cultures and retain individual employees.

Investment banks frequently are the scenes of rude, even abusive behavior, as the following example from a case study illustrates:

> An extreme example of abusive behavior occurred recently at a regional office of a national brokerage chain. A young trainee was systematically ridiculed and insulted for months by most of the senior people in his office. Some people at the firm even made a film about this and showed it as a joke at a national sales meeting of the firm. The trainee was eventually fired and has filed a lawsuit against the company. . . . Firms send a message to their employees that as long as an employee brings in revenue, he [sic] will be well paid regardless of his behavior toward others or toward the firm itself.[6]

This behavior was tolerated because of the competitive, individualistic culture typical in these companies. The only thing that matters is individual performance, being near the top of the pecking order, not the effect of any given individual and his or her behavior on others in the firm or even on the firm's overall culture. This is obviously not an environment that induces people to remain.

A second case study analyzed turnover and why it persisted, even as leaders claimed they wanted to reduce the loss of people, at Bear, Stearns & Company, another investment bank:

> Even by Wall Street standards, Bear Stearns' culture is highly competitive, independent, and entrepreneurial. . . . Because senior bankers are paid based on the transactions they attract and execute, many come to regard success as theirs alone[,] . . . dissuading loyalty. . . . This culture does little to promote the development of a solid core of junior bankers by senior managers, except to the extent they are immediately useful. Many workers come to feel like mercenaries who are discarded after each use on a specific transaction, and consequently very few junior bankers develop any loyalty to the firm.[7]

For those who claim that this is simply the nature of this industry, an inevitable consequence of the particular business and technology, there are counterexamples of firms that operate differently. Goldman, Sachs is not only one of the most consistently profitable firms in the industry, but it is also one that has a very strong, team–based culture. And, firms in the investment or money management industry, such as Barclays Global Investors, discussed in detail in the next chapter, also typically have less internally competitive cultures.

Firms with team–based cultures or that use other means to dampen internal, zero–sum competition do not suffer from the adverse consequences of a system that turns people against one another, with behavior that sometimes gets out of hand. These team–oriented firms don't as quickly or emphatically label some employees as losers and winners, and don't keep re–sorting employees so that losers quickly leave or are fired while the winners are tempted to leave for better offers at other firms. Nothing in competitive environments builds any attachment between people and their companies. The result is that investment bankers operate much like free agents in sports, often obtaining salaries that are so high as to cause their firms to earn low returns on capital and, on occasion, to lose money.

Undermining Teamwork and Creating Software Bugs at Microsoft

A study of a Microsoft business unit uncovered why teamwork is especially important to the giant software firm: "As desktop applications increase in complexity, it becomes impossible for any one person to understand everything about what the software should do, how the software functions, and what the software actually does. In order to develop these applications, employees with different backgrounds and skills must work together to produce an integrated product."[8] This case study found that Microsoft managers knew, and repeatedly said, that developing software depended on "sharing information about *what* others are doing, sharing information about *how* others are doing it, and promoting productivity within a *team setting*." Yet these known, superior practices were not implemented in the unit because "the allocation of rewards based on individual performance downplays the importance of unselfish teamwork and promotes competition . . . [that] creates barriers to the efficient sharing of information and skills."[9] As one Microsoft engineer put it:

> There are instances where a single individual may really be cranking and doing some excellent work, but not communicating . . . and working within the team toward implementation. These folks may be viewed as high rated by top management. . . . As long as the individual is bonused highly for their innovation and gutsy risk-taking only, and not on

how well the team accomplishes the goal, there can be a real disconnect and the individual never really gets the message that you should keep doing great things but share them with the team so you don't surprise them.[10]

The case study found that the company provided low base salaries in combination with bonuses that were distributed across teams and units in a forced-curve, zero-sum distribution. This structure caused people to resist helping one another. It wasn't just that helping a colleague took time away from someone's own work. The forced curve meant "Helping your fellow worker become more productive can actually hurt your chances of getting a higher bonus."[11] This competition also led to information hoarding, because everyone wanted to be an expert and be seen as more knowledgeable than internal competitors. Hoarding information obviously restricts learning about what others are doing and how they are doing it.

Microsoft is notorious for releasing software with large numbers of bugs. This case study suggests that the firm's competitive and individualistic culture fuels this problem. Because perceived individual expertise leads to high salary and bonus, there is an incentive for preventing others from uncovering your deficiencies. The head of quality assurance interviewed for the case study said she encouraged team members to swap positions occasionally because "fresh eyes" are useful for uncovering bugs. But she admitted that the competitive dynamics often meant this didn't happen because programmers didn't want other people to find their bugs.

Even though Microsoft managers understood the advantages of teamwork, this case study showed that the reward system and culture made it much harder to turn knowledge about the advantages of teams into action, at least in one business unit. Furthermore, reports from numerous other sources indicate that this continues to be a widespread problem at Microsoft. These difficulties will persist until the company eliminates management practices that encourage individualistic behavior and that limit internal learning and employee commitment to the enterprise based on anything other than money.

Undermining Knowledge Sharing:
Why Fresh Choice Didn't Learn from Zoopa

Internal competitive dynamics can also make learning from others inside the firm more difficult. This problem often occurs in firms where parallel units that perform at varying levels are expected to learn from each other, so that best practices are shared and the worse-performing units learn from those that do better. This is a case in which there is knowledge in the firm about how to work more effectively, and the goal is to spread this knowledge to all units so that its overall performance increases. This is also an instance in which new behaviors and management practices need to be acquired—learning has to happen so that people can replace old, inferior practices with new, superior ways. When learning from others inside an organization is desired, competition—especially when rewards and status are based on forced rankings—is likely to undermine knowledge sharing between parallel units. That is precisely what we observed in the Fresh Choice restaurant chain.

In May 1997, the Fresh Choice company, operating in the salad buffet restaurant business, purchased a competitor in Seattle, called Zoopa, in part to capture some of Zoopa's spirit and operational excellence. But within a few months of the acquisition, all of the general managers of the three purchased Zoopa units had left, sales in the stores were declining, and turnover in other positions increased. In one of the Zoopa units, employees were so upset that they walked out during a shift even though it was a nonunion workplace. Ironically, although learning from Zoopa once it was part of Fresh Choice was difficult, there was much evidence that earlier, when the two firms were competitors, there were many successful efforts to copy Zoopa's practices, such as its store design, "guest first philosophy," and even some of its recipes.[12] There are a number of reasons why learning from other units inside the firm can be more difficult than learning from external competitors, and internal status competition is one important explanation.

There are different consequences for status depending on where a manager gets new ideas. If the manager learns from a competitor, she or he has engaged in the high-status activity of competitive benchmarking, in the process acquiring unique and valuable (because it was difficult to obtain) information. If the manager copies someone outside the firm, he or she does not have to worry about the consequences of demonstrating that another person is superior because the two are not in direct competition inside the firm. In contrast, borrowing from an internal competitor signals to everyone inside the company that there is someone else who is better, at least on some dimensions. Therefore, copying others inside the firm can have negative career consequences. As a consequence, there is little internal learning because competition for status and management attention interferes with the transfer of better ways of doing things.

This situation is exactly what we found at Fresh Choice. The company had not performed well in the recent past and was under considerable financial pressure. There had been four CEOs in about two years. Job insecurity was rampant. Inside the company, new senior management did not have much confidence in the quality of Fresh Choice personnel, especially the quality of managers in restaurants. But they were impressed with Zoopa's people, especially with its managers. One Fresh Choice vice president commented, "They [Zoopa] brought people into the general manager role at the stores who were at least at the level of our regional managers. The people that I met up there were really sharp folks and really had a clear understanding of how service is to be done."[13]

Fresh Choice bought this competitor partly for the quality of its people. Fresh Choice senior management also acknowledged the superiority of at least some aspects of Zoopa's operations. What behavior did this provoke? In a competitive environment where people are insecure and fighting for their survival, what it will produce is not learning from the new people but rather efforts to derogate them and diminish their competence. The Fresh Choice regional manager overseeing the three restaurants downplayed the competence of the general managers:

> Restaurants Unlimited [Zoopa's previous parent company] took out some managers and put in either less experienced managers or no managers at all in some of the locations. . . . I've got to tell you in some of these cases their buildings were not great by any means, nor was the quality of operations.[14]

Our interviews with Fresh Choice people revealed that they discounted the performance and skill of Zoopa people. They made negative comments about store operations, as in the quote above, as well as disparaging comments about Zoopa's financial controls, the motivation of Zoopa people (one general manager was called "burnt out"), and their lack of control over operations. In the internal competition over status and visibility, there seemed to be at least as much interest in winning by pulling down the competitor as in winning by achieving superiority through enhancing one's own performance. "Fresh Choice managers came to see the Zoopa people as not that skilled, a feeling that was reciprocated."[15]

Undermining the Spread of "Best Practices" within General Motors: Identifying with the Unit Rather than the Organization

In Chapter 3, we showed that when people respond to new or different ways of doing things by saying, "That's not how things are done here," it is a sign that history and precedent are being used as substitutes for thinking. People often talk this way because they identify strongly with their group, having developed a self-image defined by shared and vehemently held views in their group about how they ought to think, feel, and act. A strong social identity binds people together and to the unit, creating loyalty, teamwork, and mutual commitment. But a strong social identity also causes people to readily reject knowledge and practices that are different from how people in their group think and act—even though, when they stop to reflect, they agree with the ideas and accept the evidence that underlies such knowledge.

Internal competition makes it even more difficult for people to put knowledge into action and to learn from each other. Competition causes people to see more distinctions between units than actually exist and to spend time thinking and talking about these minor or even imagined differences. As such, competition makes it more likely that ideas from other units in the firm will be rejected because they are inconsistent with the social identity of some other group or subunit. Furthermore, competition makes it even more likely that knowledge from other parts of the firm will be rejected because of the threats to status from admitting that others, elsewhere, have something to teach.

We saw this process—internal competition leading to heightened boundaries and distinct social identities that limited the ability to learn from other units within the firm—occur in case after case. One of the most striking was the relationship among divisions in General Motors. As we discussed earlier, the same physical separation that made the innovations at the Saturn division possible also created distinct and often competitive social identities within GM and its North American operations. These competitive social identities hampered knowledge transfer between GM units, and often meant that even though management in a given unit knew about better practices being used in other units and had the resources and skill to implement such knowledge in their own units, they elected not to turn this knowledge into action. One GM manager we interviewed recognized the dual-edged nature of identifying with a division within the total corporation, an identification that was encouraged by the decentralized multidivisional structure and the competition between the divisions:

> I worked for General Motors but I worked for Pontiac, and my identity was ten times stronger around Pontiac than it was General Motors. . . . So I think the very thing that was our perceived strength at this point in time started to eat you alive. Because we'd get this very proud group of people, and then somebody comes in from outside and says, "I come from the [particular division] and we do great stuff." We are probably more receptive to somebody that comes in from the outside that we hire and shares ideas with us than somebody who comes in from another unit within GM to share ideas. You say, "What the hell were you guys so good about? What gives you the right to give us advice?"

This dynamic happened with even more force at NUMMI, the Toyota–GM joint venture in California. The NUMMI plant was viewed as an internal competitor by people within GM, and most GM managers found the people at NUMMI even harder to identify with because the senior leadership of NUMMI was from Japan. It was thus even easier for the firm to claim that it had nothing to learn because of cultural and national differences. The irony, of course, is that both Saturn and NUMMI were initiated precisely so that GM *could* learn. But the distinct identities that permitted different management practices to develop made learning more difficult. This effect was exacerbated by the financial and performance problems GM was experiencing. These problems intensified internal competition and heightened the distinction between insiders and outsiders. One of the barriers to the diffusion of better management practices often cited by GM managers we interviewed was the internal competition for status. No manager wanted to admit that he or she had anything to learn from anyone else, because they were in competition with each other.

Why Organizations Continue to Foster Dysfunctional Internal Competition

The cases we reviewed above, and numerous others we encountered in our research, suggest that internal competition often undermines the ability of companies to turn knowledge into action. Yet management practices that foster internal competition continue to be widely used. Why is this so? Part of the answer is that, as we saw in Chapter 3, when people have strongly held but unexamined beliefs, they act on those beliefs without ever surfacing the underlying assumptions and asking if, indeed, their beliefs are logical and empirically sound. As we noted at the start of this chapter, beliefs in the virtues of competition are among the most deeply held and taken-for-granted assumptions in the United States. Here we challenge the underlying logic for using organizational practices that encourage internal competition, introduce additional evidence that internal competition undermines knowledge transfer and performance, and show why leaders are particularly prone to believe in and use internal competition as an organizing principle.

Doing Well Is Not the Same as Winning

The most widely used rationale for emphasizing competition in organizational reward and evaluation systems is that competition induces better performance. "Competition brings out the best in us."[16] One researcher proposed some reasons why this might be so:

> Winning and outdoing others are considered rewards that stimulate effort and productivity. One

reason that competition has been extolled is that it has been equated with motivation. . . . Competition has also been equated with achievement.[17]

In this quotation, winning a competition and performing well or succeeding are treated as if they were identical. Yet, once you start thinking about this assumption, it is obvious that dominating others in a zero-sum contest is just one form of success. Other sorts of success can be achieved without sorting people into groups of winners and losers. Alfie Kohn, in his book *No Contest: The Case Against Competition*, explained that people can achieve high goals and performance regardless of whether or not they are competing against others:

> Success and competition are not at all the same thing. . . . One can set and reach goals without ever competing. . . . I can succeed . . . in writing a book without ever trying to make it better than yours. . . . Competition need never enter the picture in order for skills to be mastered and displayed, goals set and met.[18]

Kohn's exhaustive review of the research literature on the effects of competition led him to conclude that "superior performance not only does not *require* competition; it usually seems to require its absence."[19] The failure of competition to invariably foster superior performance is readily explained: Trying to do well and trying to beat others are two different things.[20]

What does affect performance, if it isn't competition? There is a large body of research showing the power of the self-fulfilling prophecy, also called the Pygmalion effect, on performance. Independently of skill, intelligence, or even past performance, when teachers believe that their students will perform well, they do.[21] Independently of other factors, when leaders believe their subordinates will perform well, these positive expectations lead to better performance.[22]

Most of these studies show that the self–fulfilling prophecy occurs when teachers or leaders believe, or act as if they believe, that a randomly selected subset of students or employees will perform better in contrast to some average or unknown group.

The studies are compelling because they show it takes very little to convince leaders that their subordinates can and will achieve superior performance. In a study in an Israeli Army boot camp, for example, instructors were just told that based on information from a battery of tests on an incoming group of soldiers, it was possible to predict with 95 percent accuracy which one-third of the soldiers had high command potential. The other soldiers were said to have either regular or unknown potential. The soldiers were actually randomly assigned to the "high," "regular," or "unknown" conditions, and no other information was provided about command potential. Yet, at the end of 15 weeks in boot camp, soldiers who leaders believed would have high levels of performance did far better on objective performance tasks like firing a rifle, navigation, and multiple choice tests about combat tactics, administered by instructors who were not informed about the experiment. Soldiers labeled as having high command potential also had more positive attitudes toward basic training and reported that their instructors were superior leaders, compared with soldiers in the other two groups.[23]

Fortunately for our arguments that competition is not necessary to produce high levels of performance, research done in the Israeli Defense Forces shows that Pygmalion effects can be created *without* inducing contrasts between high and low performers. When platoon leaders at training camps were convinced that *all* of the soldiers in their classes had unusually high command potential, there was still a strong Pygmalion effect. This research suggests that overall performance of a group can be increased when leaders expect everyone to do well. There is apparently no need to sort people into subgroups of high–status "winners" and low-status "losers" in order to use the power of the self-fulfilling prophecy to enhance performance.[24]

It is a good thing that there is no need to sort people or groups into "winners" and "losers" to boost performance. Self-fulfilling prophecies are just as powerful in their effects in the opposite direction. When a leader believes that a person lacks skill or motivation, these negative expectations decrease performance. These effects of negative self-fulfilling prophecies help explain why internal competition can hamper performance over the long term. Once a person, group, or division has lost in a performance contest and is labeled a "loser," research suggests that subsequent performance will be *worse* because leaders and others will unwittingly act to fulfill the poor performance expectation. And, the loss of self-worth and motivation felt by those who are treated as losers leads to further decreases in their performance.

That is why quality guru W. Edwards Deming was so vehemently opposed to relative performance evaluations. Deming emphasized that forced rankings and other merit ratings that breed internal competition are bad management because they undermine motivation and breed contempt for management among people who, at least at first, were doing good work. He argued that these systems require leaders to label many people as poor performers even though their work is well within the range of high quality. Deming maintained that when people get these unfair negative evaluations, it can leave them "bitter, crushed, bruised, battered, desolate, despondent, dejected, feeling inferior, some even depressed, unfit for work for weeks after receipt of the rating, unable to comprehend why they are inferior."[25] These insidious effects of giving people negative labels are why direct sales organizations such as Mary Kay Cosmetics, Tupperware, and Avon try to praise *everyone* to success. In their awards and recognition activities, these firms assiduously avoid labeling some people as not as good because they don't outperform their peers, and thus avoid having these salespeople lose their motivation and stop trying.

Internal Competition May Seem Fair to Individuals, but the Cost to the Organization Is Usually High

Another common rationale for ranking units or people against each other and thereby establishing a competitive dynamic is that such systems are inherently fairer and more useful as incentives for desired behavior than other alternatives. Many organizations have adopted some form of relative performance evaluation in administering both performance management and compensation systems. The theory behind relative performance evaluation at first seems correct.[26] If you, as a salesperson, are on commission or are evaluated based on your absolute sales volume, you can be punished in your performance if the company has product quality problems or is lagging in product design and innovation. This can occur even though you have nothing to do with those problems that occurred in another area of the company.

In contrast, by assessing your performance in comparison to other similarly situated salespeople, these extraneous, uncontrollable factors are taken into account because people are ranked with respect to each other. Even if the company has product or manufacturing problems, presumably those problems affect all salespeople equally. So, if everyone ranked in the top 10 percent of all computer salespeople receives a bonus regardless of how much equipment is sold, no one is punished for factors outside of his or her control. As long as you perform better than your peers, you score well on the relative performance evaluation and will be rewarded and evaluated accordingly. Controllability is generally accepted as being something desirable in incentive schemes. This logic leads to recommendations to use relative performance evaluation.

Yet the strength of the system—its apparent fairness in the face of external factors over which people have no control—is also its weakness. Because people are concerned primarily about their *relative* ranking, there are incentives for them to avoid helping their peers to improve their performance and, at worst, to undermine or sabotage their peers' performance. As Deming described it, when these kinds of performance ratings are used, "Everyone propels himself forward, or tries to, for his own good, on his own life preserver. The organization is the loser."[27] We saw this in the case studies of investment banks, Microsoft, Fresh Choice, and General Motors. These systems also leave people largely unconcerned about the welfare of the whole because their rewards depend on their relative standing, not on how well the entire enterprise fares. IBM suffered a similar problem. Operating units were ranked from best to worst, a process that introduced competitive dynamics. A senior IBM executive made a presentation to the senior management team arguing that the internal competition was adversely affecting the firm's competitive capabilities: "We don't talk to the people in the other operations. They have become the competition. There is no sharing of information and limited cooperation."[28]

Management Entails Mostly Novel Intellectual Tasks, Not Routine Physical Work

The confusion between what it takes to do well in routine tasks, especially physical tasks, versus novel intellectual tasks is another reason that people develop misguided beliefs about the positive effects of competition on performance. People in business, particularly men, often draw on analogies from physical competitions such as various sports to guide their thinking about how work should be organized and rewarded. And indeed, for some physical tasks such as races, there is evidence that people, individually and in teams, perform better when racing against an opponent than when racing against a clock. But treating sports as analogous to business, which often involves novel and complex intellectual rather than routine physical tasks, is misguided. Hundreds of studies show that intellectual tasks that require learning and inventing new ways of doing things are best performed under drastically different conditions than tasks that have been done over and over again in the past.

People are better at learning new things, being creative, and doing intellectual tasks of all kinds when they don't work under close scrutiny, they don't feel as if they are constantly being assessed and evaluated, and they aren't working in the presence of direct competitors. There is, for example, a vast amount of evidence that working around others, especially outsiders who are thought to be judging one's work, enhances performance for tasks that are well learned and that do not require the acquisition of new skills or novel responses. This is called the *social facilitation effect*.[29] But these same conditions lead to worse performance on tasks that require complex mental processes and attention, the so-called *social inhibition effect* that makes it harder to learn new things or generate new ideas.[30] Related research strongly suggests that competition inhibits learning and creativity because rather than focusing on the task at hand, in conditions of competition people focus their attention too heavily on what competitors are doing, on how well they are performing in comparison, and on the reactions of third parties such as leaders and peers who are the audience for the contest. Moreover, when a task is difficult enough or complex enough that it requires help and sharing ideas with others, internal competition is especially destructive.

Interdependence, Not Independence, Is the Fact of Organizational Life

Interdependence is another important way that tasks differ. In the racing analogy that is so commonly employed, a person's speed is almost completely a function of that individual's own conditioning, ability, stamina, and mental attitude. Unless the opponent actually interferes with one's running, performance is entirely under the control of the single individual running the race. Many of the sports analogies that are also used in discussions of the benefits of competition likewise have little or no interdependence. But interdependence is what organizations are about. Productivity, performance, and innovation result from *joint* action, not just individual efforts and behavior. Chester Barnard, an early management writer who had been a senior telephone company executive, "characterized organizations as cooperative systems that depend on the coordinated activities of numerous interdependent actors. . . . *The willingness of individuals to cooperate with other members of an organization is one of the major determinants of organizational effectiveness and efficiency.*"[31]

This fact of organizational life makes using individual incentive awards for winning some internal competition of questionable value. Herbert Simon, a Nobel Prize winner in economics, perceptively noted:

> In general, the greater the interdependence among various members of the organization, the more difficult it is to measure their separate contributions. . . . But of course, intense interdependence is precisely what makes it advantageous to organize people instead of depending wholly on market transactions.[32]

Recall the Intel example from Andy Grove's book discussed at the outset of this chapter, in which he claimed that competition led to enhanced performance. The task he described was building maintenance, an activity that was likely well learned by the people doing it and one that did not require the constant acquisition of new skills or knowledge. And the facilities that were put into competition with each other were largely independent in terms of the maintenance activity, with little interdependence among the building maintenance activities across facilities. Competition is likely to be most useful for this kind of task because not much new learning is required and there is low interdependence between units.

When even modest levels of learning are required and some interdependence exists, individual incentives and internal competition discourage needed knowledge sharing, cooperation, and mutual assistance. Even Lincoln Electric, widely known for its individual piece-rate systems, depends heavily on incentives for cooperation that have been built into the system from the beginning. These incentives for cooperation include a profit-sharing system in which approximately 50 percent of an employee's pay depends on the overall success of the enterprise and a performance evaluation system in which cooperation is one of the four dimensions that supervisors use to assess employees. So, while James F. Lincoln glorified the individual and espoused the virtues of competition, he also understood that there was considerable interdependence among workers and that teamwork should be encouraged.[33]

Learning and building and leveraging intellectual capital require developing a "sharing culture." Although learning from others inside the firm can be enhanced through formal mechanisms, building a climate in which people talk and interact comfortably, in part because they aren't competing with each other, is crucial to the development and transfer of skill and wisdom. As Larry Prusak, from the IBM Consulting Group, has noted:

> Giving people the room and space to talk to each other is also important, because learning is the socialization of knowledge. People like to tell others what they are learning but they do not have the time for it. Companies spend all this money hiring smart people and then overburden them and do not allow them to share their knowledge.[34]

Not only don't people have the time, but also in many instances a competitive culture makes the sharing of information and the mutual development of skill extremely unlikely because it is so counter to individual self-interest.

Leaders Are Often Trained and Rewarded
for Valuing Internal Competition

The final reason that so many organizations establish dysfunctional internal competition is that leaders and managers, even more so than most people, have achieved their positions by winning a series of competitions, both in their corporations and during their schooling. As one article commented:

> For the most part, leaders of our companies have risen to their positions because of their ability to compete, as well as their ability to lead. Therefore, it is natural for most of them to believe that introducing competition into the work environment will increase performance.[35]

The traditional leadership model is based on a competitive dynamic that emphasizes winning a contest in which one person's success requires the failure of others. In school, success is defined in terms of class rank—a zero-sum, competitive outcome. Once on the job, the race to triumph over peers is more intense and the odds of winning are even smaller than in school. In consulting firms and investment banks, only a small fraction of each cohort rises to become partners. Even once partnership is achieved, partners' compensation frequently depends on doing better than other partners. In companies, promotion up the ladder requires winning a tournament competing against peers. And so it goes. The people in our society who have the greatest influence over how firms are organized, either because they manage them or they give advice to those who manage them, are also people who are the most heavily trained and rewarded to believe that internal competition is the best way to organize human activity. It is little wonder that internal competitive dynamics in firms are so pervasive.

Internal Competition Is Most Likely to Be Prevalent and Harmful When

- People have incentives to avoid helping others or even to undermine their work

- Leaders act as if performance comes from the sum of individual actions rather than interdependent behaviors like cooperation, knowledge sharing, and mutual assistance

- Management acts as if people in the firm are competing in a "race" or "game" in which the competitors are within the firm and there are only a few winners and many losers

- The way that work is managed distracts people from the task at hand because they feel they are under scrutiny, are constantly being compared to others, and are focused on what internal rivals in the company are doing

- Comparative or relative, rather than absolute, evaluations are emphasized

- Leaders are selected because they value competition and have a history of dominating peers in zero-sum contests

- Little attention is paid to the power of expectations and the self-fulfilling prophecy, so people are labeled as "losers" or as being part of a bad unit and feel a lack of self-worth and resentment toward the firm

Winning a competition, in school or on the job, is frequently an individual activity, a matter of individual ability and performance. But, "studies of managerial performance have found that the most critical skill . . . and one most often lacking is interpersonal competence, or the ability to deal with 'people problems.'"[36] Thus, even as we train and develop leaders in settings emphasizing internal competition, the most important skills for leadership actually entail the ability to work in teams, to collaborate, and to empathize with others. There is a striking discrepancy between what we know about leadership and what we do in many of the settings in which leadership is presumably taught and learned.

Consider, for example, the gap at Stanford Business School between knowing what an effective leadership model is and actually implementing these leadership practices, described in a case by the MBAs who experienced it. History shows it has been very difficult to introduce a team- or group-based leadership process into the student-governed public management program at Stanford. This problem recurs year after year even though the administrative director of the program and many students believe a team-based approach is a more effective leadership model for the program. The analysis of why this implementation problem persisted explicitly points to cultural beliefs in the importance of competition and individual achievement as a key barrier to introducing a more team-based way of leading and managing:

> The GSB [Graduate School of Business] is a place that worships the entrepreneur . . . who raises venture capital and ships the product. Business is about winning, not process. Shareholder value is a mantra, and whether that is achieved through teamwork or personal heroism is not a distinction that is made here. . . . The people the GSB recruits and the symbols that permeate the institution (the *View from the Top* Speaker Series most prominent among them) reinforce a culture of traditional leadership.[37]

External versus Internal Competition

We don't want to create the impression that competition is always a bad thing. Organizations such as SAS Institute, AES, The Men's Wearhouse, and Southwest Airlines are fierce competitors, not laid-back companies, which is one reason they have been so successful. It is just that their competitive juices are aimed at *external* competitors rather than at people from other locations, units, or departments within the firm, or even peers in the same unit. People in firms like these spend their time and energy trying to succeed in the marketplace, not fighting each other because they are rewarded and measured in ways that cause them to try to dominate one another rather than to help each other.

Southwest Airlines, for instance, has a collective internal orientation. The compensation system features collective rewards such as profit sharing and stock ownership; individual merit pay is eschewed. The idea of helping one another to turn planes around, to share ideas, and to build a strong, unified corporate culture is emphasized. When competitors threaten the company, the emphasis is invariably on the threat to *all* of the people of Southwest Airlines. External competitors are demonized and warlike language is used, but internally, the firm works together, as illustrated by the following excerpt from a message from CEO Herb Kelleher to his people as US Airways entered the Baltimore market:

> In 1814, at the conclusion of the War of 1812, the British forces attacking the United States were repelled at Fort McHenry in Baltimore, Maryland. . . . On June 1, 1998, the second battle of Baltimore will commence. On that date, US Airways will begin heavily bombarding Southwest airlines with an assault by its new, lower cost–lower fare operating division, MetroJet. . . . MetroJet is NOT a figment of anyone's imagination. US Airways has simply been

more discrete in its public statements concerning the aggressive interest of Metrojet than United was with respect to the aggressive intent of the Shuttle.

WHAT IS AT STAKE FOR SOUTHWEST?

The job security, profit sharing, the expansionary future and the pride of all of our Southwest Freedom Fighters! . . . The outcome of the latest attack on Southwest by another of the Big Seven Carriers is just as important to ALL of us as the result of our West Coast war with Shuttle by United. . . . Just as against the United Shuttle, the crucial elements for victory are the martial vigor, the dedication, the energy, the unity and the devotion to warm, hospitable, caring and loving Customer Service of ALL of our People ALL of the time and in EVERY place on our system. . . . Southwest's essential difference is not machines and "things." Our essential difference is minds, hearts, spirits, and souls. . . . I am betting on your minds, your hearts, your souls, and your spirits to continue our great pride and our marvelous success.[38]

How Companies Avoid Turning Friends into Enemies

There are a number of ways to overcome the problems that occur when there is too much internal competition, not enough time spent sharing information and helping others, and not enough focus on enhancing the organization's overall performance. One of the most powerful and straight-forward is to reinforce a common organizational identity and common goals and interests by highlighting external threats and enemies. This approach is illustrated by South-west Airlines' response first to the United Shuttle on the West Coast and then to US Airways' expansion of service in Baltimore. Southwest used the increased competition to enhance internal unity, energy, and focus by highlighting a common external threat that affected *all* the people in the company. Several senior managers at Southwest told us that the company benefited from the United Shuttle's entry in 1994 into the intra-California market. Their airline, Southwest, had been remarkably financially successful. Their CEO, Herb Kelleher, had appeared on the cover of *Fortune* with the text, "Is He America's Best CEO?" The company had continued to pile up service records, winning the annual triple crown (best on-time performance, fewest customer complaints, and fewest lost bags) year after year. Two problems were appearing. First, Southwest people were getting complacent. But more important, as Colleen Barrett, their executive vice president for customers, remarked, "With all this success and no apparent external enemy, we had begun fighting among ourselves. The appearance of the United Shuttle on the scene rekindled our 'warrior culture' and got people back focused on fighting the competition instead of thinking so much about each other and how they were doing compared to the others."

Similarly, in 1984 Apple Computer used the external threat of IBM to provide energy and a common enemy. In a speech Steve Jobs gave to nearly everyone in the company when he introduced the first Macintosh computer, Jobs portrayed IBM as trying to dominate the entire computer industry, the entire information age, and as posing a threat to the future freedom of the industry. This language helped to rally Apple employees in an effort to launch the Macintosh computer. The research literature going back decades is quite clear: One very effective way to reduce intergroup competition and conflict is to provide the groups struggling with each other with a common goal and a common external threat or enemy. This is a wonderful way of providing an external focus and a common social identity—us versus the outside competitors or threat.

Another way that firms reduce internal competition is to simply not tolerate it when it becomes excessive and destructive. The Men's Wearhouse, the successful off-price retailer of tailored men's clothing, pays salespeople a base salary along with commissions based on sales. These commissions are obviously individual rewards and could lead to salespeople in a store competing with each other for customers. Part of the firm's value system and strategy, however, emphasizes team selling, in which people help each other in answering customer inquiries and providing outstanding customer service. This emphasis on collaboration is at odds with the rest of the industry, where people in retailing are traditionally pitted against each other in competition for sales. Turnover is quite high throughout the industry, in part because people in stores strive to stay ahead of their co-workers, which, as we have shown, means there is no incentive for cooperation. The pressure to work collaboratively starts during employee orientation at The Men's Wearhouse Suits University. For instance, as part of the training and orientation for wardrobe consultants, Charlie Bresler, the executive vice president for human development, tells them:

> You are expected to define your success in part as only achieved when your teammates, the sales associates, the tailors, and other wardrobe consultants and management people in the store are also successful. . . . You will, over time, define your success not only in terms of your own goals, but also the goals and aspirations of the other people in your store. And that you will come to really care about them as human beings and as people who finally realize their potential, too. That is what we mean when we talk about being a . . . high quality teammate in the store.[39]

This talk is backed with action. At The Men's Wearhouse, data from the information system show the number of tickets, or transactions, each wardrobe consultant writes in a month, as well as the average sales, in dollars, per transaction.

If someone is writing a lot more sales than other colleagues in a store, say 25 percent more, this is taken as a signal that the person is probably not sharing walk-in traffic but rather is hogging business. Particularly if that person is also not writing high volumes of business per transaction, he or she is reminded about team selling and the expectation that in the company, success only comes when everyone in the store is successful. If the behavior persists, the company will fire that individual.

For example, one of the firm's most successful salespeople, measured by dollars of total sales, was fired when he refused to conform to the firm's cultural values, including the value of defining his own success in part by the success of his peers and his store. This person took more than his share of customers in the store, bad-mouthed the firm's training and culture, and disdained the idea of working to help his fellow employees. The firing showed that the company was serious about its values, particularly values about how people relate to and interact with each other. In addition to preserving the culture, this firing resulted in financial benefits. The total sales volume in the store subsequently increased significantly. No single wardrobe consultant sold as much as the person who had been fired, but the store did better collectively. The internal competitive dynamics triggered by this person's behavior had brought all of the other people in the store down. With him removed, the other wardrobe consultants felt better about themselves and the store, helped each other more, learned from each other, and as a consequence, enjoyed better collective success.

SAS Institute, the large and successful software firm, also has a culture that emphasizes internal cooperation and is willing to let people go who don't fit that style. Barret Joyner, vice president of North American sales and marketing, encourages his people to think about what they really want out of their jobs and to be open about it. He related the following incident:

> In thinking about this question, [one] employee said, "I want to be able to have performance that permits [me] to do whatever I want. When I walk down the hall, I want to feel like 'I'm the man.'" [I] told him that this sounded like a wonderful goal, and that [I] would work hard to find him a place of employment—not at SAS Institute—where he could realize the goal.[40]

Firms that are serious about building a cooperative internal culture take steps consistent with that goal. That includes being willing to fire, not hire, or encourage to leave people who may have talent but whose goals and behaviors are too competitive and individually oriented to fit. This requires making tough judgments and being willing to act on those judgments.

Firms can also reduce internal competitive dynamics by not using measures and compensation systems that emphasize success at the expense of others. Willamette Industries is one of the most successful forest products, building materials, and paper companies as measured by return on equity, return on sales, or shareholder returns compared with other firms in the industry. As a fully integrated company, cooperation across units is important for the firm's success. To encourage such cooperation, Willamette uses no short-term performance bonuses. The company's leaders believe that in an integrated, interdependent firm, such bonuses set up dysfunctional competitive dynamics. Dave Morthland, the vice president for human resources, explained the firm's compensation philosophy and its relationship to its interdependent structure:

> We control the tree literally from the time it's planted to the time our finished product leaves the shipping dock. That means we've got a lot of internal customer relationships. . . . What kind of message does it send in an integrated company where you want and need good teamwork if one side of the business is doing really well because their prices happen to be high and you're paying them big

bonuses and the person on the other side of the aisle is in the down cycle part of the business, but that person may be working harder to keep his costs down and he's getting no reward for it?[41]

The effect of zero-sum compensation schemes on behavior is not hypothetical. Mick Onustock, an executive vice president at Willamette, had come to the company from a competitor that had used individual performance bonuses parceled out in a zero-sum fashion that created internal competitive dynamics. He described the adverse effects of such a system, including the time wasted on internal battles and the need for senior leadership to continually resolve conflicts:

> Where it got to be some vicious battles was the competition that the bonus system created within the company. You found yourself competing against others in the company as opposed to pulling together and getting things done. For example, setting a transfer price—the simplest thing in the world—between a paper mill and a converting plant. Although they were both owned by the same company, a war went on over that. The guy in the converting plant didn't want the mill to screw him because his performance would look lousy if the transfer price wasn't at the proper level. . . . Often, the conflict had to go all the way up to the CEO to resolve it. It's ridiculous for a CEO to have to resolve an issue like that between two groups that were going toe to toe because it affected their bonuses.[42]

Kevin Goodwin, the CEO of SonoSite, a small company spun off from ATL in the spring of 1998 to develop and sell hand-held ultrasound systems, instituted, at the time of the company's founding, a pay system marvelous in its simplicity and powerful in its effects. All SonoSite people received generous base pay, and *all* employees in the company received stock options. That was the compensation. There were no individual or department bonuses. At a meeting we attended discussing the company, its culture, and its operations, we heard one engineering manager make the following remark about the company and how it differed from both ATL and other places he had worked: "There's less conflict and bickering here over schedules and who's responsible for what. Because the reward system makes every one at SonoSite feel like they face a common fate, they're all part of one team, everyone is more focused on working together to solve issues as they arise. Not only do we get more done because we aren't always trying to assign blame to others, but it's a much more pleasant place to work."

Finally, some companies have overcome the barriers that internal competition creates for developing and transferring knowledge by resorting to power and hierarchical authority to change the internal dynamics. General Motors has decided that it really wants and needs to implement lean manufacturing principles. So, it created a position within General Motors University, staffed by Tom Lasorda, to collect information about what was going on, develop better practices for both manufacturing and teaching and learning about manufacturing, and ensure that this knowledge was implemented. Lasorda described his role:

> My role is to pull all these folks [leaders in various plants doing lean manufacturing] together, set up a central team to help people implement, train, and coach. I now conduct leadership training for plant managers. I developed my own program based on seeing 50 plants. . . . I've got the college of lean. I'm the lean, mean, dean. . . . There was resistance on one or two initial themes until I told them that these are the facts of life. You have had your input. This is the decision. You'd better implement it. . . . You just need somebody who is the gorilla once in a while. And once you find that out, I've had no other issues after the first two. It's pretty easy once you exercise your authority.[43]

If something, such as cooperation, is crucial to an organization's success, at some point the firm has to make that clear and to enforce the message. It can be done in a nice way, but the seriousness of the effort to develop and transfer knowledge needs to be communicated and understood.

Ways of Overcoming Destructive Internal Competition

- Hire, reward, and retain people in part based on their ability and willingness to work cooperatively with others for the company's welfare.

- Fire, demote, and punish people who act only in their individual short-term self-interest.

- Focus people's attention and energy on defeating external competitive threats, not on fighting each other.

- Avoid compensation and performance measurement systems that create internal competition.

- Have measures that assess cooperation.

- Build a culture that defines individual success partly by the success of the person's peers.

- Model the right behavior via leaders acting collaboratively, sharing information, and helping others.

- Promote people to top management positions who have a history of building groups where members cooperate, share information, and provide each other mutual assistance.

- Use power and authority to get people and units to share information, to learn from each other, and to work collaboratively to enhance overall performance.

We have seen in this chapter that competition—for status, for rewards, for recognition—can hamper efforts to turn knowledge into action. It is important for leaders to carefully consider the advantages and the disadvantages of internal competitive dynamics. Competition is more useful under conditions of less interdependence and for activities that do not require much learning because the skills required are already well honed. As Dean Tjosvold, a researcher and writer on the subject of competition and cooperation, noted, "Competition stimulates, excites, and is useful in some circumstances, but those situations do not occur frequently in organizations, and the widespread use of competition cannot be justified."[44]

|7| Firms That Surmount the Knowing-Doing Gap

THROUGHOUT THIS BOOK we have not only identified causes of the knowing–doing problem, but have also provided examples from our research that show how these causes can be overcome or at least ameliorated. This chapter provides more detailed case information on three firms—British Petroleum, Barclays Global Investors, and the New Zealand Post—that have been successful at either avoiding the knowing–doing gap or transcending barriers to turning knowledge into action. Each of these more comprehensive cases shows the constellation of factors that create problems in turning knowledge into action as well as the actions and practices that help firms acquire and implement performance knowledge. The organizations are of different sizes, from different countries, operate in different industries, and confronted different challenges. This range of experience affords an excellent opportunity to learn as we consider the similarities and differences across companies.

British Petroleum

In the mid–1990s, British Petroleum (BP) was the fourth largest oil company in the world and the largest company in Great Britain, with 1995 revenues of $57 billion.[1] The late 1980s and early 1990s had been difficult for the company. Falling oil prices and an extremely diversified set of businesses that made the company almost a conglomerate had contributed to declining profits. In 1992, the company lost $811 million, its first financial loss in eight decades.[2] But just five years later, the company was enjoying excellent results, even though oil prices had remained low by historical standards. In 1997, the company earned $4.62 billion on total revenues of $71.27 billion[3] and was receiving numerous favorable mentions in the business press for its management ability.

How had the company fallen on such hard times, and what did it do to turn around? The company was old, with a great history and tradition, having been founded in 1909. Originally owned, and then partly owned, by the government, the company was the first to develop the oil reserves of the Middle East and was a leading oil producer in the North Sea and Alaska. Described as "a curious mix of dashing adventurers and stifling bureaucracy,"[4] the firm was experienced in finding, producing, and selling oil and oil products all over the world, and as a large firm in England, was able to attract outstanding talent. The problem was, to use our language, that British Petroleum was singularly incapable of transferring knowledge across its various internal units or using its expertise and its human and physical assets. In 1989,

> Turf battles, buck-passing and bureaucracy were rampant, and decision making was slow and cumbersome. Head office alone had 86 committees, and each of the six managing directors attended over 100 board or other major meetings annually. Financial proposals required fifteen signatures before they could be accepted. . . . [The] head of BP Oil described the problem: "Control had gone wrong because all of us have concentrated too much on detail. People feel they need to know the answer to every possible question just in case someone asks it. We'd lost our way."[5]

Committees, reviews, and measures provided the appearance but not the reality of effective planning and oversight. Much as at the Australian firm BHP, another natural resources company, talk substituted for action. Internal competition further hindered the ability to turn knowledge into action.

Management succession, triggered by the firm's poor financial performance, at first only made the problems worse. Robert Horton assumed the chief executive position in the spring of 1990 and immediately began to downsize the company and slash capital spending. Unfortunately, the downsizing "was accompanied by a 'proclamation of values, such as openness, care, teamwork, empowerment, and trust,'[6] that was communicated through an extensive workshop and training program."[7] We say "unfortunately" because the juxtaposition of downsizing with the emphasis on values such as care and trust made no sense at all. This transparent clash between what top management said and what they did provoked cynicism, skepticism, and anger throughout the firm. Moreover, Horton had a managerial style that inspired fear rather than affection or respect: "Horton treated everybody as though they were head gardener. People could not bear to have any more sandpaper rubbed over them."[8]

Horton's approach attacked the symptoms—too many people, resulting in operating inefficiencies—but not the cultural issues that produced the problems in the first place. Moreover, an abrasive, almost abusive management style inspired fear in the organization, an emotion not likely to motivate people to do their best or to turn knowledge into action. Horton was fired two years after his appointment, on June 25, 1992.[9] Over the succeeding years, the company was run first by David Simon and then by John Browne. Although downsizing continued, the company began to do some things to increase its ability to both capture knowledge that was being generated internally and to more effectively turn that knowledge into practice.

John Browne believed that "a critical determinant of his company's ability to compete . . . was the extent to which it could actively foster learning across units."[10] He noted:

> As a big company, we have more experiences than smaller companies. . . . So the question is "What do we do with that experience? How do we find it? How do we interpret it? How do we apply it?" . . . We *can* get leverage provided we understand how to use the experience we have. . . . If you step back and look at what BP does, it's just a few things, repeated thousands and thousands and thousands of times.[11]

British Petroleum took a number of actions to ensure that knowledge and experience would be captured and transferred within the company. First, they "developed a whole language and methodology for post–project appraisal"[12] to learn as much as they could from all of their activities, such as drilling wells, developing new oil reserves (which they call "assets"), and recovering and transporting oil. Perhaps more important, the firm implemented four mechanisms to ensure that the business units shared information among themselves and implemented what they knew: peer assists, peer groups, other federal organizations, and personnel transfers.[13]

"A peer assist was a small project in which one or several business units lent members of their staff to another business unit in order to help that business unit solve a particular problem,"[14] most frequently some technological problem. The practice had several positive benefits. First and perhaps most important, knowledge was transferred by and through actual people who had not only the explicit but also the tacit knowledge and skill required to solve complex problems. This was not just some intranet in which technical skills would be posted, but a way of actually involving people in the knowledge transfer process. Second, by directly moving people who had experience to the locale where the experience was needed, peer assists "cut through the managerial layers between the business unit leader and the technical people performing the actual work."[15]

The obvious question is why managers of these business units permitted and even encouraged key people from their units to go to other units to solve problems. This sharing of talent was particularly unlikely to occur at first glance given that BP's financial reward systems were focused on business unit performance. Sharing talented people with other units might help the firm as a whole but could negatively affect the short-term performance of the unit that had temporarily lost these skilled individuals. The amount of talent being shared was substantial. In some instances, "a large percentage of the workforce . . . could be offsite at any time."[16] One answer to why the units were so willing to help others, even at a possible short-term cost to themselves, was provided by a BP executive:

> I've never turned down anyone, because of the benefits. First, there is the benefit of goodwill, which is significant. One day you'll need the same. Second, there is the benefit that they come back better people. They know more than when they left.[17]

Peer groups involved establishing "confederations of business units that faced similar technological and strategic questions."[18] The groups met quarterly with the executive committee of British Petroleum Exploration. These quarterly meetings facilitated other interactions during the quarter because people had been together regularly and had come to know each other and better understand the business and technological issues each unit was confronting. In the peer groups, "the leader of a business unit would present his or her proposed goals for the coming year to the other members. . . . The members would critique the plan, offering information and advice."[19] Norms of reciprocity again dictated that all members participate actively. And the very establishment of these groups helped to build a common social identity that reduced the tendency for the units to view each other as only competitors.

When units faced similar operational or strategic issues that cut across peer groups, British Petroleum put together a federal group to focus on the common issues. Between the peer groups and the federal groups, a significant amount of managerial time was devoted to working collaboratively across units to solve problems, in the process both developing and transferring expertise. "John Leggate, a manager of the gas fields in the southern areas of the North Sea, estimated that roughly 50% of his time was devoted to participation in the peer group and these other asset groups, whereas the other 50% was devoted to actually running his own asset."[20]

Another example of how efforts to encourage knowledge sharing were implemented is seen in the pilot test for the Virtual Teamwork Program. The initiative was designed to build a network of knowledgeable people who could work together to learn and solve actual problems in real time as they happened. The experimental program was implemented in five groups over an 18-month period in BP Exploration between 1994 and 1996. The program made heavy use of modern information technology such as desktop video conferencing equipment, multimedia e-mail, shared electronic chalkboards, scanners, and a web browser. These technologies allowed rich real-time communication and the joint solving of problems by geographically dispersed people. But the program's designers did not make the common mistake of treating knowledge as a "thing" stored away for later use. Rather, the goal of the program was to "build a network of people" across different parts of BP and "to let knowledgeable people talk to each other, not to try to capture or tabulate their expertise."[21] The project team also encouraged using technologies that would create rich communication between people in order to duplicate "as much as possible the nuances, variety, and human dimension of face-to-face communication" because these designers "understood that the value of individual expertise resides largely in just those subtleties and intuitions, which words alone cannot convey."[22]

The program was supported by a group of "coaches" on a "knowledge management team." These coaches were expected to spend only 20 percent of their time training people how to use the technical systems. They were expected to spend the rest of the time working with people to discover how the information technology could be used to help them do their work in faster, better, and less expensive ways. The level of use, participant enthusiasm, and savings in time and money indicated that this program was successful in four of the five groups where it was tried. The group where it failed was the only one that did not spend the money to hire coaches. The success of the pilot program led BP executives to approve plans for expanding the program to other parts of the company in 1996 and to weave it into other efforts to create real knowledge sharing among units.

The following incident illustrates how the systems used by people in the Virtual Teamwork Program enabled them to share knowledge between different parts of the organization that enabled BP to save time and money:

> When equipment failure brought operations to a halt on a North Sea mobile drilling ship one day in 1995, the ship's drilling engineers hauled the faulty hardware in front of a tiny video camera connected to one of British Petroleum's Virtual Teamwork stations. . . . They dialed up the Aberdeen office of a drilling equipment expert who examined the malfunctioning part visually while talking to the shipboard engineers. He quickly diagnosed the problem and guided them through the necessary repairs. In the past, a shutdown of this kind would have necessitated flying an expert out by helicopter or sending the ship (leased at a cost of $150,000 a day) back to port. . . . The shutdown only lasted a few hours.[23]

Within the exploration division of British Petroleum, there was also an emphasis on moving personnel geographically to facilitate knowledge development and the transfer of wisdom. As with peer assists, the company recognized that it was not likely to be in any business unit manager's short-term interests to move competent personnel to other units. This was true even if such movement benefited other units, enabled people who moved to learn and transfer new knowledge, and helped the firm as a whole because performance knowledge was spread more quickly and completely among business units. So, the firm established some formal mechanisms to ensure geographic mobility of people. "Once a year, business unit leaders met at a worldwide forum to help facilitate the geographic mobility of engineers. At this forum, individual people and individual jobs were discussed."[24] The meeting forced management to collectively assume responsibility for personnel movement and ensured that such movement and the resulting people development and knowledge sharing actually occurred.

All of these formal mechanisms required people at BP to develop a sense of shared social identity and a spirit of cooperation rather than unrestrained rivalry, particularly the unit managers. The senior leadership was conscious of this requirement and took steps to build a more cooperative culture that recognized the interdependence among the various units and their leaders. Nick Butler, policy advisor to the chief executive, put it this way:

> In so many organizations there is a tendency for individuals to hoard knowledge and to think they are making themselves more powerful by doing so. Our aim has been to change this mental model by encouraging people to see that if they are open—both receptive to new ideas and willing to share their own knowledge—they will be recognized and rewarded.[25]

The British Petroleum experience shows that knowledge transfer and knowledge use can be important to a firm's financial performance. It also demonstrates the importance of using formal mechanisms for encouraging such transfer, and the need for knowledge to be carried by *people*, not just by and in management information systems. And the BP case shows the importance of actions by senior leaders. Those actions and what leaders said helped establish cultural norms that favored cooperation and a set of recognition and reward practices that reinforced cooperative behavior. Senior management's willingness to try new ideas like the Virtual Teamwork Program also reinforced the message that, to move toward a culture of knowledge sharing, people were expected to experiment with new ways of working, to fail sometimes, and to keep learning from such trials and errors. The very different BP experiences under Robert Horton and John Browne also show that leaders who provoke fear and exhibit abusive behavior create organizational situations in which people focus on avoiding blame and punishment and concentrate on their own individual survival rather than the collective good. Leaders who induce fear discourage their people from turning knowledge into action and instead create organizations in which people learn it is better to do nothing or to keep doing things in less effective ways than to turn their performance knowledge into organizational action.

Barclays Global Investors

Barclays Global Investors (BGI) faced a different set of challenges than British Petroleum. Rather than trying to overcome knowing–doing gaps that were fueling declining performance, BGI faced challenges that were due, in large part, to the firm's impressive financial performance and rapid growth throughout the world.

Barclays Global Investors is the largest manager of tax-exempt investments in the world, with more than $550 billion under management. The firm was founded in the early 1970s as part of Wells Fargo Bank's trust department. The intent was to apply quantitative techniques and modern portfolio theory, being developed in universities, to the money management business. The unit later became a wholly owned subsidiary and profit center of Wells Fargo, and then was owned by a joint venture between Wells Fargo and the Japanese securities firm Nikko. In 1996, what was then called Wells Fargo Nikko Investment Advisors was purchased by Barclays, the large United Kingdom bank, for a price in excess of $400 million. The company has maintained its strong roots in academic finance and quantitative financial analysis. As a matter of ideology, people at Barclays do not believe in picking individual stocks, which one executive described as "get a hunch, buy a bunch, go to lunch."

Barclays Global Investors faced three major management challenges in the 1990s: (1) significant and rapid growth, from about 350 people in 1993 to about 1,400 people in 1997; (2) the need to become a truly global firm, integrating significant operations in Japan, the United Kingdom, Australia, and Canada while trying to build and maintain a "one firm firm" culture and orientation; and (3) a change in corporate ownership from a joint venture between Wells Fargo Bank and Nikko Securities to Barclays Bank. Most significantly, BGI was involved in taking over the investment management activities of the firm that had bought them—sometimes referred to as a reverse takeover. The means that BGI used to meet these challenges provide several key lessons about how other firms can use their accumulated wisdom and experience and turn knowledge into action.

The heart of BGI's business is turning knowledge into action. Fred Grauer spent almost 20 years in the company, including many years as either chairman or co-chair. He defined BGI's core activities in this way:

Investment performance is actually not only about knowledge, it's about action. It's the ability to acquire the ideas and translate them into forms that deliver investment performance. . . . What you buy and sell is part of the process. . . . They [the pension fund managers] have a need to explain to others what you have done on their behalf. . . . And if you fall down in any part, there is an inference that you may fall down in other parts and put your entire relationship at risk. All of that is by way of saying that whether it's knowledge or action, whether it is an investment return or the service proposition, all of it is governed by people. Our job was to very rapidly create an attitude that enabled people to gain knowledge and convert knowledge into action with a purpose of having our clients really feel as though they had experienced first-rate investment performance, not just the plus sign in front of the investment return.[26]

Two of the three challenges BGI faced, the global expansion and growth in personnel, had similar consequences for the firm: It was becoming more difficult to transact business on the basis of long-standing personal relationships that were mediated largely by face-to-face interaction. Janet Campagna, a group leader in the asset allocation group, commented:

The bigger you grow and the faster you grow, with all the attendant structural changes that occur, the more difficult it is to maintain the kinds of relationships that allow you to find your way through the maze. And with the growth also came the loss of people and that makes maintaining relationships much harder. Because if you lose two or three of your key relationships and you're now in this much bigger place, you lose a lot of your support system. And with the attendant growth that tends to keep you very, very busy, it's harder to reach out and establish

> relationships. Trying to establish those relationships
> and have them work with the distance and the cul-
> tural differences has its own unique challenges.

Commenting on the challenge of operating as a global firm, Garrett Bouton, head of BGI's human resources function as well as a business unit manager and member of the management committee, noted:

> Just shortly after I arrived [in October 1996] it
> became clear to all of us in the top management . . .
> that we weren't organized like a global firm needed
> to be organized. We were still run as a U.S. business,
> and a relatively small U.S. business. . . . We were very
> much U.S.–centered. The merger with Barclays
> required that we suddenly think quite differently.

BGI was and continues to be committed to operating according to a set of common values as well as a core set of principles that govern their investment work. This goal to be a "one firm firm" made the task of quickly integrating new people essential. Diane Lumley, the chief of staff, commented: "We wouldn't be who we are if we said it's okay to have a confederation of different investment managers with different philosophies and different principles, because that's not us."

The change in ownership compounded the problems of growth and operating on a global basis. This change was largely initiated by BGI because its top management believed it needed a different corporate parent to succeed in the future. Fred Grauer argued:

> We'd gotten to the point where what Wells Fargo
> could realistically contribute to the business and
> what we could realistically contribute to Wells was
> very modest. There's no fundamental reason why we
> needed each other. . . . The competitive environment
> was definitely changing from being a national busi-

ness to being a global business. And we had a parent
that didn't have a global perspective or global motivation or a global culture. . . . There was a need to
find ourselves.

Although Barclays Bank, the parent company, was
global, operating in 16 countries around the world, this
London–based bank had a very different culture from the
entrepreneurial spirit of BGI. Barclays was quite bureaucratic and had never had a major subsidiary with its headquarters outside of England. The company was run by
committees and had lots of meetings. Most important, the
people at Barclays' headquarters in England felt as if they
should be in control, since they had been the acquirers. But
that was not how it was to be. Fred Grauer and Pattie Dunn,
the co–chairs of Wells Fargo Nikko, were put in charge of
the combined entity, and its headquarters remained in San
Francisco. Although some people from Barclays' asset management group became managing directors in the new,
combined entity, most of the managing directors came
from the original Wells Fargo Nikko because it was much
more successful in the investment management business,
was larger, and had a longer history in that business. So, the
change in ownership, accompanied by the requirement to
integrate the investment management part of Barclays with
what had been Wells Fargo Nikko, brought the issues of
globalization and building a single firm culture to the fore.
Garrett Bouton stated:

> There was definitely an "us and them" feeling around
> the world. The British and the Americans definitely
> were in kind of a standoff. . . . And that was compli-
> cated by the fact that the British had come into this
> as the acquirers. And they had assumed that they
> were going to tell us what to do. . . . Suddenly the
> Americans had been empowered to tell them what to
> do . . . so it was doubly hard to take.

BGI had a number of underlying characteristics that helped it meet these various challenges, and the firm also took a number of explicit, planned steps that helped them further. One attribute the company had in its favor was a long culture and tradition of action orientation and self-reliance. For instance, when in the past the human resources function didn't have the capacity to develop and deliver some badly needed training, "people took training into their own hands," said Diane Lumley. "It became, let's get people together from different areas and have them put on presentations for people and walk them through the investment process, rather than waiting for somebody else to do it for you. People started to organize on their own." Describing the integration of Barclays' asset management business, Fred Grauer noted, "A lot of businesses find themselves in some sense being molded by the sequence of events. They are reacting to events as opposed to driving events. And we wanted to come to grips with our future by driving events as opposed to being driven by them." Diane Lumley concurred, "It's like, 'we've got to know it, we've got to do it, it's got to be done by February.' So, you had to charge ahead."

This action orientation, this cultural characteristic of not allowing talk to substitute for action, helped BGI to address issues as soon as they emerged. Because people were used to acting and taking responsibility, they were better able to meet new challenges. This culture of action meant that people did not sit around waiting to be told what to do, denying that issues existed or hoping that the issues would somehow disappear. This action orientation also had costs. Several BGI people told us that the drive for action caused occasional problems when people worked at cross-purposes or did not coordinate sufficiently. But this was a small price to pay for the ability to quickly identify and address issues.

Another part of the firm's cultural heritage that served it in good stead was a tradition of excellence. People at all levels of BGI had always expected the highest levels of effort and performance from one another. People talked about having to recommit periodically to the performance demands of the company. This emphasis on excellence was accompanied by clear views about the kinds of people the firm wanted to hire and develop. This clarity about what individual qualities were important, which included the ability to work collaboratively, led BGI to hire for both technical skills and cultural fit. When people came to the firm through an acquisition or the Barclays ownership change, they had not necessarily signed on to the culture, or the firm to them. So, BGI was, in the words of BGI co-chair Pattie Dunn, "ruthless" in weeding out people who would not sign up for the company's values and business principles. Garrett Bouton described the firm's commitment to its core values and principles and how that affected its personnel decisions:

> One of the things we discovered was that there are certain basic things—values, vision, the culture of the firm—that are not up for discussion. You can discuss it in the sense of explaining it and understanding it, but it's not something that is going to be changed. It's important for people to understand that. When you become part of BGI, this is what you are signing up for. . . . And quite frankly, we've still got a small hard core of our managing directors that still are questioning it. . . . So we are at the point of saying to them, "Well, maybe it's best that you go someplace else, because these things aren't up for discussion."

BGI's clarity on values and principles helped the company sort fairly rapidly through people who fit and who didn't. It made both hiring and retention decisions easier. This emphasis on values and principles had existed for a long time, so BGI had groomed a large and influential core group who shared a set of investment business principles. These core values could be transmitted to others because they were well understood and had stood the test of time, helped bind the geographically dispersed firm together, and provided a foundation for the task of building a single, unified, global firm. The cultural values and shared business ideas also helped people decide what was important and what was not.

Another positive attribute of the firm that helped it meet the various challenges was that its leaders were held to the same standards as everyone else. BGI's leaders consciously tried to model behaviors that they were encouraging others to do and that they believed were central to the firm's culture. The welfare of the firm came first, before considerations of ego or internal competition. Fred Grauer, when he was chairman of the firm, elevated Patricia Dunn to the position of co–chair. This was done voluntarily, to strengthen the senior leadership structure, not because of some pressure from the corporate parent. All the evidence suggests that the co–leadership structure worked quite well, as the two individuals had complementary skills as well as a great deal of mutual respect for each other.

The firm's leadership was also committed to building a sense of security as well as high performance expectations. BGI's leaders believed that driving out fear, especially the fear of failure, was crucial to the company's long–term success. Fred Grauer explained:

> One has to be prepared to accept criticism. . . . One has to be proactive in getting at the problems. . . . Vulnerability is part of the tool kit of leadership. . . . Modeling that behavior is important. It's OK to be vulnerable. It's OK to make mistakes, and it starts at the top. Nobody gets fired around here for being vulnerable. It makes you approachable. There is less pretense in the way in which people interact. Hopefully, the time required to get to the real issue is reduced.

Besides having some existing characteristics that helped it, senior BGI executives also took a number of specific actions to leverage the company's core culture and capabilities to proactively attack the three challenges the firm faced. One thing they did was to reduce the number of job titles, changing from a long list of titles such as senior vice president, vice president, deputy manager, and senior deputy manager to just three corporate titles: managing director, principal, and associate. Diane Lumley, the firm's chief of staff, said, "There was a lot of debate about this. Do you have senior principal, junior principal, senior associate, and so forth? And we said we didn't want to make the lines between people more apparent than they already are, and those are the three titles and positions." By reducing the distinctions among people and having as few status categories as possible, competition for status was downplayed and the structure emphasized building a shared identity within the firm. People felt they had a shared fate, that they were in it together, and there was less of a feeling of difference across classes or categories of people.

Another action the firm took was to build a global intranet, with a home page for the two co-chairs of the firm. This was a way of sharing information across large distances quickly. The firm also started a quarterly newsletter. BGI had always had meetings to bring people together. Now, the firm changed the number, composition, and most important, the content of what was discussed in the meetings. All the managing directors come together twice a year. There had previously been managing director meetings, but the focus of the discussion changed. Garrett Bouton stated, "Previously, we were talking about new investment ideas and talking about where the industry in the U.S. was headed and those types of things. Now, we're talking about a much different type of topic, organizational and management issues, organizational culture, and what constitutes good management." Management issues, including the core activity of turning knowledge into action, received much more focus at the senior leadership levels.

BGI also formed a management committee in January 1997. The committee is a global team, with people from BGI offices throughout the world, that meets in person once each month. The face–to–face interaction has helped to build relationships and to develop a stronger firm culture. To further encourage communication throughout the firm, Garrett Bouton said, "We asked that each of the members of the management committee have an executive committee of their direct reports. And that those committees meet on a regular basis, and that they would discuss the critical issues for their business or global functions in a way that empowered the people at that level to feel as though they were really part of the management team." This structural innovation helped to involve more people in the decision-making process. It was critical for getting people through-out the firm to recognize and accept responsibility for solving the firm's management challenges.

Finally, BGI hired an outside consultant, David Zenoff, to run a series of workshops titled "Reaching for Number One." The workshops were designed to bring people together around a common learning experience, creating an opportunity for them to consider other business exam-ples and models and also to focus on BGI management and leadership issues. This experience was remarkably success-ful in assisting in the organizational development of the firm. Garrett Bouton, who suggested this course of action in the first place, described the various outcomes:

> We needed to bring the senior team together, as a team, as quickly as possible, to create a feeling of leadership throughout the management committee. Once our managing directors had completed that course, they were saying things like "This was a life-changing experience for me and I think it changed my whole attitude towards BGI."
>
> There were a couple of common threads in their comments. One was that the managing directors hadn't really accepted that they were the top man-agement of this firm. There was still an attitude that if things weren't going right, you look for somebody

to blame. . . . And I think that was one of the most
important things that came out of this. People at the
top of the firm realized that, in fact, there was no one
else to point at. They were the ones who were
responsible, and they had to make it work. . . .

The second thing that was really important was
that . . . we forced an integration of people from
around the world. For the first time, the management group began to really appreciate each other's
views, and they were forced to sit there and listen
to what the other people believed. . . . So we managed to come together as a global team in a way that
wasn't happening previously.

The firm then implemented a similar type of program for
160 midlevel managers the following year. An important fea-
ture of this second program was the mixing of people from
different offices. The model was a training program in two
parts, the first part occurring in the person's home country
and the second in one other country around the world. This
sent the important symbolic message that all offices were
important and that BGI was a global, not a U.S.–centric, firm.

BGI has done a number of other things to facilitate the
integration of the different offices and to help build a
strong, unified culture:

- There is one global bottom line and one global
  bonus pool. People therefore have an economic
  interest in helping the entire firm succeed and in
  learning enough about other offices and other
  departments to do so successfully.

- There is one review process using the same criteria and
  the same time frame for all people around the world.

- BGI moves people around a lot to other offices. This
  began almost immediately after the acquisition and
  has continued since that time. This practice helps
  build better networks and social relations across the
  various offices.

The available evidence suggests that the BGI interventions were quite successful. At the most basic level, BGI was valued at more than $1.3 billion within three years after Barclays purchased it for $400 million, an extraordinary return. As significant, voluntary turnover in the highly competitive asset management business actually declined. Relations with the various offices around the world improved. People from Barclays were integrated into BGI, and Barclays Bank developed a good working relationship with the senior leadership. The BGI story is about building a one firm firm and a truly global, integrated business. It entailed bringing leaders together to develop a common understanding of the business as a whole, with the intent of enabling people in various functions and offices to work together more effectively. Some events in 1998 illustrate the success of this effort and provide concrete evidence of effective integration of offices and functions.

In 1998, BGI spent seven months preparing for the introduction of the new European currency, the euro, on January 1, 1999. This was a large and important challenge. Jennifer Campbell, head of the European Economic and Monetary Union (EMU) team in Tokyo, noted that the shift to the euro affected everything BGI does. "When you look at the assets affected and the investment process, and carry through to taking the order from the client, to the broker, to trade operations, to trust accounting, to portfolio accounting . . . it's the full investment process once you analyze where it reaches." In the San Francisco office alone, the conversion project involved 167 funds, 99 clients, more than 900 accounts, and affected 30 system applications and more than 15 operational departments that had to modify their procedures.

When the conversion date came, it was, according to Diane Lumley, "a non–event. Everything worked perfectly. In fact, we are already prepared for the rest of the currency conversion that will occur over the next three years." Lumley noted that in the past, the firm had failed at large–scale projects. She maintained that the tremendous success of this project reflected the ability of numerous functions and offices of the firm to work together effectively. This was a concrete indicator of the success of the training, the meetings, the communication, and all the other things that had occurred to knit the firm together.

A second event that demonstrated the effective integration of the firm occurred during the early fall of 1998. As the Asian markets fell, a large European client of the firm wanted to move $500 million out of Japanese markets and into Canada and Australia. This activity involved staff in London, Tokyo, San Francisco, Sydney, and Toronto, working across five different time zones and using multiple computer systems. "It took absolute teamwork and people who are all dedicated to making BGI a global company to pull this off," according to Signe Curtis, senior contract officer in San Francisco. Commenting on this transaction, Diane Lumley said, "It never would have happened as effectively before, without a doubt." As yet another example, the firm developed investment products that outperform various indexes in the countries in which the firm invests. Although operated out of different offices, the products all use the same investment model. Again, people at BGI said this would not have been possible in the past.

Perhaps the most important indicator of success in meeting the various challenges BGI had faced was this: Fred Grauer, a leader in the firm for years, someone who had so personified the firm that an article about it in *Fortune* had featured his picture on the cover, resigned in the summer of 1998. The firm continued without missing a beat, although people were obviously sorry to see him step down. The organization's ability to readily handle an important succession provides additional evidence of the strength of its management practices and its culture, built through the actions we have described.

The BGI example is, first of all, very much concerned about turning knowledge into action. The fundamental business involves turning investment knowledge into products and services that are sold in the marketplace, turning knowledge of theoretical finance into investment product development actions. And the case illustrates how meeting challenges really entails the ability to act on knowledge about what to do. The challenges facing the firm were, at some level, not unusual or arcane—growth, global integration, combining two different firms successfully. Yet many firms fail at these basic tasks. How many firms have failed at managing rapid growth? How many firms have failed to build a global organization? How many firms have failed at merger integration? Unfortunately, probably many more have failed than have succeeded. These failures come not so much from not knowing what to do than from not doing it.

Think about what BGI did. Having meetings and off-site training, setting up both structural and other mechanisms to enhance communication, being clear about values and principles, holding high performance expectations and admitting mistakes, encouraging authenticity and vulnerability in interpersonal interactions—none of this is rocket science. The lessons from BGI are that these straightforward actions are effective and provide tremendous leverage in building an organization in which knowledge develops and is transformed into action. The specifics of BGI's actions are no less important because they appear to be so simple and straightforward. They worked, and for good reasons.

The New Zealand Post

British Petroleum found ways to increase its ability to leverage learning and put knowledge into action throughout a geographically dispersed firm. Barclays Global Investors used its action-oriented culture and its skilled people to meet some demanding challenges. The New Zealand Post, our third case, faced perhaps the greatest challenge of all—

reinventing itself as an essentially new organization with mostly the same people who had been part of the old organization. In this process, the Post took steps that offer additional lessons on how organizations can turn knowledge into action. Perhaps the most important lesson, from both the Post and British Petroleum, is that you don't have to necessarily get it right from the start. These examples both show that it is possible, even for large and rather bureaucratic organizations, to make broad and deep changes in how people think and act despite daunting obstacles.

In 1986, when it was still a government department, the New Zealand postal system lost about $38 million (this and all subsequent figures are in New Zealand dollars) and faced the prospect of continuing losses into the indefinite future. The Post delivered only about 80 percent of the mail within the targeted delivery time. As a government department and an employer of last resort, this postal system had too many people, arcane work rules, a civil service mentality, and poor relations with its customers and its employees. In April 1987, the Post became a state–owned enterprise. This change meant that it was no longer a government department but was a corporation, expected to operate efficiently and to earn money for its shareholders, in this instance, the New Zealand government.

The Post's transformation in operating results is remarkable and provides a dramatic backdrop as we consider what the firm did to achieve this substantial change. The story also suggests that profound organizational transformations need not take a long time to accomplish. In 1991, just four years after becoming a state–owned enterprise and beginning the process of change, the New Zealand Post was named "Government Enterprise of the Year." In 1994, it was named by the Deloitte & Touche accounting and management consulting firm and *Management* magazine as the "Company of the Year," the most prestigious business recognition award in New Zealand. These plaudits reflected substantial improvements in nearly every aspect of the firm's operations.

By the mid-1990s, between 97 percent and 99 percent of the mail (depending on the type of mail) was delivered by the Post on time. This resulted in some 86 percent of respondents in a quarterly survey reporting that they were satisfied with the service they received. In the mid-1990s, the company implemented a "Quality Service standard that requires at least 95% of customers to wait no longer than two minutes before being served."[27] The company measures performance on this standard and has mostly achieved it in every transaction.

The Post's financial and operating results were equally impressive. Between 1987 and 1995, the company delivered 30 percent more mail, had achieved a 30-percent reduction in real unit costs, and had improved its labor productivity by 100 percent. The gains in productivity were achieved in part by eliminating positions that weren't needed. Employment was cut from about 12,500 at the time of the change in the governance structure to 8,700 people in the mid-1990s. The company became profitable almost immediately, earning $72 million in its first year. In 1995, the company earned approximately 16 percent on total assets and in excess of 30 percent on shareholder's equity. And the Post accomplished these outstanding financial results while *decreasing* the price of a stamp and becoming among the most efficient postal systems in the world. For instance, in 1994 it cost 45 New Zealand cents to mail a standard first-class letter in New Zealand. Comparable figures (in New Zealand currency) were 52 cents in the United States, 57 cents in Australia, 65 cents in the United Kingdom, 70 cents in France, and 105 cents in Japan.[28] Since that time the comparisons with other postal systems have grown more favorable, as New Zealand has not raised postage rates in the interim.

The operating principles used by the Post during its transformation included a simultaneous focus on common sense and simplicity and not relying on precedent, or even what other postal systems did, when those actions contradicted common sense and simplicity. For example, almost every postal system in the world prices mail by weight, and so did the old New Zealand postal service. The New Zealand Post analyzed this practice and found that (1) if a letter did not have enough postage, the company could either return it to the sender or try to collect the postage due, but both of these activities were costly; and (2) the biggest determinant of the costs of transporting a letter was not the weight of the letter but the *size* of the envelope—bulk was a more critical cost factor than weight. So the Post eliminated weight-based charges and instead introduced three postal rates based on the size of the letter or package.

The Post also defied conventional wisdom and common practice by taking over nearly all of its transportation infrastructure, including planes and trucks. Virtually every other postal system in the world contracts out at least some part, and in some instances almost all, of the delivery task, such as carrying mail by plane. New Zealand is a country that has many places that are difficult to reach and that frequently has stormy weather. The Post found that when its mail was carried on commercial flights, such flights were often late and occasionally cancelled during poor weather. Late flights made scheduling mail center operations difficult, and cancelled flights meant delays in delivering the mail, especially express mail. So the Post's executives decided that to meet its service commitments, the company would build its own transportation system. In 1994, the firm had 600 vans, 100 trucks, and in a joint venture with Airwork New Zealand, owned three Metroliners and two Friendship F-27 aircraft and leased two other planes.[29] This investment in building its own transportation infrastructure not only helped the Post meet its service delivery targets, but also demonstrated to its union that even at a time of employment retrenchment, the Post would do things to grow employment when those activities made sense in light of the firm's mission.

The Post made many other changes in its operations. It instituted a "clear floor" policy and redesigned postal stations and mail sorting centers so that leftover mail would be visible to all employees. The policy stated that at the end of a shift, all of the mail should be sorted or delivered—in other words, that nothing should be left to be done by the next shift. It changed the scheduling of people to put them on fixed, as contrasted with rotating, shifts. This change helped employee retention and labor relations, because rotating shifts make adjusting one's lifestyle to accommodate working different hours almost impossible. The Post implemented what were essentially lean manufacturing operations practices, reducing buffers and emphasizing involving people in enhancing operations efficiency. The company continually sought ways to rationalize the process of providing postal service to reduce its costs, all the while maintaining a commitment to outstanding customer service so it could build its market.

But perhaps the most important changes the Post made were in its management practices. In a speech given in 1989, Harvey Parker, the Post's managing director at the time, stated:

> The transformation from an unprofitable government department to the cost-conscious, dynamic, customer-oriented and profit making enterprise the New Zealand Post has become required, and can largely be credited to, significant changes in management style and practices. . . . A new decentralized style and form of management was instituted, vesting accountability for operational decisions and resources at a local management level, at the closest point to the customer.[30]

The Post is committed to recruiting outstanding talent. To best accomplish this objective, recruiting is localized. Individual managers in each location get to control the hiring process, not some central human resources function that may not be as familiar either with the specific jobs or with local labor market circumstances. The firm pays competitively and offers performance-based incentives. It has positive, collaborative relations with its union. As part of that collegial relationship, information about all aspects of the company's business plans and operations is shared with the union and with all of the people in the company. The Post is committed to implementing the best business practices it can and to that end engages in extensive educational and developmental activities, using resources both in New Zealand and throughout the world. The Post accomplished a radical transformation in a short period of time with a workforce, including managers, who for the most part have spent their entire careers in the organization. It did this by rethinking everything and relying on common sense and business judgment, not on precedent or what other firms were doing. Harvey Parker explained:

> Local managers were very quickly given authority to hire, promote and discipline their own staff and also clear accountabilities for managing, developing and recognising staff performance and for communicating the company's business directions to their teams.
>
> In decentralizing Personnel decisions it was not merely a case of changing the responsibility levels of the policies used by the NZPO. . . . To support achievement of New Zealand Post's business goals and effect real change in its staff management practices a complete rethink was required—the start point was a blank page.[31]

Staff reductions were made humanely in ways that decreased rather than magnified fear.[32] People could volunteer to leave, and some who the Post had intended to keep left so that others could stay. The company offered generous severance benefits. People left with dignity. There were parties, and people had an opportunity to say good-bye. Most important, the reductions in force were accomplished quickly and with plenty of notification and open discussion about what was occurring and why, getting the pain over and permitting the organization to focus on future growth and development.

The Post also encouraged its managers to experiment and innovate in building high-performance work arrangements. It has changed its organizational structure frequently, both to make substantive improvements and to forestall people from becoming entrenched in existing routines. Managers from throughout the firm meet regularly to exchange ideas. Elmar Toime, the current managing director, has encouraged opening more of the firm's markets to external competition as a way of continuing to encourage people at the Post to improve performance. In a speech in 1995, he made the following points about the Post:

> We put a premium on high productivity and performance. It justified the restructuring we have carried out over the years, with all the attendant pain people have withstood. We wish to keep prices down, so that we can encourage volume growth . . .
>
> One of our challenges is coping with success. . . . Our profitability this year will better that of last year, even though we reduced some prices significantly. . . . Competition will keep us at the leading edge . . . It is not that we are arrogant about competition. We are just fired up.[33]

The lessons from the New Zealand Post case are consistent with those of the other cases. The essential elements for turning knowledge into action are not complex. Don't get stuck in the past. This was a company that made a fresh start and that reexamined every policy and practice to see if it made sense. When it didn't, the Post changed, regardless of the past or what other postal systems were doing. Don't be afraid to do what your managers think is best, even if it goes against conventional wisdom. The Post has sought deregulation, eschewed outsourcing, and actively involved its labor unions in the transformation process—none of these decisions fitting the mold. Involve people so that, just as in the British Petroleum and BGI cases, the firm gets the benefit of all of the knowledge and skill inside it and, more important, so that people are motivated to help each other.

None of these firms, or the others we have described in this book, is perfect. They all have things they can do better. They make mistakes. They face reversals of fortune. They are, after all, human, fallible entities. Nevertheless, these three examples offer some important lessons about turning knowledge into action. And, if nothing else, they should help convince you that it is possible to do so, even in large organizations that must break with the past.

|8| Turning Knowledge into Action

W E HAVE SEEN THAT THE knowing–doing gap is a pervasive and important problem. Organizational performance often depends more on how skilled managers are at turning knowledge into action than on knowing the right thing to do. Knowledge and information are obviously crucial to performance. But we now live in a world where knowledge transfer and information exchange are tremendously efficient, and where there are numerous organizations in the business of collecting and transferring best practices. So, there are fewer and smaller differences in *what firms know* than in their *ability to act* on that knowledge. It is widely recognized that many firms have gaps between what they know and what they do, but the causes have not been fully understood. Harlow Cohen, the president of a Cleveland, Ohio, consulting firm, has called this gap between knowing and doing the *performance paradox*: "Managers know what to do to improve performance, but actually ignore or act in contradiction to either their strongest instincts or to the data available to them."[1]

Our research, reported in this book, has uncovered a set of understandable and often controllable factors that help account for the knowing–doing gap and why some organizations suffer from it more than others. Recognizing these causes, and seeing examples of firms that are better able | 243 to implement their knowledge, can help firms in which there is enough motivation to overcome these problems. But, as the following example illustrates, knowledge—even of why knowledge may not be implemented—is not always enough.

In the summer of 1998, one of us gave a workshop to a group of executives from the retail industry. The topic was high-performance management practices and putting people first—a subject of obvious importance in a service industry where service is still largely delivered by people. Sears, in an example discussed previously in this book, dramatically improved its financial results by first discovering that employee attitudes influenced turnover, which in turn affected customer satisfaction. Customer satisfaction can directly affect store sales and profitability. The company then acted on this understanding by taking actions that made Sears a more compelling place to work and shop. Financial performance improved substantially.

At the end of the seminar, a manager from Macy's, the department store chain, came up and, after recounting how useful she felt the morning had been, described all the obstacles to actually implementing any of the ideas she had heard. The CEO, she said, had no interest in or appreciation for the people aspects of the operation. When he came to the stores, all he wanted to do was to see the merchandise and the displays. Sometimes he wouldn't even meet with many people in the stores or say hello to them as he walked through. And, in addition to the leadership's emphasis on merchandising, all the assessments and measurements of the stores and store performance were strictly by the accounting numbers. There was no measurement of employee attitudes, customer satisfaction, or customer retention. This manager asked how she could possibly get Macy's to focus on people, the data from Sears and other studies in the service industry notwithstanding? There was not really much to say. Short of a change in top management and massive changes in culture and work practices, such a change did not seem possible.

Then, walking to the car, we encountered a group of executives from Trader Joe's, a privately owned, rapidly growing, and highly profitable $1 billion retailer of food items, particularly wine and gourmet items. The company locates interesting foods and wines, negotiates a good price, and offers the merchandise to the public through advertisements and by getting customers to return to the stores to see what's new and tasty. Trader Joe's is located primarily on the West Coast, but it has recently begun a significant expansion in the East. Although the company had already implemented many aspects of a high-performance work environment, and had done so since its founding, four executives from the firm had attended the seminar and, looking very serious, had taken notes and during lunch sat together and talked to each other. Passing their car, we made polite conversation. "I hope you enjoyed and benefited from the day," we said to one executive. This executive was still quite serious as he pointed to a person talking on a cellular telephone. "See him. He's talking to corporate headquarters. Although we do a lot of what you talked about, we have not done as good a job as we can in sharing information with our associates so they can better serve the customers and understand the business. During the day we got some ideas from what you were talking about. He's on the phone now telling people what we learned. It will be implemented by Monday [the talk was on a Tuesday]."

So there it is: At one organization, we see a futile struggle to turn knowledge into action, an attitude of defeat almost at the outset, and a sense of resignation that the past will be carried into the future—even though there are people in the firm who know what needs to be done. At another organization we see that knowledge—new and old— is turned into action with an immediacy that is startling. Which one would you bet on?

Eight Guidelines for Action

As we noted at the outset, there are no simple analyses or easy answers for the knowing–doing problem. The problem is not just costs, or leadership, or some single organizational practice that can be changed to remedy the problem. The knowing–doing gap arises from a constellation of factors and it is essential that organizational leaders understand them all and how they interrelate. Nonetheless, there are some recurring themes that help us understand the source of the problem and, by extension, some ways of addressing it.

1. Why before How: Philosophy Is Important.

Why has General Motors in the past had so much difficulty learning from Saturn or NUMMI? Why have executives from so many firms toured Toyota's facilities but failed to comprehend the essence of the Toyota Production System? Why have so few firms copied The Men's Wearhouse, SAS Institute, Whole Foods Market, AES, PSS/World Medical, Kingston Technology, or the many other successful firms that people read about, visit, but then fail to learn from? One reason is that too many managers want to learn "how" in terms of detailed practices and behaviors and techniques, rather than "why" in terms of philosophy and general guidance for action. Skip LeFauve was president of Saturn for much of its history and is now in charge of General Motors University. This internal university is expected to take the lessons from Saturn and the best practices and knowledge from throughout the company and diffuse them throughout GM. LeFauve said this about learning the lessons from Saturn:

> It's a process, it's not an answer. I think a lot of people got misled when they started to study Saturn. They thought it was an answer, when, in fact, it's fundamentally a process you could use whether you

are going to fry chickens or make cars. The process is founded in this focus on people and their need to understand before they can do it. And the thing that came out of it was this focus on leadership teaching. When you came into the organization, the first thing the leaders did was to introduce themselves to everyone who came into the company. And, the leaders taught the new people who the leaders are and what our philosophies are, what our background was, and what we hoped we would be able to achieve. We laid the philosophical base. That's the first thing you get when you join Saturn.

I can't tell you how many people from General Motors who came to Saturn and said, "I've been with General Motors for 25 years and I have never met a plant manager, let alone the president of the company." So I would tell them that their input is important. That they have a responsibility to understand, so that when they do something, they'll understand not only *what* to do but *why* they are doing it. If you don't understand how and you ask questions, it's okay. This is a learning organization, and the leaders will teach.[2]

Saturn, Toyota, Honda, IDEO Product Development, AES, the SAS Institute, The Men's Wearhouse, and many of the other organizations we have discussed begin not with specific techniques or practices but rather with some basic principles—a philosophy or set of guidelines about how they will operate. AES has a set of four core values—fun, fairness, integrity, and social responsibility—that guide its behavior. It also has a set of core assumptions about people that it tries to implement in its management approach: that people (1) are creative, thinking individuals, capable of learning; (2) are responsible and can be held accountable; (3) are fallible; (4) desire to make positive contributions to society and like a challenge; and (5) are unique individuals, deserving of respect, not numbers or machines.[3] SAS Institute has a philosophy of treating everyone fairly, equally, and with trust and respect—treating people in accordance with the firm's stated belief in their importance to the organization. The Men's Wearhouse philosophy comes from founder George Zimmer's background: "He'd grown up in the mid–sixties to early seventies . . . and was definitely interested in alternative forms of social organization."[4] Zimmer believes very strongly that there is tremendous untapped human potential and that it is his company's job to help people realize that potential. "What creates longevity in a company is whether you look at the assets of your company as the untapped human potential that is dormant within thousands of employees, or is it the plant and equipment? . . . If you ask me how I measure the results of my training program, I can't. I have to do it on . . . trust in the value of human potential."[5] That is why Zimmer has stated that the company is in the people business, not the suit business.

These firms learn and change and do things consistent with implementing their general principles to enhance organizational performance. Operating on the basis of a general business model or theory of organizational performance, a set of core values, and an underlying philosophy permits these organizations to avoid the problem of becoming stuck in the past or mired in ineffective ways of doing things just because they have done it that way before. They don't let precedent or memory substitute for thinking. No particular practice, in and of itself, is sacred. What is constant and fundamental are some basic business and operating principles. Consequently, these firms are able to learn and adapt, to communicate with newcomers and across large geographic distances, and to do so in ways consistent with their basic understanding of what creates success and high performance in their particular business.

2. Knowing Comes from Doing and Teaching Others How.

In a world of conceptual frameworks, fancy graphics presentations, and, in general, lots of *words*, there is much too little appreciation for the power, and indeed the necessity, of not just talking and thinking but of *doing*—and this includes explaining and teaching—as a way of knowing. Rajat Gupta, managing director of McKinsey since 1994, had this to say about the importance of apprenticeship and experience in developing leadership within the firm: "The notion of apprenticeship and mentoring is that you learn by observation, learn from doing together with someone who's done it before. . . . You [also] learn a lot when you're thrown into a situation and you don't have a lot of help."[6] Tom Lasorda, a senior executive at General Motors, said it well:

> Where we go from an awareness stage to a real knowledge is where we have problems. We are aware of it [for instance, standardized work or lean manufacturing] but we don't have the knowledge because we've never had to teach it or implement it. And I see that's a huge gap, where people don't engage in the learning process by teaching. And where companies are doing that I think we are seeing far greater results on an operational level. Because now you understand it. You're committed because you're teaching it, and you're coaching people in the implementation.[7]

Teaching is a way of knowing, and so is doing the work, trying different things, experimenting. As David Sun of Kingston Technology said, "If you do it, then you will know." Honda's emphasis on putting people where they could see the actual part and the actual situation reflects the idea that seeing and touching, being closely involved in the actual process, is imperative for real understanding and learning.

The notion that learning is best done by trying a lot of things, learning from what works and what does not, thinking about what was learned, and trying again is practiced with religious zeal at IDEO Product Development, the largest and most successful product design consulting firm in the world. CEO David Kelley likes to say that "enlightened trial and error outperforms the planning of flawless intellects." As in the other action-oriented firms we studied, Kelley doesn't just talk about the virtues of learning through trial and error. They live it at IDEO. As engineer Peter Skillman puts it, "Rapid prototyping is our religion. When we get an idea, we make it right away so we can see it, try it, and learn from it." Kelley, Skillman, and many others at IDEO also regularly teach classes to managers, engineers, and artists in which they explain their philosophy and have students enact it by designing, building, demonstrating, and pitching their inventions to others.

What an out-of-fashion idea—being in proximity to what you are learning, using experience as a teacher, learning by doing and teaching! We live in an era of distance learning. We have companies that sell CD-ROMS so that people can learn things alone by interacting with their computers. We have a plethora of seminars in which people sit and listen to ideas and concepts. We human beings can learn some things those ways—mostly specific cognitive content. But many things, about organizations, operations, and people, can only be learned by firsthand experience. The tangible, physical, material aspects of knowledge acquisition and knowledge transfer, learning by doing, learning by coaching and teaching, are critical. A senior executive in charge of the quality initiative at a large financial services institution described that firm's evolution to understanding the importance of learning through experience:

> When we started out, we probably didn't do our training right. We did it the way we had all been taught. . . . If you have facts to transmit, you stand up and transmit facts. Then you say, "what are your questions," and you dialogue around the questions and close the book. At the end, you assume people will go off and do something with it. That's just dead wrong. And so we combined the experiential learning with some of the textbook learning. And the training got a little better. . . . What really matters is if you can get a team together around a business process that

> they think is really important in their business and
> have them participate in activities that show them
> what these tools [of the quality process] are about.

Knowing by doing is, unfortunately, a less cost–efficient way of transmitting knowledge. There is less ability to leverage the Internet or to put lots of people in a large room with one instructor, which are, unfortunately, the modes of instruction at most business schools today. But both the evidence and the logic seem clear: Knowing by doing develops a deeper and more profound level of knowledge and virtually by definition eliminates the knowing–doing gap.

3. Action Counts More Than Elegant Plans and Concepts.

A number of years ago, Tom Peters and Robert Waterman talked about the virtues of a "ready, fire, aim"[8] approach to running organizations. We have seen that this principle of acting even if you haven't had the time to fully plan the action has two advantages. First, it creates opportunities for learning by doing. Without taking some action, without being in the actual setting and confronting the actual "part," learning is more difficult and less efficient because it is not grounded in real experience. Second, the idea of "firing" and then "aiming"—or doing and then planning—helps to establish a cultural tone that action is valued and that talk and analysis without action are unacceptable.

Greg Brenneman, the COO of Continental Airlines and one of the architects of its successful turnaround, attributed the turnaround to an action orientation: "If you sit around devising elegant and complex strategies and then try to execute them through a series of flawless decisions, you're doomed. We saved Continental because we acted and we never looked back."[9] In a world where sounding smart has too often come to substitute for doing something smart, there is a tendency to let planning, decision making, meetings, and talk come to substitute for implementation. People achieve status through their words, not their deeds. Managers come to believe that just because a decision has been made and there was discussion and analysis, something will happen. As we have seen, that is often not the case.

Although architects live in the world of plans, Walter Gropius, one of the twentieth century's greatest architects, asserted that being action oriented, rather than just enamored with plans and theories, was crucial to success in his occupation also:

> I have found throughout my life that words, and particularly theories not tested by experience, can be much more harmful than deeds. When I came to the U.S.A. in 1937, I enjoyed the tendency of Americans to go straight to a practical test of every newborn idea, instead of snipping off every shoot by excessive and premature debate over its possible value.[10]

A while ago we worked with the World Bank as it was trying to transform its culture. One of the problems the bank faced was a set of human resource policies and practices that clashed with the culture the bank thought it wanted and that it needed to implement to fulfill its evolving role in the world economy. So the bank embarked on an effort to change those practices. But what this particular change effort largely entailed, and this was true in many other instances of change in the bank, was preparing a white paper laying out options, providing rationales, talking about implementation plans, and providing supporting data. The white paper on human resource practices was then critiqued by senior officials and revised on the basis of those critiques. And the process continued—analysis, writing, critique, and revision. There was great concern to produce an outstanding paper about human resource policies and practices, but much less concern with actually making any changes. This sort of process came naturally in an environment of people with advanced degrees who had learned to write journal articles in precisely this way—write, get comments, revise, and produce yet another draft. But behavior that may be useful for writing articles in scientific journals can be quite unproductive for organizations trying to change. In the time it took the people at the bank to analyze, document, propose, and revise descriptions of possible changes to management practices, they could have implemented many actual changes, learned what worked and what did not and why, and could have made revisions based on that experience numerous times.

4. There Is No Doing without Mistakes. What Is the Company's Response?

In building a culture of action, one of the most critical elements is what happens when things go wrong. Actions, even those that are well planned, inevitably entail the risk of being wrong. What is the company's response? Does it provide, as PSS/World Medical does, "soft landings"? Or does it treat failure and error so harshly that people are encouraged to engage in perpetual analysis, discussion, and meetings but not to do anything because they are afraid of failure?

Warren Bennis and Burt Nanus defined learning as an extension of the word *trying* and asserted that "all learning involves some 'failure', something from which one can continue to learn."[11] They proposed a general rule for all organizations: "Reasonable failure should never be received with anger," which they illustrated with the following story about Thomas Watson Sr., IBM's founder and CEO for many decades:

> A promising junior executive of IBM was involved in a risky venture for the company and managed to lose over $10 million in the gamble. It was a disaster. When Watson called the nervous executive into his office, the young man blurted out, "I guess you want my resignation?" Watson said, "You can't be serious. We just spent $10 million dollars educating you!"[12]

At AES, there is a culture of forgiveness, in keeping with the firm's values and beliefs. Roger Sant, one of the co-founders and currently the chairman of the company, noted, "You would be amazed at how quickly people support and forgive one another here." Dennis Bakke, the other co-founder and current CEO, commented, "It is okay to make most mistakes. We are all human. It's part of AES's values to accept mistakes, as long as people own up to them."[13]

5. Fear Fosters Knowing-Doing Gaps, So Drive Out Fear.

Fear in organizations causes all kinds of problems. Greg Brenneman, COO of Continental Airlines, noted: "Pressure and fear often make managers do erratic, inconsistent, even irrational things."[14] No one is going to try something new if the reward is likely to be a career disaster. The idea of rapid prototyping—trying things out to see if they work and then modifying them on the basis of that experience—requires a culture in which failure is not punished because failure provides an opportunity for learning. Clayton Christensen, a professor at Harvard Business School, has said, "What companies need is a forgiveness framework, and not a failure framework, to encourage risk taking and empower employees to be thinking leaders rather than passive executives."[15] Fear produces sentiments like the following, which we often hear when we teach executives about high-performance work cultures and ask why their firms don't implement these ideas: "We may not be doing very well, but at least our performance is predictable. And, no one has gotten fired for doing what we're doing. So why should we try something new that has risk involved?"

That is why firms that are better able to turn knowledge into action drive out fear. They don't go on missions to find who has erred, but rather attempt to build cultures in which even the concept of failure is not particularly relevant. Livio DeSimone, Minnesota Mining and Manufacturing's CEO, commented: "We don't find it useful to look at things in terms of success or failure. Even if an idea isn't successfully initially, we can learn from it."[16] Such firms put people first and act as if they really care about their people. If they have too many people—as the New Zealand Post did or as Continental Airlines did when it began paring back its routes— those who are redundant are treated humanely, with dignity and respect. At Continental, many managers had come in under Frank Lorenzo, CEO and hostile takeover king. Many of these managers were replaced because they drove fear *in* rather than out of the organization, clashing with the new culture. As routes were restructured, other people had to leave. But, "cleaning house needn't be a brutal or humiliating experience. . . . If you fire people inhumanely, you'll be left with a bunch of employees who don't trust the company or their coworkers."[17]

Putting people first and driving out fear are not just ideas to be implemented when times are good. You can downsize, you can even close a facility, but do it in a way that maintains employee dignity and well-being and, as a consequence, productivity and performance. The people at the Newcastle Steelworks of the Australian firm BHP learned in April 1997 that the works would have to be closed. There was overcapacity in steel making within BHP and this particular plant required excessive capital for modernization. Extensive evidence suggests that "at least half of the plants facing closure experience between limited to extreme productivity losses."[18] A case study of the Newcastle plant, however, revealed that in the time after the closing announcement, the plant enjoyed *higher* productivity, better quality, and better safety. Why did this occur? The plant management did a number of things right, many of the same things that Levi Strauss did when it implemented the plant closings we described in Chapter 4. One of the most important was to make and keep a commitment to look after the employees. The company implemented a program called Pathways, "a structured set of initiatives aimed at assisting employees both to decide their future direction (path) after leaving . . . and to receive intensive support to achieve it."[19] That program, coupled with open communication and lots of employee and union involvement, created an atmosphere of trust and mutual respect. If this success in both performance and maintaining employee morale and spirit can be achieved under the difficult and demanding experience of a plant closure, think what can be achieved under more favorable circumstances by organizations committed to building a workplace in which people aren't afraid of the future.

Fear starts, or stops, at the top. It is unfortunate, but true, that a formal hierarchy gives people at the top the power to fire or harm the careers of people at lower levels. Fear of job loss reflects not only the reality of whether or not one can readily find another job, but also the personal embarrassment that any form of rebuke causes. Organizations that are successful in turning knowledge into action are frequently characterized by leaders who inspire respect, affection, or admiration, but not fear. Jim Goodnight, CEO of SAS Institute, has a modest and unassuming personal style that includes driving a station wagon to work, sitting in an office with the door open (he has a chair in front of the door, so it's not even clear it could be closed), dressing informally, and taking every opportunity to speak informally to people in the company. Herb Kelleher of Southwest Airlines is notorious for his antics such as dressing up as Elvis, Ethel Merman, or Corporal Klinger from M*A*S*H, attending parties with his people, and taking opportunities to talk to everyone in the company he sees. Dennis Bakke of AES likes to visit power plants and talk to operators in the middle of the night. George Zimmer of The Men's Wearhouse attends more than 30 Christmas parties and also seizes every opportunity to visit the stores, a norm that the company encourages for all of its leadership.

Hierarchy and power differences are real. But firms can do things to make power differences less visible and, as a consequence, less fear-inducing. This is possibly one of the reasons why removing status markers and other symbols that reinforce the hierarchy can be so useful and important. Those symbols of hierarchy serve as reminders that those farther down have their jobs, their salaries, and their futures within the firm mostly at the sufferance of those in superior positions. Although to some extent this is always true, removing visible signs of hierarchy—things such as reserved parking spaces, private dining rooms, elaborate, separate offices, differences in dress—removes physical reminders of a difference in hierarchical power that can easily inspire fear among those not in the highest-level positions.

6. Beware of False Analogies: Fight the Competition, Not Each Other.

Cooperation has somehow developed a bad reputation in many organizations. Collaborative, cooperative organizations, where people worry about the welfare of each other and the whole instead of just themselves, seem to remind some people of socialism. Yet, cooperation means that "the result is the product of common effort, the goal is shared, and each member's success is linked with every other's. . . . Ideas and materials, too, will be shared, labor will sometimes be divided, and everyone in the group will be rewarded for successful completion of the task."[20] There is a mistaken idea that because competition has apparently triumphed as an economic system, competition *within* organizations is a similarly superior way of managing. This is not just a sloppy use of analogies, but has real consequences that hurt real people and real organizations. Following this suspect logic, firms establish all sorts of practices that intensify internal rivalry: forced-curve performance rankings, prizes and recognition for relatively few employees, raises given out in a zero-sum fashion, and individual rewards and measurements that set people against each other.

We have shown that these ideas and the practices they produce almost certainly undermine organizational performance as well as employee well-being. British Petroleum enjoyed a turnaround in the 1990s because it encouraged business units to learn from each other and had senior leaders that worked to build a culture of cooperation that made doing so possible. The Men's Wearhouse has succeeded in selling clothes by emphasizing team selling and the fact that employees succeed only as their colleagues succeed. "The customer doesn't care about who gets the commission. All he remembers is the store's atmosphere. That's why we use 'team selling.' One wardrobe consultant can offer the customer a cup of coffee; another can offer to press his clothing while he's in our dressing rooms; and another can take his kids to watch the videos we keep in some of our stores."[21] One of the reasons that SAS Institute's turnover is so low is that people actually prefer working in a place where they don't have to always look over their shoulder to see who is doing them in. In contrast, learning within Fresh Choice, particularly following the Zoopa acquisition, was inhibited by the competition for internal status and related feelings of insecurity and fearfulness. Learning within General Motors was similarly hampered by unproductive internal competition that left people reluctant to learn from each other or to share their knowledge with internal competitors.

There is also much evidence that people prefer collaborative and cooperative work arrangements. For instance, a study of 180 people from five organizations found that "employees with compatible goals had high expectations, exchanged resources, and managed conflicts. Cooperative interactions improved the work relationship, employee morale, and task completion."[22] John F. Donnelly, the president of Donnelly Mirrors, noted:

> People can get satisfaction from a group effort as well as from individual effort. This is a good thing for business, because in an industrial organization

it's group effort that counts. . . . You need talented people, but they can't do it alone. They have to have help.[23]

Turning knowledge into action is easier in organizations that have driven fear and internal competition out of the culture. The idea that the stress of internal competition is necessary for high levels of performance confuses *motivation* with *competition*. It is a perspective that mistakes internal competition and conflict, accompanied by a focus on "winning" internal contests, for an interest in enhancing *organizational* performance and winning the battle in the marketplace.

7. Measure What Matters and What Can Help Turn Knowledge into Action.

"The foundation of any successfully run business is a strategy everyone understands coupled with a few key measures that are routinely tracked."[24] But this simple notion is frequently ignored in practice. Organizations proliferate measures. "Mark Graham Brown, a performance-measurement consultant based in Los Angeles, reports working with a telecommunications company that expected its managers to review 100 to 200 pages of data a week."[25] The readily available computer hardware and software that make data capture and analysis easy also make it hard to resist the temptation to confuse data with information and to measure more and more things.

The dictum that what is measured is what gets done has led to the apparent belief that if a company measures more things, more will get done. But that is not at all the case. Southwest Airlines focuses on the critical measures of lost bags, customer complaints, and on-time performance—keys to customer satisfaction and therefore to success in the airline industry. AES focuses on plant utilization (uptime), new business development, and environmental and safety compliance, the factors that are critical to success in the electric power generation business. SAS Institute measures employee retention, important in an intellectual capital business. A few measures that are directly related to the basic business model are better than a plethora of measures that produce a lack of focus and confusion about what is important and what is not.

Organizations tend to measure the past. Typical information systems can tell you what has happened—how much has been sold, what costs have been, how much has been invested in capital equipment—but the systems seldom provide information that is helpful in determining *why* results have been as they have or what is going to happen in the near future. We sit in too many meetings in which too much time is spent discussing what has occurred but too little time is spent on discussing why or, more important, what is going to be done to create a different and better future.

Organizations tend to measure outcomes instead of processes. We know what the quality of our output is, but we don't know why it is so good or so bad. One of the important lessons of the quality movement is the importance of measuring processes so that process improvement is possible. As we saw, when General Motors became more serious about implementing lean or flexible manufacturing, attention switched to enhancing measures of intermediate outcomes and in-process indicators.

Even fewer organizations measure knowledge implementation. Typical knowledge management systems and processes focus instead on the stock of knowledge, the number of patents, the compilation of skills inventories, and knowledge captured on overheads or reports and made available over some form of groupware. Holding aside whether these systems even capture the tacit, experiential knowledge that is probably more important than what can be easily written down, such systems certainly don't capture whether or not this knowledge is actually being used. Organizations that are serious about turning knowledge into action should measure the knowing–doing gap itself and do something about it.

8. What Leaders Do, How They Spend Their Time and How They Allocate Resources, Matters.

The difference between Barclays Global Investors, IDEO, or British Petroleum in the late 1990s and the many organizations that have greater difficulty in turning knowledge into action is not that one set of firms is populated by smarter, better, or nicer people than the other. The difference is in the systems and the day–to–day management practices that create and embody a culture that values the building and transfer of knowledge and, most important, acting on that knowledge. Leaders of companies that experience smaller gaps between what they know and what they do understand that their most important task is not necessarily to make strategic decisions or, for that matter, many decisions at all. Their task is to help build systems of practice that produce a more reliable transformation of knowledge into action. When Dennis Bakke of AES says that in 1997 he only made one decision, he is not being cute or facetious. He understands that his job is not to know everything and decide everything, but rather to create an environment in which there are *lots* of people who both know and do. Leaders create environments, reinforce norms, and help set expectations through what they do, through their actions and not just their words.

When Dave House left Intel to become CEO of Bay Networks, a company that was experiencing extremely poor performance, he knew he had to change the existing culture and do so quickly. The company suffered from its creation through a merger of two competitors, Synoptics and Wellfleet Communications, two firms of about equal size, one headquartered on the East Coast and one on the West. Following the merger, the company had tried to take on the best products and ideas of both companies, but what had resulted was product proliferation and slow decision making in a rapidly moving market. "Bay engineers were working on twice as many new products as the company had the resources to ship."[26] What House did was create a set of courses to teach business practices he believed could help the company, and House taught many of the sessions himself. By actually delivering the material, House showed he was serious about the ideas and about making change happen. Larry Crook, Bay's director of global logistics, described the impact of House's training sessions: "They blew my mind. . . . He showed us that he was serious about how we conducted ourselves—and that if we wanted to be successful, we had to get down to basics."[27]

Skip LeFauve told us that the CEO of General Motors teaches in GM University, reinforcing the importance of the knowledge building and sharing activity. David Kearns, when he was CEO at Xerox, applied quality principles to the top management team as he encouraged their implementation throughout the company. For instance, he and his colleagues thought about who their customers were and realized that these were managers one and two levels below who looked to them for advice and for strategic direction. So Kearns instituted practices to gather information on how well the senior leadership was actually helping executives below them to do their jobs.

The remarkable success of the product development firm IDEO is not simply because the firm has somehow been able to attract "better" designers. Its success is dependent in large measure on a set of management practices that come from a philosophy that values an "attitude of action" and the importance of learning by trying new things. For instance, David Kelley believes that, even when a designer knows a lot about a product, there are advantages in trying to feel and act "stupid." By pretending to be naïve and asking "dumb" questions, and even trying to design solutions that are known to be wrong, product designers can overcome the hazards of being too knowledgeable. The ability of product designers at IDEO to think and act in this fashion comes from the fact that this is how Kelley himself behaves and from his efforts to create consistent norms for management behavior throughout the company.

Knowing about the Knowing-Doing Gap Is Not Enough

We now have a better understanding of some of the organizational processes and factors that hinder efforts to turn knowledge into action. But even if we do understand something more about why organizations fail to turn knowledge into action, these insights are insufficient to solve the problem. *Knowing* about the knowing-doing gap is different from *doing* something about it. Understanding causes is helpful because such understanding can guide action. But by itself, this knowing is insufficient—action must occur.

We have provided numerous examples both of the knowing-doing problem and of possible remedies to address its causes. We have provided a lot of talk. Now it is up to you and your colleagues to turn this knowledge into action—to not just read, think about, and discuss the interesting issues involved in the difference between knowing and doing, but to take action to do something about this important and pervasive problem. If you take action to turn knowledge into action, you will learn even more about the knowing-doing gap. We hope you will share your knowledge and insights, gained from experience—always the best teacher—with us and with others.

Appendix:
The Knowing-Doing Survey

The Underlying Idea

THE IDEA BEHIND THIS survey is simple. Company leaders often have an accurate view of what management practices are most important for achieving success, a view developed on the basis of experience, reading, training, and discussions with consultants and other industry participants. Even though leaders *know* what needs to be done to affect performance, they may be relatively uninformed about the extent to which this knowledge is actually being implemented in the actions occurring in the company. Identifying the gaps between what leaders know should be done and what is actually going on in the company provides an agenda for action. In fact, we maintain that one of the best ways to evaluate training efforts is to monitor over time the extent to which this gap between knowing and doing is reduced. If it isn't reduced, then the training isn't accomplishing much.

Although there are obviously surveys, such as the Gallup Workplace Audit, that measure general employee attitudes and opinions and have results that are related to performance measures, such surveys often have two problems. First, they measure attitudes and other outcomes rather than | 265 management practices, so it is hard to know what, specifi-cally, to change to improve survey results. Second, one of the strengths of these surveys is also their weakness: Imple-mented across a wide range of companies and industries, they are necessarily quite general in the questions asked.

Our recommendations are straightforward: Ask about specific management practices and behaviors, to the extent possible, and tailor the questions to the specific company and industry context to reflect what leaders believe is related to performance. Ask knowing questions of senior management. Ask doing questions of senior management and people throughout the firm. Then measure the gaps between (1) what senior leaders know and what they think is happening, (2) what senior leaders think is happening and what people in the organization report is going on, and (3) what senior leaders think affects performance and what is actually occurring in the company. These three gaps are likely to affect performance—firms that don't implement what they know will perform less well than those that do.

The items listed below come from interviews in the restaurant industry for the research that we reported in Chapter 1. Although the items also reflect general manage-ment practices, your company will want to add and delete items to reflect the environment in which you operate. The main idea is to ask (1) what people believe affects perfor-mance, and (2) what is actually going on in the company.

The Survey

This survey of restaurant managers was part of a telephone interview, which included completing a form that con-tained knowing or doing questions and faxing it back to the interviewer. We read the following instructions to the managers for the knowing survey:

> Now I would like you to look at the following prac-
> tices and consider to what extent you agree or dis-
> agree that each one is important for the performance
> of your restaurant. First, please go through the list
> and mark with a 1 the practices you *strongly disagree*
> with (i.e., the practice is not at all important for the
> performance of your restaurant). Next, please review
> the list again, this time labeling with a 6 the practices
> you *strongly agree* are important to your restaurant's
> performance. Finally, please use the rest of the scale
> (2–5) to rate the remaining practices according to the
> extent to which you agree or disagree that they are
> important for the performance of your restaurant.

We read the following instructions to the managers for
the doing survey:

> Now I would like you to look at the following prac-
> tices and consider to what extent you agree or dis-
> agree that each one describes what actually occurs
> in your restaurant. First, please go through the list
> and mark with a 1 the practices you *strongly disagree*
> with (i.e., the practice is not employed in your
> restaurant). Next, please review the list again, this
> time labeling with a 6 the practices you *strongly agree*
> are used in your restaurant. Finally, please use the
> rest of the scale (2–5) to rate the remaining practices
> according to the extent to which you agree or dis-
> agree that they occur at your restaurant.

Both knowing and doing questions were rated on the
following scale:

1	2	3	4	5	6
Strongly Disagree	Disagree	Disagree Somewhat	Agree Somewhat	Agree	Strongly Agree

The following items were rated with the above scale for
both the knowing and the doing interview, and were faxed
back to the interviewer:

1. Restaurant management sets high but realistic goals for employee performance

2. Sharing information about your restaurant's financial performance with all your employees

3. Managers in your restaurant getting good ideas from other restaurants in the chain

4. Training employees to do each other's jobs ("cross-training")

5. A detailed assessment process for hiring new employees

6. Working in teams

7. An active suggestion program

8. The managers in your restaurant protect it from unproductive corporate practices and policies

9. Posting all job openings internally

10. Devising contests and other promotions to motivate your employees

11. Reducing in-house training in response to poor economic conditions

12. Using peer evaluations of managers' performance

13. The managers in your restaurant know which corporate resources to use—and which to ignore—to enhance financial performance

14. Getting good ideas from customers

15. Restaurant management provides employees with frequent feedback

16. Training employees to understand the company's operations

17. Managers in your restaurant talk openly about learning from their own mistakes

18. Paying below the median for similar jobs in your area

19. Allowing your employees to change how their work is done without prior management approval

20. Managers in your restaurant always on the floor helping employees when they're "in the weeds"

21. Restaurant management has both the responsibility for your unit's financial performance and the authority to make changes deemed necessary to improve it

22. Employees in your restaurant getting good ideas from other restaurants in the chain

23. Corporate red tape hindering restaurant management when it tries to implement new ideas

24. The managers in your restaurant make it a fun place to work

25. Selecting employees on the basis of their fit with the [company name] culture

Notes

Chapter 1

[1]Blurb Buddies, *Fast Company*, December 1998, 54.

[2]Robert G. Eccles and Nitin Nohria, *Beyond the Hype* (Boston: Harvard Business School Press, 1992).

[3]Mark Zbaracki, "The Rhetoric and Reality of Total Quality Management," *Administrative Science Quarterly* 43 (1998): 602–636.

[4]Blurb Buddies, 54.

[5]"Electra: An Electrical Utility Not Ready for Deregulation" (unpublished paper, June 1998).

[6]Morgan W. McCall Jr., Michael M. Lombardo, and Ann M. Morrison, *The Lessons of Experience* (Lexington, MA: Lexington Books, 1988), 19.

[7]Ibid.

[8]See, for instance, Jeffrey Pfeffer, *The Human Equation: Building Profits by Putting People First* (Boston: Harvard Business School Press, 1998); Department of Labor, Office of the American Workplace, *High Performance Work Practices and Firm Performance* (Washington, DC, August 1993); Mark A. Huselid, "The Impact of Human Resource Management Practices on Turnover, Productivity, and Corporate Financial Performance," *Academy of Management Journal* 38 (1995): 635–672; and Brian E. Becker and

Mark A. Huselid, "High Performance Work Systems and Firm Performance: A Synthesis of Research and Managerial Implications," *Research in Personnel and Human Resource Management* 16 (1998): 53–101.

[9]John T. Dunlop and David Weil, "Diffusion and Performance of Human Resource Innovations in the U.S. Apparel Industry," working paper, Harvard University, Cambridge, MA, 15 December 1994. See also John T. Dunlop and David Weil, "Diffusion and Performance of Modular Production in the U.S. Apparel Industry," *Industrial Relations* 35 (July 1996): 334–355.

[10]See, for instance, John Paul MacDuffie, "Human Resource Bundles and Manufacturing Performance: Organizational Logic and Flexible Production Systems in the World Auto Industry," *Industrial and Labor Relations Review* 48 (1995): 197–221.

[11]Frits K. Pil and John Paul MacDuffie, "The Adoption of High-Involvement Work Practices," *Industrial Relations* 35 (1996): 434.

[12]For a further discussion of this issue, see Pfeffer, *Human Equation.*

[13]"The Fast Track Is Where to Be, If You Can Find It," *Fortune,* 20 July 1998, 152.

[14]W. Bruce Chew, Timothy F. Bresnahan, and Kim B. Clark, "Measurement, Coordination, and Learning in a Multi-plant Network," working paper, Harvard Business School, Japan Management Association, Boston, MA, 1986.

[15]Richard Ricketts, "Survey Points to Practices that Reduce Refinery Maintenance Spending," *Oil and Gas Journal,* 4 July 1994, 38.

[16]Deone Zell, *Changing by Design: Organizational Innovation at Hewlett-Packard* (Ithaca, NY: ILR Press, 1997), 56.

[17]Quoted in Carla O'Dell and C. Jackson Grayson, "If Only We Knew What We Know: Identification and Transfer of Internal Best Practices," *California Management Review* 40 (spring 1998): 154.

[18]Ibid., 155.

[19]Andrew Hargadon, "Firms as Knowledge Brokers," *California Management Review* 40 (spring 1998): 209–227.

[20]See, for instance, Kevin Frieberg and Jackie Frieberg, *Nuts! Southwest Airlines' Crazy Recipe for Business and Personal Success* (New York: Bard Press, 1996).

[21]Leon Mann, Danny Samson, and Douglas Dow, "A Field Experiment on the Effects of Benchmarking and Goal Setting on Company Sales Performance," *Journal of Management* 24 (1998): 82.

[22]Ibid., 92–93.

[23]Ibid., 93.

[24]John Paul MacDuffie and Susan Helper, "Creating Lean Suppliers: Diffusing Lean Production through the Supply Chain," *California Management Review* 39 (summer 1997): 118–150.

[25]Ibid., 138.

[26]Robert E. Cole, "Introduction," *California Management Review* 40 (spring 1998): 16.

[27]Thomas A. Stewart, "Knowledge, the Appreciating Commodity," *Fortune*, 12 October 1998, 199.

[28]Don Cohen, "Toward a Knowledge Context: Report on the First Annual U.C. Berkeley Forum on Knowledge and the Firm," *California Management Review* 40 (spring 1998): 23.

[29]Douglas Harper, *Working Knowledge: Skill and Community in a Small Shop* (Chicago: University of Chicago Press, 1987).

[30]"The Real Meaning of On-the-Job Training," *Leader to Leader* (fall 1998): 61.

[31]The Conference Board, *HR Executive Review* 5, no. 3 (1997): 3.

[32]Samuel Greengard, "How to Make KM a Reality," *Workforce*, October 1998, 90.

[33]Samuel Greengard, "Storing, Shaping and Sharing Collective Wisdom," *Workforce*, October 1998, 84.

[34]Conference Board, 6.

[35]Corey Billington, interview by Andrew Hargadon and Robert Sutton, Palo Alto, California, July 1996.

[36]Cohen, "Toward a Knowledge Context," 24.

[37]Ikujiro Nonaka and Noboru Konno, "The Concept of '*Ba*': Building a Foundation for Knowledge Creation," *California Management Review* 40 (summer 1998): 40–41.

[38]Alex Taylor III, "How Toyota Defies Gravity," *Fortune*, 8 December 1997, 100–108.

[39]Ibid., 102.

[40]MacDuffie and Helper, "Creating Lean Suppliers," 123.

[41]David Castelblanco, Michel Kisfaludi, and Gagan Verma, "Do It, Then You Will Know" (Graduate School of Business, Stanford University, Stanford, CA, 4 June 1998).

[42]John Paul MacDuffie, "The Road to 'Root Cause': Shop-Floor Problem-Solving at Three Auto Assembly Plants," *Management Science* 43 (April 1997): 492.

[43]Richard Pascale, "Fight. Learn. L*E*A*D," *Fast Company*, August 1996, 65.

[44]McCall, Lombardo, and Morrison, *Lessons of Experience*, 19.

[45]See, for instance, Melvin Konner, *Becoming a Doctor: A Journey of Initiation in Medical School* (New York: Penguin, 1984).

Chapter 2

[1]We heard David Kelley say this at a speech he gave to a group of executives at the Graduate School of Business, Stanford University, Stanford, CA, in July 1996. He told us that he has made this argument to dozens of other groups of executives in speeches he has made in the past few years.

[2]George W. Bohlander and Marshall H. Campbell, "Problem-Solving Bargaining and Work Redesign: Magma Copper's Labor-Management Partnership," *National Productivity Review* 12 (1993): 531.

[3]Leonard A. Schlesinger and Amy B. Johnson, "Xerox Corporation: Leadership Through Quality (A)," Case 490–008 (Boston: Harvard Business School, 1989).

[4]Ibid., 10–11.

[5]Ibid., 10.

[6]Todd D. Jick, "Xerox Corporation: Leadership Through Quality (B)," Case 492–045 (Boston: Harvard Business School, 1992), 3.

[7]Ibid., 1.

[8]Todd D. Jick, "Xerox Corporation: Leadership Through Quality (C)," Case 492–046 (Boston: Harvard Business School, 1992), 2.

[9]See, for instance, James C. Collins and Jerry I. Porras, *Built to Last: Successful Habits of Visionary Companies* (New York: HarperBusiness, 1994); Charles A. O'Reilly and Jennifer A. Chatman, "Culture as Social Control: Corporations, Cults, and Commitment," in *Research in Organizational Behavior*, vol. 18, ed. Barry M. Staw and Larry L. Cummings (Greenwich, CT: JAI Press, 1996), 157–200; and Christopher Kenneth Bart and Mark C. Baetz, "The Relationship Between Mission Statements and Firm Performance: An Exploratory Study," *Journal of Management Studies* 35 (November 1998): 823–853.

[10]Eileen Shapiro, *Fad Surfing in the Boardroom* (Reading, MA: Addison–Wesley, 1995), 15.

[11]"Case Analysis: Financial Analyst Program" (Graduate School of Business, Stanford University, Stanford, CA, June 1998).

[12]Michael Santoli, "Electrifying," *Barron's*, 4 January 1999, 23.

[13]Henry Mintzberg, *The Rise and Fall of Strategic Planning* (New York: Free Press, 1994), 134.

[14]See, for instance, Richard D. Arvey and James E. Campion, "The Employment Interview: A Summary and Review of Recent Research," *Personnel Psychology* 35 (1982): 281–322; B. M. Springbett, "Factors Affecting the Final Decision in the Employment Interview," *Canadian Journal of Psychology* 12 (1958): 13–22; and David J. Schneider, Albert J. Hastorf, and Phoebe C. Ellsworth, *Person Perception* (Reading, MA: Addison–Wesley, 1979).

[15]Teresa Amabile, "Brilliant but Cruel: Perceptions of Negative Evaluators," *Journal of Experimental Social Psychology* 19 (1983): 146–156.

[16]See, for instance, R. F. Bales, *Interaction Process Analysis* (Cambridge, MA: Addison–Wesley, 1951); and Bernard M. Bass, *Bass and Stogdill's Handbook of Leadership*, 3rd ed. (New York: Free Press, 1990), particularly pages 90–94.

[17]Randall Collins, "On the Micro Foundations of Macro Sociology," *American Journal of Sociology* 86 (1981): 984–1013.

[18]George Maclay and Humphrey Knipe, *The Pecking Order in Human Society* (New York: Delacorte Press, 1972), 97.

[19]Robert Reid, "The Battle for Air," chap. 5 in *Year One: An Intimate Look Inside the Harvard Business School* (New York: Avon Books, 1994); see also Peter Robinson, *Snapshots from Hell: The Making of an MBA* (New York: Warner Books, 1994).

[20]Steve Mariucci, keynote speech given at Ernst & Young's Northern California Entrepreneur of the Year Award Banquet, San Francisco, California, 28 June 1998, notes taken by authors.

[21]C. Wright Mills, *The Sociological Imagination* (New York: Oxford University Press), 218.

[22]John Paul MacDuffie and Susan Helper, "Creating Lean Suppliers: Diffusing Lean Production through the Supply Chain," *California Management Review* 39 (summer 1997): 147.

[23]Andre Millard, *Edison and the Business of Innovation* (Baltimore: Johns Hopkins University Press, 1990). Edison is sometimes portrayed as an ineffective manager because a high percentage of his lab's inventions were not commercial successes and many of the companies based on individual technologies developed in his laboratories subsequently went out of business. Millard disputes this stereotype of Edison because, overall, Edison's inventions made money

and he continued to attract numerous investors to
support his operations. Millard asserts that Edison's
critics miss the point—a high failure rate, punctu-
ated by an occasional great success, is endemic in
organizations based on new technologies. Most of
the ideas that come out of modern research and
development labs are not commercialized. Only a
minority of the firms funded by even the most successful venture capitalists are financially successful.
As Millard implies, critics sometimes confuse businesses in which it is difficult to succeed without a
high failure rate with bad management.

[24]Jeffrey Pfeffer, "SAS Institute: A Different Approach to
Incentives and People Management Practices in the
Software Industry," Case HR–6 (Stanford, CA: Gradu-
ate School of Business, Stanford University, 1998), 13.

[25]Greg Brenneman, "Right Away and All At Once: How We
Saved Continental," *Harvard Business Review* 76 (September–October 1998): 164.

[26]Ibid., 170.

[27]Robert G. Eccles and Nitin Nohria, *Beyond the Hype: Redis-
covering the Essence of Management* (Boston: Harvard
Business School Press, 1992).

[28]Ibid., 32.

[29]Ronald N. Ashkenas and Todd D. Jick, "From Dialogue to
Action in GE Work–Out: Developmental Learning in
a Change Process," in *Research in Organizational Change
and Development*, vol. 6, ed. William A. Pasmore and
Richard W. Woodman (Greenwich, CT: JAI Press,
1992), 269.

[30]Janet Lowe, *Jack Welch Speaks: Wisdom from the World's Greatest Business Leader* (New York: John Wiley, 1998),
133–134.

[31]Ibid., 131.

[32]Ibid., 135.

[33]Ashkenas and Jick, "From Dialogue to Action," 274, 276.

[34]Ibid., 269–270.

35Ibid., 281.

36Lowe, *Jack Welch Speaks*, 130.

37Ashkenas and Jick, "From Dialogue to Action," 281.

38Richard Pascale. "Fight. Learn. L*E*A*D," *Fast Company*, August 1996, <http://www.fastcompany.com/online/04/wargames.html>.

39See, for instance, Elliot Aronson, "Self-Justification," chap. 4 in *The Social Animal* (San Francisco: W. H. Freeman, 1972); Daryl Bem, *Beliefs, Attitudes, and Human Affairs* (Belmont, CA: Brooks/Cole, 1970); and Robert B. Cialdini, "Commitment and Consistency," chap. 3 in *Influence*, 2d ed. (Glenview, IL: Scott, Foresman, 1988).

40Jeffrey Pfeffer, *Managing with Power* (Boston: Harvard Business School Press, 1992), 204.

41Ibid.

Chapter 3

1Ellen J. Langer, "Minding Matters: The Consequences of Mindlessness–Mindfulness," in *Advances in Experimental Social Psychology*, ed. Leonard Berkowitz (New York: Academic Press, 1989), 137–173.

2David Beardsley, "This Company Doesn't Brake for (Sacred) Cows," *Fast Company*, August 1998, 66.

3"Confession of a CEO" (Department of Industrial Engineering, Stanford University, Palo Alto, CA, December 1998).

4Trey Pruitt and Willie Quinn, "Recruiting and Training at Children's Hospital Los Angeles Foundation" (Graduate School of Business, Stanford University, Stanford, CA, June 1998), 4.

5Ibid.

6Ibid., 6.

7Robert B. Cialdini, *Influence: The Psychology of Persuasion* (New York: Quill), 1993

8Ibid.

9Quoted in Cialdini, *Influence*, 7.

[10]See, for instance, William G. Ouchi, *Theory Z* (Reading, MA: Addison–Wesley, 1981); and John Kotter and James Heskett, *Corporate Culture and Performance* (New York: Free Press, 1992).

[11]The values are described in numerous Hewlett–Packard internal documents, including one entitled "The HP Way." They are also discussed in writings about the company; for instance, in Deone Zell, *Changing by Design: Organizational Innovation at Hewlett-Packard* (Ithaca, NY: ILR Press, 1997), 16.

[12]Zell, *Changing by Design*, 106.

[13]See, for instance, Meryl Reis Louis and Robert I. Sutton, "Switching Cognitive Gears: From Habits of Mind to Active Thinking," *Human Relations* 44 (1991): 55–76.

[14]Langer, "Minding Matters," 139.

[15]Jeffrey Pfeffer, "The Fresh Choice Company: Acquiring and Transferring Knowledge," Case HR–7 (Stanford, CA: Graduate School of Business, Stanford University, 1998), 1.

[16]Ibid., 6–8.

[17]Jeffrey Pfeffer, Tanya Menon, and Robert I. Sutton, "Knowledge Transfer within and across the Boundaries of a Restaurant Chain: Why It Is Sometimes Easier to Learn from Outsiders than Insiders," working paper, Graduate School of Business, Stanford University, Stanford, CA, 1998, p. 29.

[18]Ibid., 30.

[19]Barry M. Staw, Lloyd E. Sandelands, and Jane E. Dutton, "Threat–Rigidity Effects in Organizational Behavior: A Multilevel Analysis," *Administrative Science Quarterly* 26 (1981): 501–524.

[20]Robert I. Sutton, Kathleen Eisenhardt, and James V. Jucker, "Managing Organizational Decline: Lessons from Atari," *Organizational Dynamics* 14 (1986): 17–29.

[21]Gary High, Director, Human Resource Development, People Systems, Saturn Corporation, interview by Jeffrey Pfeffer and Robert Sutton, Detroit, Michigan, 25 March 1998.

[22]Ibid.

[23]Anna Kretz, General Motors, interview by Jeffrey Pfeffer and Robert Sutton, Detroit, Michigan, 25 March 1998.

[24]Ibid.

[25]Mike Bennett, Saturn, interview by Jeffrey Pfeffer and Robert Sutton, Spring Hill, Tennessee, 24 March 1998.

[26]Tom Lasorda, General Motors, interview by Jeffrey Pfeffer and Robert Sutton, Detroit, Michigan, 25 March 1998.

[27]Arie W. Kruglanski and Donna M. Webster, "Motivated Closing of the Mind: 'Seizing' and 'Freezing,'" *Psychological Bulletin* 103 (1996): 264.

[28]Ibid.

[29]Randy Kennedy, "Private Group Offers Educator Bonus Plan," *New York Times*, 27 January 1998, sec. A, p. 20.

[30]Steve Stecklow, "Apple Polishing: Kentucky's Teachers Get Bonuses, but Some Are Caught Cheating," *Wall Street Journal*, 2 September 1997, sec. A, p. 1.

[31]Burt Schorr, "School's Merit-Pay Program Draws Gripes from Losers—and Winners," *Wall Street Journal*, 16 June 1983, sec. B, p. 31.

[32]Winslow Ward, *The Making of Silicon Valley: A One Hundred Year Renaissance* (Palo Alto, CA: Santa Clara Historical Society, 1995).

[33]See, for example, Edward W. Lawler III, *High-Involvement Management* (San Francisco: Jossey-Bass, 1986).

[34]See, for example, Michael Beer, "Human Resources at Hewlett-Packard (A)," Case 9-495-051 (Boston: Harvard Business School Publishing, 1995).

[35]Beardsley, "This Company Doesn't Brake," 66.

[36]Ibid.

[37]These figures come from J. Burgess Winter, "Magma: A High Performance Company" (paper presented at the Copper 95-Cobre 95 International Conference, Santiago, Chile, November 1995), 1.

[38]Ibid., 3.

[39]Ibid., 1.

⁴⁰The following material comes from a telephone inter-
view by Robert Sutton with Annette Kyle on 17 Sep-
tember 1998. This section also relies on information
from a technical report by Gerald Ledford and Susan
Cohen, "The Wow Program at the Bayport Terminal,
Los Angeles," Center for Effective Organizations,
Graduate School of Business, University of Southern
California, Los Angeles, July 1996.

⁴¹Tom Peters, *The Pursuit of Wow! Every Person's Guide to Topsy-
Turvy Times* (New York: Vintage Books, 1994).

⁴²Winter, "Magma," 4.

⁴³Jeffrey Pfeffer, "Human Resources at the AES Corpora-
tion: The Case of the Missing Department," Case
SHR–3 (Stanford, CA: Graduate School of Business,
Stanford University, 1997), 4.

⁴⁴AES Corporation, *Annual Report* (Arlington, VA: 1997), 9.

⁴⁵"Power to the People," *CFO*, March 1995, 41.

⁴⁶Pfeffer, "Human Resources at the AES Corporation," 15.

⁴⁷AES, *Annual Report*, 10.

⁴⁸Paul C. Nystrom and William H. Starbuck, "To Avoid
Organizational Crises, Unlearn," *Organizational Dynamics* (spring 1984): 53.

Chapter 4

¹W. E. Deming, *Out of the Crisis* (Cambridge, MA: Massachusetts Institute of Technology, Center for Advanced
Engineering Study, 1986).

²Matt Krantz, "How Sweet It Is: Al Dunlap Gets Sunbeam
Deal," *Investor's Business Daily*, 23 July 1996, sec. A, p. 4.

³"For Markets, A Good Quarter on Paper," *Investor's Business
Daily*, 1 October 1996, sec. A, p. 1.

⁴On October 27, 1998, Dunlap, in a conversation with Paul
Reist of Stanford Business School, claimed he had
spoken at 14 major business schools, including the
ones listed, in the past year.

⁵Holman W. Jenkins Jr., "When CEOs Can't Add Up the Numbers," *Wall Street Journal*, 19 August 1998, sec. A, p. 19.

[6]"'Chainsaw' Al Cuts Up for MBAs," *Chicago Tribune*, 12 January 1998, sec. C, p. 3.

[7]Albert J. Dunlap, *Mean Business* (New York: Times Books, 1996), 169.

[8]Ibid., 232.

[9]Ellen Joan Pollock and Martha Brannigan, "The Sunbeam Shuffle, or How Ron Perelman Wound Up in Control," *Wall Street Journal*, 19 August 1998, sec. A, p. 1.

[10]Patricia Sellars, "Can Chainsaw Al Really Be a Builder?" *Fortune*, 12 January 1998, 118–120.

[11]Anne Fisher, "Tom Peters, Professional Loudmouth," *Fortune*, 29 December 1997, 274.

[12]Andrew S. Grove, *Only the Paranoid Survive* (New York: Currency Doubleday), 117, emphasis added.

[13]The site can be found at http://www.igc.apc.org/faceintel/.

[14]Princeton Survey Research Associates, *Worker Representation and Participation Survey: Report on the Findings* (Princeton, NJ: Princeton Survey Research Associates, 1994), 5.

[15]Ibid., 9.

[16]Ibid., 19.

[17]Ibid., 40.

[18]Francis Harris, "Nasty or Nice?" *World Link*, September–October 1996, 39.

[19]Ibid.

[20]For example, Edward Lazear's explanation of seniority-based wage systems maintains that paying people less than what they have produced earlier in their career and more when they are older motivates effort because there are now incentives for more senior people not to shirk. If they shirk, are caught, and are fired, they will lose the deferred compensation inherent in seniority-based wages. Similarly, younger workers are motivated not to shirk because otherwise they will lose the opportunity to get paid more than the value of what they are producing as they become more senior. Edward P. Lazear, "Agency,

Earnings Profiles, Productivity, and Hours Restrictions," *American Economic Review* 71 (1981): 606–620.

[21]For studies of the negative effects of monitoring, see, for instance, B. C. Amick and M. J. Smith, "Stress, Computer-Based Work Monitoring and Measurement Systems: A Conceptual Overview," *Applied Ergonomics* 23 (1992): 6–16; J. R. Aiello, "Electronic Performance Monitoring," *Journal of Applied Psychology* 23 (1993): 499–507; and R. Grant and C. Higgins, "Monitoring Service Workers Via Computer: The Effect on Employees, Productivity, and Service," *National Productivity Review* 8 (1989): 101–112. On the negative consequences of punishment, see F. Luthans and R. Kreitner, *Organizational Behavior Modification* (Glenview, IL: Scott, Foresman, 1975).

[22]John D. Sterman, Nelson P. Repenning, and Fred Kofman, "Unanticipated Side Effects of Successful Quality Programs: Exploring a Paradox of Organizational Improvement," *Management Science* 43 (April 1997): 505.

[23]Ibid., 506.

[24]Ibid., 514.

[25]Deone Zell, *Changing By Design: Organizational Innovation at Hewlett-Packard* (Ithaca, NY: ILR Press, 1997), 82.

[26]Ibid., 82–83.

[27]Thomas H. Davenport, "The Fad That Forgot People," *Fast Company*, November 1995, 71–74.

[28]See, for instance, "Re-engineering with Love," *The Economist*, 9 September 1995, 69–70; David A. Garvin, "Leveraging Processes for Strategic Advantage," *Harvard Business Review* (September–October 1995): 80–81; and James P. Womack, review of *The Reengineering Revolution: A Handbook*, by Michael Hammer and Steven A. Stanton, and *Reengineering Management: The Mandate for New Leadership*, by James Champy, *Sloan Management Review* 36 (summer 1995): 99–100.

[29]Zell, *Changing by Design*, 23.

[30]M. R. Leary, *Self-Presentation: Impression Management and Interpersonal Behavior* (Boulder, CO: Westview), 30.

[31]H. S. Schwartz, *Narcissistic Process and Corporate Decay* (New York: New York University Press), 89.

[32]James Charlton, *The Executive's Quotation Book* (New York: St. Martin's Press), 77.

[33]Grove, *Only the Paranoid*, 118–119.

[34]Patrick Kelly, *Faster Company* (New York: John Wiley, 1998), 24.

[35]Ibid., 96.

[36]Ibid., 154.

[37]Comments from a talk by David F. Russo to a class at the Graduate School of Business, Stanford University, Stanford, California, 5 May 1998.

[38]Jeffrey Pfeffer, "SAS Institute: A Different Approach to Incentives and People Management Practices in the Software Industry," Case HR–6 (Stanford, CA: Graduate School of Business, Stanford University, 1998), 4.

[39]Jeffrey Pfeffer, "The Men's Wearhouse: Success in a Declining Industry," Case HR–5 (Stanford, CA: Graduate School of Business, Stanford University, 1997), 1.

[40]AES Corporation, *Annual Report*, (Arlington, VA: 1997), 17.

[41]Ibid., 9.

[42]Charles L. Bosk, *Forgive and Remember* (Chicago: University of Chicago Press, 1979).

[43]Stephen E. Frank, "Citicorp to Lay off 9,000 in Revamping," *Wall Street Journal*, 22 October 1997, sec. A, p. 3.

[44]Kathleen DesMarteau, "Levi Closes 11 U.S. Plants," *Bobbin*, January 1998, 14–16.

[45]For a discussion of how these factors can reduce the harmful effects of distressing events, see Robert I. Sutton and Robert L. Kahn, "Prediction, Understanding, and Control as Antidotes to Organizational Stress," in *Handbook of Organizational Behavior*, ed. Jay Lorsch (Englewood Cliffs, NJ: Prentice Hall, 1987), 272–285.

[46]For other material on how the two companies dealt with their layoffs, see Mike Verespej, "How to Manage Adversity," *Industry Week*, 19 January 1998, 24; "A

Community Affair," *Apparel Industry Magazine*, September 1998, 84ff.; and Stephen E. Frank, "Citicorp's Reed Received Raise of 15% in 1997," *Wall Street Journal*, 9 March 1998, sec. B, p. 10.

[47]Jerald Greenberg, "Employee Theft as a Reaction to Underpayment Inequity: The Hidden Cost of Pay Cuts," *Journal of Applied Psychology* 75 (1990): 561–568.

Chapter 5

[1]Discussions of the importance of measurement and its effects on organizational behavior have a long history. Most of the research indicates that measurement in and of itself, even without incentives attached to the measures, affects behavior. See, for instance, Peter M. Blau, *The Dynamics of Bureaucracy* (Chicago: University of Chicago Press, 1955); and V. F. Ridgway, "Dysfunctional Consequences of Performance Measurements," *Administrative Science Quarterly* 1 (1956): 240–247.

[2]A. T. Kearney, "Workforce Initiative Discussion Document" (presentation sponsored by Silicon Valley Joint Venture, 25 August 1998), 4.

[3]Frederick F. Reichheld, *The Loyalty Effect* (Boston: Harvard Business School Press, 1996), 217.

[4]See, for instance, Thomas J. Peters and Robert H. Waterman, Jr., *In Search of Excellence* (New York: Harper and Row, 1982); and William G. Ouchi, *Theory Z* (Reading, MA: Addison–Wesley, 1981).

[5]See, for instance, Shelly Branch, "The 100 Best Companies to Work for in America," *Fortune*, 11 January 1999, 122; and Robert Levering and Milton Moskowitz, "The 100 Best Companies to Work for in America," *Fortune*, 12 January 1998, 85.

[6]"Have We Lost Our 'Way'?" (Department of Industrial Engineering, Organizational Behavior and Management Knowing–Doing Case Study, Stanford University, Palo Alto, CA, December 1998).

[7]Ibid.

[8]Ibid.

[9]"Final Project Paper" (Graduate School of Business, Stanford University, Stanford, CA, 2 June 1998), 2.

[10]Ibid., 3.

[11]Ibid., 4.

[12]Ibid., 6.

[13]For a comprehensive discussion of the balanced scorecard, see Robert S. Kaplan and David P. Norton, *The Balanced Scorecard: Translating Strategy into Action* (Boston: Harvard Business School Press, 1996).

[14]Robert Simons and Antonio Dávila, "Citibank: Performance Evaluation," Case 198–048 (Boston: Harvard Business School Publishing, 1997), 7.

[15]Ibid., 3.

[16]Ibid., 4.

[17]G. A. Miller, "The Magical Number Seven, Plus or Minus Two: Some Limits on Our Capacity for Processing Information," *Psychological Review* 63 (1956): 81–97.

[18]Interview by Jeffrey Pfeffer and Robert Sutton, Detroit, Michigan, 25 March 1998, emphasis added.

[19]Ibid.

[20]Wainwright Industries, *Leader's Guide, Sincere Trust and Belief in People: The Wainwright Story* (St. Louis: Wainwright Industries, 1998), 7.

[21]Ibid., 20.

[22]Quoted in Jeffrey Pfeffer, "The Men's Wearhouse: Success in a Declining Industry," Case HR–5 (Stanford, CA: Graduate School of Business, Stanford University, 1997), 27.

[23]Ibid., 15.

[24]Ibid., 20–21.

[25]Jeffrey Pfeffer, "SAS Institute: A Different Approach to Incentives and People Management Practices in the Software Industry," Case HR–6 (Stanford, CA: Graduate School of Business, Stanford University, 1998), 3–4.

[26]Ibid., 5.

[27]Ibid., 8.

[28]Ibid., 11.

[29]Gina Imperato, "How to Give Good Feedback," *Fast Company*, September 1998, 147.

[30]The material in this section is taken from "Intuit: A Company That Identifies and Attacks Gaps" (Department of Industrial Engineering, Stanford University, Palo Alto, CA, December 1998).

[31]Roger Hallowell, James I. Cash, and Shelly Ibri, "Sears, Roebuck and Company (A): Turnaround," Case 9-898-007 (Boston: Harvard Business School, 1997), 3.

[32]Anthony J. Rucci, Steven P. Kirn, and Richard T. Quinn, "The Employee–Customer–Profit Chain at Sears," *Harvard Business Review* (January–February 1998): 84.

[33]Hallowell, Cash, and Ibri, "Sears (A)," 3.

[34]Ibid.

[35]Ibid. See, for instance, the data from the customer surveys on p. 22.

[36]Ibid., 24.

[37]Rucci, Kirn, and Quinn, "Employee–Customer–Profit Chain," 91–94.

Chapter 6

[1]Alfie Kohn, "Is Competition Inevitable?" chap. 2 in *No Contest: The Case Against Competition*, rev. ed. (Boston: Houghton Mifflin, 1992).

[2]Dean Tjosvold, *Working Together to Get Things Done* (Lexington, MA: D. C. Heath, 1986), 34.

[3]Norman Berg and Norman Fast, "The Lincoln Electric Company," Case 376-028 (Boston: Harvard Business School, 1975), 3.

[4]Andrew S. Grove, *High Output Management* (New York: Random House, 1983), 170.

[5]Kohn, *No Contest*, 4.

[6]"Knowing versus Doing on Wall Street" (Graduate School of Business, Stanford University, Stanford, CA, June 1998), 3.

[7]"Employee Turnover at Bear, Stearns & Co." (Graduate School of Business, Stanford University, Stanford, CA, June 1998), 3–4.

[8]"Promoting Teamwork and Cooperation within a Culture of Individuals: A Case Study of a Microsoft Business Unit" (Stanford University School of Engineering, Palo Alto, CA, December 1996), executive summary.

[9]Ibid.

[10]Ibid., 2.

[11]Ibid., 4.

[12]Jeffrey Pfeffer, "The Fresh Choice Company: Acquiring and Transferring Knowledge," Case HR–7 (Stanford, CA: Graduate School of Business, Stanford University, 1998).

[13]Jeffrey Pfeffer, Tanya Menon, and Robert I. Sutton, "Knowledge Transfer within and across the Boundaries of a Restaurant Chain: Why It Is Sometimes Easier to Learn from Outsiders than Insiders," working paper, Graduate School of Business, Stanford University, Stanford, CA, 1998, 37.

[14]Interview by Tanya Menon, 1997.

[15]Pfeffer, Menon, and Sutton, "Knowledge Transfer," 38.

[16]Ibid., 45.

[17]Tjosvold, *Working Together*, 34.

[18]Kohn, *No Contest*, 45–46.

[19]Ibid., 47.

[20]Ibid., 55.

[21]R. Rosenthal and L. Jacobson, *Pygmalion in the Classroom: Teacher Expectations and Pupils' Intellectual Development* (New York: Holt, Rinehart, and Winston, 1968).

[22]See, for instance, J. Sterling Livingston, "Pygmalion in Management," *Harvard Business Review* 47 (1969): 81–89; and Dov Eden, "Self-Fulfilling Prophecy as a Management Tool: Harnessing Pygmalion," *Academy of*

Management Review 9 (1984): 64–73. An excellent
review of the literature can be found in Dov Eden,
*Pygmalion in Management: Productivity as a Self-Fulfilling
Prophecy* (Lexington, MA: Lexington Books, 1990).

23D. Eden and A. B. Shani, "Pygmalion Goes to Boot Camp:
Expectancy, Leadership and Trainee Performance,"
Journal of Applied Psychology 67 (1982): 194–199.

24Dov Eden, "Pygmalion without Interpersonal Contrast
Effects: Whole Groups Gain from Raising Expectations," *Journal of Applied Psychology* 75 (1990): 394–398.

25W. Edwards Deming, *Out of the Crisis* (Cambridge, MA:
Massachusetts Institute of Technology Center for
Advanced Engineering Study, 1986), 102.

26An excellent discussion of the benefits and costs of rela-
tive performance evaluation can be found in Robert
Gibbons and Kevin J. Murphy, "Relative Performance
Evaluation for Chief Executive Officers," *Industrial and
Labor Relations Review* 43 (February 1990): 30-S–51-S.
The ideas underlying the advantages of relative per-
formance evaluation can be found in Edward P.
Lazear and Sherwin Rosen, "Rank-Order Tourna-
ments as Optimum Labor Contracts," *Journal of Politi-
cal Economy* 89 (1981): 841–864.

27Deming, *Out of the Crisis*, 102.

28Robert Crow, "Institutionalized Competition and Its
Effects on Teamwork," *Journal for Quality and Participation* 18 (June 1995): 47.

29For a discussion of the social facilitation idea, see Robert
B. Zajonc, "Social Facilitation," *Science* 149 (1965):
269–274. A comprehensive review of many studies of
the social facilitation effect can be found in C. F. Bond
Jr. and L. J. Titus, "Social Facilitation: A Meta-Analysis
of 241 Studies," *Psychological Bulletin* 94 (1983): 265–292.
See also John R. Aiello and Carol M. Svec, "Computer
Monitoring of Work Performance: Extending the
Social Facilitation Framework to Electronic Presence,"
Journal of Applied Social Psychology 23 (1993): 537–548.

[30]Kohn, *No Contest*, chap. 3. For other studies and reviews of the effects of competition and cooperation on learning, see David W. Johnson, Geoffrey Maruyama, Roger Johnson, Deborah Nelson, and Linda Skon, "Effects of Cooperative, Competitive, and Individualistic Goal Structures on Achievement: A Meta-Analysis," *Psychological Bulletin* 89 (1981): 47–62; Abaineh Workie, "The Relative Productivity of Cooperation and Competition," *Journal of Social Psychology* 92 (1974): 225–230; and Morton Goldman, Joseph W. Stockbauer, and Timothy G. McAuliffe, "Intergroup and Intragroup Competition and Cooperation," *Journal of Experimental Social Psychology* 13 (1977): 81–88.

[31]Roderick M. Kramer, "Cooperation and Organizational Identification," in *Social Psychology in Organizations: Advances in Theory and Research*, ed. J. Keith Murnighan (Englewood Cliffs, NJ: Prentice-Hall, 1993), 245, emphasis added.

[32]Herbert A. Simon, "Organizations and Markets," *Journal of Economic Perspectives* 5 (1991): 33.

[33]A mathematical simulation by a trio of economists showed that a piece-rate system like Lincoln's would cause excessive self-interested behavior without these incentives for cooperating and for supporting the firm as a whole. See George Baker, Robert Gibbons, and Kevin J. Murphy, "Subjective Performance Measures in Optimal Incentive Contracts," *Quarterly Journal of Economics* 109 (1994): 1125–1156.

[34]Conference Board, "Leveraging Intellectual Capital," *HR Executive Review* 5, no. 3 (1997): 5–6.

[35]Crow, "Institutionalized Competition," 47.

[36]Morgan W. McCall Jr., Michael M. Lombardo, and Ann M. Morrison, *The Lessons of Experience: How Successful Executives Develop on the Job* (Lexington, MA: Lexington Books, 1988), 19.

[37]Brian Trelstad, "Group Leadership or Organizational Anrchy: The Case of Stanford's Public Management

Program" (Graduate School of Business, Stanford University, Stanford, CA, June 1998), 9.

[38]Excerpts from memorandum sent by Kelleher to the people of Southwest Airlines, forwarded through someone at United Airlines.

[39]Jeffrey Pfeffer, "The Men's Wearhouse: Success in a Declining Industry," Case HR–5 (Stanford, CA: Graduate School of Business, Stanford University, 1997), 15.

[40]Jeffrey Pfeffer, "SAS Institute: A Different Approach to Incentives and People Management Practices in the Software Industry," Case HR–6 (Stanford, CA: Graduate School of Business, Stanford University, 1998), 6–7.

[41]Jeffrey Pfeffer, "Willamette Industries 'No Pay at Risk' Compensation Practices," Case HR–9 (Stanford, CA: Graduate School of Business, Stanford University, 1998), 7.

[42]Ibid., 8.

[43]Tom Lasorda, General Motors, interview by Jeffrey Pfeffer and Robert Sutton, Detroit, Michigan, 25 March 1998.

[44]Tjosvold, *Working Together*, 35.

Chapter 7

[1]Joel Podolny, John Roberts, and Andris Berzins, "British Petroleum: Performance and Growth (A)," Case S–1B–16A (Stanford, CA: Graduate School of Business, Stanford University, 1998).

[2]Ibid., 1.

[3]Joel Podolny, John Roberts, and Andris Berzins, "British Petroleum: Focus on Learning (B)," Case S–1B–16B (Stanford, CA: Graduate School of Business, Stanford University, 1998), 1.

[4]"British Petroleum (A)," 1.

[5]Ibid., 5–6.

[6]"When Toughness Is Not Enough," *Financial Times*, 26 June 1992.

[7]"British Petroleum (A)," 8.

[8]"Blood in the Boardroom," *Sunday Telegraph*, 28 June 1992, quoted in "British Petroleum (A)," 8.

[9]"British Petroleum (A)," 9.

[10]"British Petroleum (B)," 1.

[11]Ibid., 2.

[12]Ibid., 4.

[13]Ibid.

[14]Ibid.

[15]Ibid.

[16]Ibid., 5.

[17]Ibid., 6.

[18]Ibid.

[19]Ibid.

[20]Ibid., 7.

[21]Thomas H. Davenport and Laurence Prusak, *Working Knowledge: How Organizations Manage What They Know* (Boston: Harvard Business School Press, 1998), 20.

[22]Ibid.

[23]Ibid., 21.

[24]"British Petroleum (B)," 7–8.

[25]Ibid., 8.

[26]All quotations in the Barclay's Global Investors section come from interviews by Jeffrey Pfeffer, San Francisco, California, 12 February 1998.

[27]New Zealand Post, *Annual Report* (Wellington, New Zealand: 1994), 10.

[28]Ibid.

[29]Ibid., 5.

[30]Harvey Parker, "New Zealand Post—Using the Personnel Function to Promote Excellence in Management" (unpublished ms, January 1989), 4.

[31]Ibid., 5

[32]Jeffrey Pfeffer, *The Human Equation: Building Profits by Putting People First* (Boston: Harvard Business School Press, 1998).

[33]Elmar Toime, "The Case for Postal Deregulation" (paper presented at the Utility Markets Summit, Wellington, New Zealand, 27 April 1995), 4, 6.

Chapter 8

[1]Harlow B. Cohen, "The Performance Paradox," *Academy of Management Executives* 12 (1998): 30.

[2]Skip LeFauve, interview by Jeffrey Pfeffer and Robert Sutton, Detroit, Michigan, 25 March 1998.

[3]Jeffrey Pfeffer, "Human Resources at the AES Corporation: The Case of the Missing Department," Case SHR-3 (Stanford, CA: Graduate School of Business, Stanford University, 1997), 3–4.

[4]Jeffrey Pfeffer, "The Men's Wearhouse: Success in a Declining Industry," Case HR-5 (Stanford, CA: Graduate School of Business, Stanford University, 1997), 2.

[5]Ibid., 4.

[6]"McKinsey's Value Chain," *World Link*, September–October 1998, 30–32.

[7]Tom Lasorda, interview by Jeffrey Pfeffer and Robert Sutton, Detroit, Michigan, 25 March 1998.

[8]Thomas J. Peters and Robert H. Waterman, Jr., *In Search of Excellence: Lessons from America's Best-Run Companies* (New York: Harper and Row, 1982).

[9]Greg Brenneman, "Right Away and All At Once: How We Saved Continental," *Harvard Business Review* 76 (September–October 1998): 164.

[10]Walter Gropius, *Scope of Total Architecture* (New York: Macmillan, 1970).

[11]Warren Bennis and Burt Nanus, *Leaders: Strategies for Taking Charge* (New York: HarperBusiness, 1997), 60.

[12]Ibid., 70.

[13]Suzy Wetlaufer, "Organizing for Empowerment: An Interview with AES's Roger Sant and Dennis Bakke," *Harvard Business Review* 77 (January–February 1999): 119.

[14]Brenneman, "Right Away," 166.

[15]"Forgive Don't Forget," *World Link*, September–October 1998, 47.

[16]"Interview," *World Link*, September–October 1998, 49.

[17]Ibid., 170.

[18]"Managing Major Organizational Change: Transition to Closure at Newcastle Steelworks," BHP Newcastle Steelworks Case Study (Melbourne, Australia: Broken Hill Proprietary, 1998), 6. See also Coopers and Lybrand, *Closing Plants: Planning and Implementation Strategies* (Morristown, NJ: Financial Executive Research Foundation, 1986).

[19]Ibid., 26–27.

[20]Alfie Kohn, *No Contest: The Case Against Competition* (Boston: Houghton Mifflin, 1992), 50–51.

[21]Eric Ransdell, "They Sell Suits with Soul," *Fast Company*, October 1998, 68.

[22]Dean Tjosvold, *Working Together to Get Things Done* (Lexington, MA: D.C. Heath, 1986), 26. See also Dean Tjosvold, "Testing Goal Linkage Theory in Organizations," *Journal of Occupational Behavior* 7 (1986): 77–88.

[23]Quoted in Tjosvold, *Working Together*, 11.

[24]Brenneman, "Right Away," 166.

[25]"Using Measurement to Boost Your Unit's Performance," *Harvard Management Update* 3 (October 1998): 1.

[26]Michael Warshaw, "Have You Been House-Trained?" *Fast Company*, October 1998, 48.

[27]Ibid., 46.

Index

accountability, 65, 239
accounting measures and
    practices, 159–160,
    161, 166, 171, 173, 174,
    244
acquisitions, 78–80
AES Corporation, 41–42, 53,
    76, 103–106, 130–131,
    202, 246, 247, 254, 256,
    259, 261
Allan, Kelly, 166
Amabile, Teresa, 45
ambiguity, 88
Analog Devices, 119
analysis
    of information, 88, 259
    quantitative, 56
Andersen Consulting, 13
andon cords, 23
antitrust concerns, 167
Apple Computer, 80, 204
apprenticeship, 249
Association of Executive
    Search Consultants, 8
A. T. Kearney, 141
Atari Corporation, 80
ATL, 208, 209
audits, 160
Avon, 193

Bakke, Dennis, 53, 104, 130,
    254, 256, 261
balanced scorecard systems,
    52, 147, 148–153, 154, 158,
    161, 251
Baldrige Award (Malcolm
    Baldrige National
    Quality Award), 9, 37,
    124, 161
Barclays Bank, 222, 225, 232
Barclays Global Investors (BGI),
    182, 213, 221–234, 241, 261
Barnard, Chester, 197
Barrett, Colleen, 204
Bay Networks, 261–262
Bear, Stearns & Company, 182
Behar, Howard, 23
behavior in organizations, 88,
    147, 151
    acquiring new, 185
    drivers of, 153, 154, 156, 168
    inconsistency of, 73–74
    individual control over,
        157–159
    of leadership, 88, 200, 210,
        221
    tracked through employee
        surveys, 167–168
benchmarking, 14, 15, 186

benchmarking (*continued*)
   from project–based struc-
      ture, 31
Bennett, Mike, 86
Bennis, Warren, 253
best practices, 5, 14, 15, 95,
      239
   implementation of, 13–14
   sharing/transfer of, 9, 13,
      18, 185, 243
   undermining of, 187–190
BGI. *See* Barclays Global
      Investors (BGI)
BHP. *See* Broken Hill
      Proprietary (BHP)
bidding systems, 71
Billington, Corey, 19
bonuses, 131, 150, 158, 165,
      183–184, 194, 208
   elimination of, 208–209
   See also employee(s): com-
      pensation
Bosk, Charles, 132–133
Boston Philharmonic, 131
Bouton, Garrett, 224, 225, 229,
      230–231
brainstorming, 63
Brenneman, Greg, 60, 251, 254
Bresler, Charlie, 59, 130,
      162–163, 205
British Petroleum (BP), 213–221,
      234, 241, 258, 261
Broken Hill Proprietary (BHP),
      34–35, 37, 41, 96, 215,
      255–256
Brown, Mark Graham, 259
Browne, John, 215, 221
Bucknell University survey, 114
budget targets, 143, 145, 146
Buehler, William, 9
build–from–within policies, 73
Burdick, Paul, 105
business models. *See* philoso-
      phy of business
business process reengineer-
      ing, 52

business schools/business
      education, 1, 3–4, 38, 47,
      110–111, 112
business units
   cooperation among,
      216–218, 220, 258
Butler, Nick, 220

Campagna, Janet, 223
Campbell, Jennifer, 232
Campbell, Marsh, 96
capitalism, 177
capital market interests, 160
career systems, 51, 56
cash management account
      (CMA), 66, 67
Center for Workplace
      Development, 18
change
   benefits of, 100–101
   drivers, 64, 153, 154, 156, 168
   organizational, 2
   resistance to, 87, 98
   threat of, 77–80, 88
chaos theory, 52
Christensen, Clayton, 254
Cialdini, Robert, 73
Citibank, 134–135
   measures and measurement
      systems, 147, 148–149,
      150, 158
cognitive closure, 88, 91
Cohen, Don, 16, 21
Cohen, Harlow, 243
collective good concept,
      126–127, 221, 257
commission sales, 194
common sense, 53, 55, 56, 59,
      140, 148, 236, 237, 239
communication(s), 9, 55, 83,
      233, 234, 248
   of action plans, 102
   distortion of, 59
   encouragement of, 133,
      229–230
   interpersonal, 166, 229, 234

technological networks, 218–219

compassion, 134, 135, 136. *See also* employee(s): corporate attitude toward

competition (general discussion)
across firms, 179
benefits and necessity of, 177, 179, 190, 197, 198, 211, 216
innovation and, 177
knowing–doing gap and, 22, 259
measures and measurement systems and, 170–171
product market, 167
versus success, 190–193
zero–sum, 179, 182, 191, 199, 208, 257

competition within firms, 146, 257–259
avoidance of, 203–211
business units and, 216–220
cost to the organization, 194–195
doing well versus winning, 190–193, 259
efficiency and, 177
employee turnover and, 180–183
encouragement of, 190, 199–201
external threats and, 203–204, 210
external versus internal, 202–203, 210, 211
goal attainment and, 178–179
innovation and, 177, 196
interdependence and, 196–198, 211
knowing–doing gap created by, 180–190, 257–259
knowledge sharing under-

mined by, 185–187, 190, 195, 196, 198, 200, 209
management practices and, 179–180, 185, 190, 195–196, 199–201, 257–259
organizational perform-ance and, 177, 180, 190, 194–195, 257–259
as organizing principle, 177, 190–201
peer groups and, 216–218, 220
teamwork undermined by, 183–185
zero–sum compensation schemes and, 208, 257

competitive advantage, sus-tainable, 53, 54

complexity concept, 51–55, 56, 59–60, 248–249
measures and measurement systems and, 147–153

Conference Board, 18

consistency, pressure for, 72–75

consulting, 13, 230. *See also* man-agement consulting firms

Continental Airlines, 59–60, 251, 254, 255

continuous improvement con-cept, 15

contract labor, 144–145

control, 134–135, 136, 156, 157–159, 160, 194

conventional wisdom. *See* knowledge: conven-tional wisdom

conversational marketplace concept, 47. *See also* talk

cooperation/collaboration, 197–198, 200, 201, 205, 210, 221, 227, 239, 258
among business units, 216–218, 220, 258
knowledge-to-action process and, 257–259
technology, 16

co–op learning, 26
core operating principles, 38,
        168, 173, 174. *See also* val-
        ues: core
core processes, 58, 59, 62
corporate identity, 81, 91,
        203–204
cost structures, 71
creativity. *See* innovation and
        creativity
criticism, 45–46, 57, 228
Crook, Larry, 262
cross–training, 105
CSC Index, 121
cultural fit concept, 54–55,
        72–73, 75, 82–83, 227–228
culture, 84, 85, 97
    action–oriented, 226, 234,
        250, 251–253, 262
    continuity of, 75–77, 231,
        232
    global, 224–225
    high–performance, 254
    long– versus short–term
        performance and, 140,
        217, 220
    transformation of, 252, 261
    See also mission and vision
        statements
Curtis, Signe, 233
customer
    loyalty, 2
    needs, 61–62
    retention, 244
    services and satisfaction, 2,
        5, 12, 58–59, 124, 158–159,
        161, 162–164, 171, 205,
        238, 244, 259
cycle time, 8

DaPrile, Mike, 23
data systems, 19, 259. *See also*
        information
data warehouses. *See* knowledge:
        repositories (intranets,
        data warehouses)

day care, on–site, 65–66
decentralization, 54, 189, 238,
        239
    of decision making, 103, 128
    radical, 103–105
decision making, 19, 37, 42, 74,
        87, 88, 90, 144
    creative, 106
    decentralization of, 103, 128
    delegation of, 54–55
    employee involvement in,
        230
    follow–up processes for, 57,
        60–65
    implementation of deci-
        sions, 57
    inaccurate bases for, 91, 92,
        261
    individual control of,
        157–159
    by leadership, 63, 261
    operational, 238
    precedent and, 79
    as substitute for action,
        30–33, 37, 54
    See also problem solving
defect density concept, 8
Deloitte & Touche, 235
Deming, W. Edwards, 109, 112,
        125, 193
deregulation, 240
DeSimone, Livio, 254–255
Destec, 131
direct sales organizations, 193
distributed intelligence, 42
distrust, 109
    creation of knowing–doing
        gap through, 118–127
    as management technique,
        110, 137
    pervasiveness of, 113–115,
        116, 118
    See also trust
documents and reports
    as substitutes for action,
        35–37, 41, 50, 54, 252–253

Donnelly, John F., 258–259
Donnelly Mirrors, 258
downsizing. *See* personnel
    practices: firings and
    downsizing
Dunlap, Albert, 110–112,
    125–126
Dunn, Pattie, 225

Early, Dennis, 120
economic theory of human
    behavior, 90
Edison, Thomas, 57
education programs. *See* train-
    ing programs
efficiency
    competition within firms
        and, 177
    undermining of, 121,
        123–125, 127
employee attitude surveys,
    102, 167–168, 172, 265
employee(s), 3
    behavior/attitudes, 69, 188,
        244
    career progression, 51, 56
    compensation, 40, 106, 145,
        165, 179, 184, 194–195,
        199, 208
    corporate attitude toward,
        54–55, 115, 133, 136–137,
        144, 161, 164–166, 181,
        244, 247–248, 255–256
    cultural fit into firm, 54–55,
        72–73, 75, 82–83, 227–228
    evaluations/performance
        appraisals, 42–47, 51, 54,
        163, 165–166, 179, 190,
        194–195, 200, 231
    feedback from, 26
    interviews, 102
    labor shortages, 113
    layoffs and downsizing,
        119–121
    loyalty, 75, 114, 130, 144, 183,
        188

morale, 168, 171
motivation, 114, 115, 118,
    119, 142–143, 172, 178, 191,
    193, 259
    of new organizations, 95
    part-time, 171
    promotion from within, 56,
        128
    quality, 11–12
    recognition of, 36–37
    retention, 83, 228, 260
    rights, 114
    sharing information with,
        10–11, 183–185, 216–217
    temporary workers,
        144–145, 146
    transfer of, 216–217, 220, 231
    turnover, 5, 12, 39, 58, 65,
        72–73, 75, 78, 84, 123, 141,
        143, 166, 180–183, 185,
        205, 232, 244, 258
    use of information by, 88,
        155–156, 157
    work methods, 31
    See also bonuses; incentive
        systems; management:
        employee relations;
        personnel practices;
        reward systems
Ephlin, Donald, 81
Ernst & Young, 16, 19–21
ethical business practices, 146.
    See also information: fal-
    sification of
European Economic and
    Monetary Union (EMU),
    232
evaluations
    based on smart talk, 42–47
excellence tradition, 226–227

FACE–Intel website, 113
failures and mistakes
    admitting to, 130–131, 133,
        228, 234
    avoidance of, 132, 133

failures and mistakes (*continued*)
corporate response to,
253–154
covering up, 184
learning from, 19, 27, 64, 93,
128–129, 131–132, 133,
169, 241, 253–255, 262
repetition of, 110
fatigue, 88
fear, 88, 107, 109–110
creation of knowing–doing
gap through, 109–110,
118–127, 136, 254–257
as deliberate management
technique, 110–118,
125–126, 136–137, 215, 221
elimination of, 127–137, 169,
254–257
external, 113–118
of job loss, 118, 121–124,
124–126, 254
long– versus short–term
performance and,
124–126
pervasiveness of, 113–118
self–preservation versus
collective good and,
126–127, 133, 134, 221
feedback, 10, 123
from employees, 26, 145,
166, 168
Feynman, Richard, 122
financial analyst programs,
38–40
financial measurement systems, 170, 244
flexible manufacturing, 7–8,
86, 154
focus groups, 218
follow–up processes, 54, 57,
60–65
forced curve rankings, 184, 185,
193, 194, 257
Fresh Choice company, 77–80,
185–187, 195, 258

frustration, 155
fund–raising, 72–73, 75

Gallup Workplace Audit, 265
General Electric, 28
Work–Out Process, 61–65
General Motors (GM), 81, 83,
84–86, 93, 195, 246–247,
249, 258, 262
Business Plan Deployment
Strategy, 156
lean manufacturing at,
209–210, 260
measures and measure-
ment systems, 154–156,
260
Powertrain Group, 166
undermining spread of
best practices within,
188–190
See also New United Motor
Manufacturing
(NUMMI); Saturn
geographic concentration/dis-
persing of, 8, 76
Glenroy, Inc., 166
goal attainment
competition and, 178–179
goals
high–performance, 14, 94
team, 101
Goldman, Sachs, 182
Goldwyn, Samuel, 123
Goodnight, James, 58, 129,
164–165, 166, 256
Goodwin, Kevin, 208
Grauer, Fred, 222, 226, 228, 233
Greenberg, Jerald, 135
Gropius, Walter, 252
group dynamics, 46
Grove, Andrew, 112, 123,
178–179, 197
growth of organizations,
221–223, 234
Gupta, Rajat, 249

Haas, Robert, 134
Hackborn, Dick, 94
Harvard Business School, 48,
    148–149, 177, 254
health benefits, 66
Hewlett–Packard (HP), 9, 94,
    120–121, 124–125
  "HP Way," 75–77, 142, 143
  long– versus short–term
    performance problem
    at, 142–147
  Strategic Planning,
    Analysis, and Modeling
    group, 21
hierarchal structures, 59, 62,
    106, 209, 256–257
High Output Management
    (Grove), 178
high performance
  firms, 116
  goals, 14, 94
  management practices, 5, 94
Hoechst Celanese Corporation,
    98–102
Honda, 23, 26–27, 55, 247, 249
  BP program, 15
Horton, Robert, 215, 221
hostile takeovers, 255
House, Dave, 261–262
human behavior, 88, 89–93,
    157

IBM, 93, 195, 204, 253
IBM Consulting Group, 198
IDEO Product Development,
    29, 106, 132, 247, 249,
    250, 262
implementation
  barriers and problems, 32,
    52, 67
  of best practices, 13–14
  of knowledge, 4–5, 8, 14, 21,
    25, 26, 46
  of knowledge manage-
    ment, 22

versus understanding,
    53–55
incentive systems, 89–90, 118,
    159, 165, 170, 183–185,
    194–195, 200
  for cooperation, 198
  individual, 158
  performance–based, 90, 239
  piece–rate, 177, 198
information, 243
  codification of, 16, 18, 22
  dissemination of, 59, 134,
    135, 136
  falsification of, 123–124,
    125–126, 146
  financial, 159–160
  gathering/capture, 42, 259
  hoarding, 184, 220
  market for, 13
  processing/analysis of, 88,
    259
  screening of negative,
    121–123
  sharing/transfer of, 10, 18,
    42, 54–55, 159, 183–185,
    203, 210, 216, 229, 239,
    243, 245
  storage, 88
  technology, 16–17, 19,
    218–219
  use of, by employees, 88,
    155–156, 157, 161
  See also knowledge *listings*
Informix (database software
    company), 125
innovation and creativity, 97,
    116
  competition and, 177, 196
  knowing by doing and, 103,
    104–107, 254
  in management practices,
    240
  organizational, 10
  rewards for, 129, 133
  technological, 9

insecurity, 116, 186–187
integrity in firms, 115
Intel, 112–113, 123, 178, 197,
     261
intellectual capital, 15, 18,
     57–58, 79–80, 142, 164,
     166, 198, 260
intellectual property, 16
interdependence, 196–198, 200,
     207, 211
Internet, 167, 251
internships, 26
interviews, 102
intimidation, 111. *See also* dis-
     trust; fear
intranets (data warehouses),
     229. *See also* knowledge:
     repositories (intranets,
     data warehouses)
Intuit, 166–168, 169, 172, 174
investment banking, 38, 39, 40,
     180–183, 195
investment management,
     221–234

Jobs, Steve, 204
job titles, 228
joint ventures, 222
Joyner, Barrett, 165

kaizen, 15
kanban, 23
Kearns, David, 36, 37, 262
Kelleher, Herb, 130, 202–203,
     204, 256
Kelley, David, 29, 106, 249–250,
     262
Kelly, Patrick, 128
Kentucky school systems, 89, 90
Kingston Technology, 26, 246,
     249
Kmart, 170
Knipe, Humphrey, 47
knowing by doing, 19, 25–28,
     64, 65, 103–107, 118

in action-oriented cultures,
     251–253
knowing-doing gap and,
     248–251, 263
knowledge-to-action
     process and, 248–251
of leadership, 56, 58
knowing-doing survey,
     265–269
knowledge, 5, 12, 181
acquisition, 26–27, 215
codification of, 16–17, 19
collection and storage, 13,
     21–22, 24–25
conceptions of, 16, 22
conventional wisdom,
     72–75, 175, 220, 237, 240
creation and development,
     15, 19, 26, 42, 209–210
enhancement through
     measures and measure-
     ment systems, 160–173
implementation barriers
     and problems, 32, 52, 85
implementation of, 4–5, 8,
     14, 21, 25, 26, 46, 87, 94,
     103, 125, 128, 244, 245,
     254, 260
investment in, 16–17, 19
organizational action from,
     16–17, 22, 25, 42, 47, 50,
     68, 221, 245
past, 88
performance and, 243
repositories (intranets, data
     warehouses), 16, 18, 19,
     22
risk based on, 110
sharing/transfer of, 8, 9, 13,
     19–21, 22, 26, 81, 84, 118,
     127, 185–188, 190, 198,
     209–210, 214, 216,
     218–221, 243, 251, 261
sharing undermined by
     competition within

firms, 185–187, 190, 195, 196, 198, 200, 209
tacit, 19, 22, 153, 260
technical, 23, 181
working, 18
See also information
knowledge brokers, 13
knowledge management, 19
implementation of, 22
knowing–doing gap and, 15–24
philosophy of, 21–22, 23, 24
See also management practices
knowledge-to-action process, 22, 58, 67, 102, 103, 159, 233–234, 241, 243–245, 261
through accumulated wisdom, 222–223
barriers to, 5–6, 29, 42, 53, 56, 70, 139, 180, 181, 184, 213, 215–216
competition within firms and, 188–189, 257–259
complexity and, 55
decision making in, 30–33
effect of fear-based management on, 121–124, 254–257
encouragement of, 132
failure of, 6, 109, 123, 132
guidelines for, 246–262
knowing by doing and, 248–251
management and, 229–230, 261–262
measures and measurement systems and, 139, 142, 169, 173–175, 259–261
organizational, 16–17, 22, 25
organizational performance and, 243
philosophy of business and, 246–248

planning, 30, 251–253
precedent, 76–77
through proper use of language, 59, 60–61
reinventing organizations and, 233–241
knowledge workers, 140–141
Kohn, Alfie, 191
Kretz, Anna, 83, 84–85
Kyle, Annette, 98–102, 112

labor market, 239
Langer, Ellen, 77
language
action-oriented, 57, 60–65, 68, 250
simplicity of, 56, 59
Lasorda, Tom, 86, 154–156, 209–210, 249
leadership, 56, 102, 201, 233
behavior, 88, 200, 210, 221, 244–245, 256, 262
competition within firms encouraged by, 199–201
decision making by, 63, 261
development, 27, 249
of groups/teams, 46–47, 201
implementation problems and, 52, 265
knowing by doing and, 56, 58
knowing–doing gap and, 266
measures and measurement systems and, 141, 266
power of, 256–257
qualities and skills, 51, 58, 152, 262
rationalization of actions by, 11–12
resource allocation by, 261–262
standards for, 228
training programs, 1–2, 48, 59, 209

lean manufacturing/production, 7, 27, 86, 154, 209–210, 249, 260
lean suppliers, 23
learning. *See* information; knowing by doing; knowledge
learning organizations, 52, 103, 107, 247
LeFauve, Skip, 246–247, 262
Leggate, John, 218
Levi Strauss, 134–135, 255
licensing agreements, 164–166
Lincoln, James F., 177, 198
Lincoln, John C., 178
Lincoln Electric Company, 177–178
Lockheed Corporation, 71
Lockheed-Martin, 71
Lorenzo, Frank, 255
Loyalty Effect, The (Reichheld), 141
Lumley, Diane, 224, 226, 229, 232–233

Macintosh, 80, 167, 204
Maclay, George, 47
Macy's, 244
Magma Copper, 33–34, 96, 97–98, 102–103, 112
management, 4, 51, 54
   authority of, 239
   build-from-within policies and, 73
   decentralization of, 54, 103–105, 189, 238, 239
   development, 59
   employee relations, 102, 109, 112, 117
   evaluation of, 147
   fear-based, 109, 110–118, 121–126, 136–137, 215, 221, 254–257
   implementation problems and, 52
   information systems, 221
   isolation of, 122–123
   knowledge-to-action process and, 229–230
   middle, 49
   organizational performance and, 243
   of people, 7, 24, 127, 150–151, 153
   sanction-based, 119
   teams, 99–100, 230–231
   training programs, 59
management consulting firms, 1, 2–3, 4, 47, 56, 121
   substitutes for action and, 48–51
management education, 1, 26, 48–51, 56, 177. *See also* business schools/business education
management practices, 6, 9, 76, 81, 127, 157, 158, 185, 261–262, 265–266
   Asian, 25
   barriers to improvement of, 189–190
   carried from past to future, 97
   changes in, 4, 155, 238
   competition within firms and, 179–180, 185, 190, 195–196, 199–201
   enlightened, 109
   high-commitment/high-performance, 5, 10, 94, 240, 244, 245
   innovation in, 240
   knowing-doing gap and, 6, 7–12, 254–257, 260
   knowledge about, 13, 55
   long- versus short-term performance and, 140, 142–147, 217, 220
   novel versus routine tasks, 195–196

precedent and, 74, 91
principles of, 24–28, 136
as reflection of firm's cul-
    ture, 75, 136, 262
to resist mindless action,
    103–107, 161
as substitute for thinking, 79
talk as substitute for
    action, 31–32
techniques, 110–113
workplace, 33, 34
See also balanced scorecard
    systems; knowledge
    management; measures
    and measurement
    systems
manufacturing practices, 5,
    7–8, 15, 119–120
flexible, 7–8, 86, 154
outsourcing, 144–145, 240
See also lean manufactur-
    ing/production
Mariucci, Steve, 50–51
marketing, 5
Martinez, Arthur, 171
Martin Marietta, 71
Mary Kay Cosmetics, 193
Maxfield, Bob, 93
Mayo, Rick, 23
McKinsey & Company, 13, 249
McMillen, Dave, 104
Mean Business (Dunlap), 110
measures and measurement
    systems, 139–140, 215
balanced scorecard, 52, 147,
    148–153, 154, 158, 161, 251
categories of, 148–149, 150,
    173
changing nature of, 173–174
complexity of, 139, 147–153,
    174
counterproductive/flawed,
    139, 244, 257–258
as drivers of change,
    169–173

as focusing mechanism,
    166–168, 260
implementation of, 148, 153,
    174
ineffective, persistent use
    of, 147, 156–160
in-process versus outcome,
    154–156, 173, 260
knowing-doing gap and,
    139, 141–142, 157, 257,
    260, 265
knowledge enhancement
    through, 160–173
knowledge-to-action
    process and, 139, 142,
    160, 169, 173–175, 257,
    259–260
organizational action
    resulting from, 139–140,
    173, 175
problems created by,
    140–156
time scale of, 147
memory
customs/history as, 69–70,
    74–75, 87, 88, 91, 245,
    248, 260
knowing-by-doing prob-
    lems, 69–70
precedent and, 69–70,
    72–75, 87
standard operating proce-
    dures as, 69, 74–75, 244
as substitute for thinking,
    69–71, 74, 248
wise use of, 106
Men's Wearhouse, The, 3, 24,
    76, 129–130, 202, 246,
    247–248, 256
measures and measure-
    ment systems, 162–164,
    169, 175
team selling strategy, 58–59,
    162–164, 205–206, 258
mentoring, 249

mergers, 234, 261. *See also*
　　Barclays Global
　　Investors (BGI)
Merrill Lynch, 66, 67
Microsoft, 167
　　reward system at, 183–185,
　　195
Mills, C. Wright, 52
Minnesota Mining and
　　Manufacturing, 254
Mintzberg, Henry, 42
mission and vision state-
　　ments, 81–82, 237
　　as substitute for action,
　　37–40, 42, 54
mistakes. *See* failures and
　　mistakes
Mitel Corporation, 70, 95–96,
　　102
modernization, 255
monitoring systems, 119
Montessori, Maria, 129
Morthland, Dave, 207–208
motivation, 114, 115, 136, 242
　　knowing–doing gap and,
　　90, 259
　　lack of, 193
　　morale and, 142–143
　　for problem solving, 244
Motorola, 28
MUM effect, 121–122

Nanus, Burt, 253
NASA space shuttle disaster, 122
networks, 16
Newcastle Steelworks. *See*
　　Broken Hill Proprietary
　　(BHP)
Newmont company, 96
New United Motor
　　Manufacturing
　　(NUMMI), 59, 189, 246
New York City schools, 89, 90
New Zealand Post, 213,
　　234–241, 255
Nikko Securities, 222, 225

*No Contest: The Case Against
　　Competition* (Kohn), 191
NUMMI. *See* New United
　　Motor Manufacturing
　　(NUMMI)
Nystrom, Paul, 106

Only the Paranoid Survive (Grove),
　　110
Onustock, Mick, 208
operating principles/values,
　　38, 167, 168, 173, 174, 224,
　　236, 238, 248
Oracle (database management
　　company), 125
organizational action, 251–253
　　from knowledge, 16–17, 22,
　　25, 42, 47, 50, 68, 221, 263
　　from measures and meas-
　　urement systems,
　　139–140, 173, 175
organizational learning, 180
organizational performance, 4,
　　5, 12, 158, 161
　　changing, 97–98
　　effect of fear–based man-
　　agement on, 118, 221
　　enhancement/improve-
　　ment of, 14, 87
　　knowing–doing gap and,
　　12–15, 88, 90, 258, 259
　　knowledge-to-action
　　process and, 243, 258
　　management and, 243
　　precedent and, 77
　　predictability of, 254
　　talk as substitute for action
　　and, 27
　　theories of human behav-
　　ior and, 90–91
　　training programs and, 248
　　undermining of, by fear
　　and distrust, 109, 221
　　undermining of, by man-
　　agement practices, 119,
　　122–123, 257–259

See also competition within
  firms
organizational practices, 5, 7,
  247
organizational restructuring.
  See restructuring; turnarounds
organizations
  action-oriented, 226, 234, 250
  breaking from the past in,
    95–103
  building of new, 92, 93–95
  infrastructure changes, 237
  resisting mindless action
    in, 103–107, 161
outsourcing, 144–145, 240
ownership, corporate, 222

Parker, Harvey, 238, 239
Pecking Order in Human Society,
  The (Maclay and Knipe),
  47
peer groups, 216–218, 220
Penn Manor school district,
  Pittsburgh,
  Pennsylvania, 89–90
Pennsylvania school systems,
  89–90
performance, 161
  business unit, 216–217
  demands, 227
  differences within firms,
    8–9
  enhancement/improve-
    ment of, 171, 197, 203,
    210, 240, 243, 248
  expectations, 97, 234
  indicators, 171–172, 265
  individual versus collec-
    tive, 126–127, 221
  information, sharing of,
    54–55
  knowledge and, 243
  long- versus short-term,
    124–126, 140, 142–147, 217
  motivation and, 90, 240

reward and incentive sys-
    tems and, 90, 239
  self-fullfilling prophecy
    concept of, 191–193, 200
  undermining of, by com-
    petition within firms,
    190–193, 194–195
  See also measures and
    measurement systems
performance knowledge, 13,
  181, 220
  implementation of, 69, 90,
    153
  knowing–doing gap and,
    213, 266
performance management,
  194
performance measures, 37,
  265–266
permanence tendency, 88
personality, 6
personnel practices
  costs of, 141
  cultural fit considerations,
    54–55, 72–73, 75, 82–83,
    227–228
  demotions, 125
  in expanding firms,
    223–224
  firings and downsizing, 114,
    118, 130, 134–135, 206,
    215, 236, 239–240,
    255–256
  hiring policies, 3–4, 8, 11, 12,
    39, 43, 56, 72–73, 75, 95,
    171, 186–187, 210, 227
  humane, 134–135
  interviews, 43
  negative reputation of
    firms and, 39
  pay cuts, 125, 134, 135
  promotions, 56, 210
  recruiting policies, 39,
    49–50, 54–55, 82–84,
    140–141, 144, 146, 167,
    238–239

personnel practices (*continued*)
    transfers and plant clos-
        ings, 125, 134–135
    See also employee(s)
Peters, Tom, 100, 112, 251
philosophy of business, 84, 87,
    260
    core operating principles,
        38, 168, 173, 174
    employee involvement in,
        86
    knowing–doing gap and,
        246–248
    knowledge management,
        21–22, 23, 24
    knowledge-to-action
        process and, 246–248
    long- versus short-term,
        175, 217, 220
    measures and measure-
        ment systems and,
        147–148, 162–164,
        169–173
    performance as reflection
        of, 147–148
    training programs for, 250
planning
    action, 64, 68, 99–101
    knowledge-to-action
        process and, 30, 251–253
    as substitute for action,
        40–42, 54, 215, 251–253
Platt, Lew, 9
precedent, 76, 236, 239
    decision making and, 79
    knowledge-to-action
        process and, 76–77
    management practices and,
        74, 91
    memory and, 69–70, 72–75,
        87
    organizational perform-
        ance and, 77
    problem solving and, 80
    reliance on, 102

    as substitute for action, 80
    as substitute for thinking,
        69–71, 87–88, 92–107,
        187–188
    wise use of, 105–106
prediction, 134, 135, 136
presentations
    identity of the organization
        and, 68
    as substitute for action,
        33–35, 41, 50, 56, 248–249
Princeton Survey Research
    Associates, 113–114
private branch exchanges
    (PBX), 70
problem solving, 69
    motivation for, 244
    precedent and, 80
    through teamwork, 217,
        218, 219
    See also decision making
product
    design, 145
    development process, 30–33
    life cycles, 142
    teams, 58
production
    flexible, 7–8, 86, 154
    strategies, 84
    See also lean manufactur-
        ing/production
productivity, 236
profits, 97, 244
profit-sharing systems, 198,
    202
project-based organization,
    30–33
promotions. *See* personnel
    practices: promotions
Prusak, Larry, 198
PSS/World Medical, 3, 127–129,
    246, 253
psychology
    individual, 6
    social, 88, 121–122, 157, 257

punishment, 119, 127, 129, 132, 133
    See also reward systems
Pygmalion effect (self-fullfilling prophecies), 191–193, 200

quality circles, 23
quality concerns, 161, 260
Quesnelle, Stephen, 70
quit forms, 82–83

reciprocity norm, 130
reconfiguration. *See* restructuring
reengineering, 121, 252
reframing, 65–68. *See also* restructuring
Regan, Donald, 66–67
Reichheld, Frederick, 141
Reid, Robert, 48
reinventing organizations, 233–241. *See also* restructuring
relative performance evaluation, 194–195. *See also* employee(s): evaluations/performance appraisals
resource allocation, 261–262
responsibility, 220, 226
Restaurants Unlimited, 187
restructuring, 114, 120, 235, 240
reward systems, 31, 34, 36–37, 90, 129, 134, 140, 143, 183–185, 195, 208–209, 217
    collective, 202, 221, 257
    competition within firms and, 183–185, 190, 195, 211, 257
rigidity, 77–80
risk, job, 118, 121
risk-taking, 83–84, 110, 117, 133, 183, 253, 254

Rogers Commission, 122
ROLM corporation, 93
Rucci, Anthony, 170
Russo, David, 23–24, 55, 65, 66, 129, 165

salaries. *See* employee(s): compensation
sales-driven organizations, 59, 162–164
sales/sales forces, 41, 125, 244
    commission, 165, 194, 205
Sant, Roger, 254
SAS Institute, 3, 24, 55, 57–58, 65–66, 76, 129, 175, 202, 246, 247–248, 256
    cooperative culture at, 206–207, 258
    measures and measurement systems, 164–166, 169, 259–260
Saturn, 59, 81–87, 92, 93–95, 188, 189, 246–247
Scott Paper, 110, 111
Sears, 169–173, 175, 244
securities firms, 38, 39, 40
self-esteem, 110, 130, 193
self-reliance, 226
seniority, 83
ServiceMaster, 3
severance packages, 134, 135, 239
Shapiro, Eileen, 38
shared fate concept, 102–103
shareholders, 111, 157
Sharp, Barry, 104
shifts, fixed versus rotating, 238
Shore, Andrew, 112
Simon, David, 215
simplicity concept, 54, 55, 56, 59–60, 61–62, 237
Skillman, Peter, 250
skills, 54–55, 130, 211
    development of, 19, 26

skills (*continued*)
    group, 83
    lack of, 6, 193
    leadership, 152
    management, 200–201
    sharing/transfer of, 87, 159,
        183–185, 198
    talk as, 56
    testing, 83
social facilitation effect, 196
social identity of firms, 87, 188,
    218, 220
social inhibition effect, 196
social psychology, 88, 121–122,
    157, 257
SonoSite, 208–209
Southwest Airlines, 3, 13–14,
    76, 130, 202–204, 256,
    259
specialization, 62, 105
SRI, 66
standard operating proce-
    dures, 69, 74–75, 244, 249
Stanford Business School, 201
Starbuck, William, 106
Starbucks, 3, 76
Starbucks International, 23
status, 252
    seeking, 51–52, 53, 140, 185,
        186, 190, 211, 257, 258
    threats to, 188
Staw, Barry, 80
Stewart, Tomas, 16
stock options, 165, 208
stock ownership plans, 202
stress, 88, 102, 155, 259
substitutes for action
    analytical processes, 37, 41
    avoidance of, 56, 92–107,
        226
    decision making, 30–33, 37,
        54, 251
    documents and reports,
        35–37, 41, 50, 54, 252–253
    meetings, 37, 251, 252

    memory, 69
    mission and vision state-
        ments, 37–40, 42, 54
    planning, 40–42, 54, 215,
        251–253
    precedent and, 93, 103
    presentations, 33–35, 41, 50,
        56, 248–249
    talk, 27, 29–30, 31–32, 37, 40,
        42–43, 43, 54, 56–68, 215,
        226, 251–252
substitutes for thinking
    avoidance of, by breaking
        from the past, 92,
        95–103
    avoidance of, by building
        new organizations, 92,
        93–95
    avoidance of, by resisting
        mindless action, 92–93,
        95–103, 161
    corporate identity, 91
    management practices, 71,
        79
    memory/precedent, 69–71,
        87–88, 92–107, 187–188,
        248
    need for cognitive closure
        and, 88, 91
Sun, David, 26, 249
Sunbeam, 110, 111, 125–126
supplier–partner relationships,
    23, 62, 79
supply chain management, 19
Synoptics, 261

talk
    criticism and negativity,
        45–46, 54
    informal, 56
    organizational dialogue, 62
    as reflection of stature,
        46–47
    smart, 42–47, 48–51, 54, 56,
        58

smart actions resulting
from, 43–45, 56
status seeking through,
51–52, 53, 54
as substitute for action, 27,
29–30, 31–32, 37, 42–43,
56–68
Target, 170
teaching, 249, 250–251
teams, 86, 239, 250–251
compensation, 40
culture-based, 182
management, 99–100,
230–231
multidisciplinary/multi-
functional, 29, 63
product development, 58
project, 31
self-managing, 120
See also Men's Wearhouse,
The: team selling strat-
egy
team spirit, 163–164
teamwork, 158, 201, 205, 233,
258–259
as core value, 40, 205,
207–209, 210
problem solving through,
217, 218, 219
undermining of, through
competition within
firms, 183–185, 195, 198,
200, 201, 258
technology, 9
communications, 218–219
core, 58
information, 16–17, 19,
218–219
knowledge management,
19
process, 9
sharing/transfer of, 18–19
temporary workers, 144–145,
146
threat–rigidity effect, 80

Tjosvold, Dean, 211
Toime, Elmar, 240
Total Quality Management
(TQM), 2, 35, 119–120
town meeting formats, 63, 64
Toyota, 155, 247
Production System (TPS),
23, 246
See also New United Motor
Manufacturing
(NUMMI)
Trader Joe's, 245
training programs, 4, 24, 36,
97–98, 102, 120, 171, 231,
233, 234, 262
cost of, 141
cross-training, 105
ineffectiveness of, 27, 28,
265
investment in, 83, 130, 162
leadership, 1–2, 48, 59, 209
organizational perform-
ance and, 248
for philosophy of business,
250
for team strategies, 205
trust, 114, 117, 119, 247, 255. See
also distrust
Tu, John, 26
Tupperware, 193
turnarounds, 59–60, 78,
171–173, 214, 251. See also
British Petroleum (BP);
Continental Airlines;
New Zealand Post

understanding, 134, 135, 136
unions, 33, 81–82, 84, 239, 241
strikes, 86
United Auto Workers, 81, 86
United Shuttle, 14, 203–204
U.S. Army, 27–28
After Action Reviews, 64,
65
US Airways, 202–203

values
  continuity of, 75–77
  core, 38, 39–40, 205,
    207–209, 210, 224,
    227–229, 247, 248
  corporate cultural, 37, 56,
    88–89, 144, 160, 162–164,
    168, 205, 215, 224, 261
  in management processes,
    24
  operating, 167, 224
View from the Top Speaker
    Series, 201
virtual organization, 52

Wainwright Industries, 161
Wal-Mart, 3, 170
Waterman, Robert, 251
Watson, Thomas, Sr., 253
Welch, Jack, 61, 65
Wellfleet Communications, 261
Wells Fargo Bank, 222, 224

Whitehead, Alfred North, 74
Whole Foods Market, 3, 246
Willamette Industries, 207–208
Winter, Burgess, 33–35, 96–98,
    102–103, 112
workplace learning, 18
workplace rights, 114
World Bank, 252

Xerox, 9, 262
  Leadership Through
    Quality initiative, 35–37,
    65

Zander, Benjamin, 131–132
Zbaracki, Mark, 2
Zell, Deone, 120
Zenoff, David, 230
Zimmer, George, 24, 59, 130,
    248, 256
Zoopa food chain, 78–80,
    185–187, 258

About the Authors

Jeffrey Pfeffer is the Thomas D. Dee Professor of Organizational Behavior in the Graduate School of Business, Stanford University, where he has taught since 1979. He received his B.S. and M.S. from Carnegie–Mellon University and his Ph.D. in business from Stanford. Dr. Pfeffer has served on the faculties at the University of Illinois, the University of California at Berkeley, and as a visiting professor at the Harvard Business School. He has taught executive seminars in 22 countries throughout the world and was Director of Executive Education at Stanford from 1994 to 1996. He serves on the board of directors of Portola Packaging, Resumix, and SonoSite, as well as on numerous editorial boards of scholarly journals. He is the author of *The Human Equation, New Directions for Organization Theory, Competitive Advantage through People, Managing with Power, Organizations and Organization Theory, Power in Organizations,* and *Organizational Design,* and co-author of *The External Control of Organizations,* as well as more than 100 articles and book chapters.

Robert I. Sutton is Professor of Organizational Behavior in the Stanford Engineering School, where he is Co–Director of the Center for Work, Technology, and Organization and Research Director of the Stanford Technology Ventures Program. He received his Ph.D. in organizational psychology from The University of Michigan and has served on the Stanford faculty since 1983. Dr. Sutton has also taught at U.C. Berkeley's Haas Business School and has been a Fellow at the Center for Advanced Study in the Behavioral Sciences. He has given many executive seminars, consulted to numerous corporations, and currently directs the Management of Innovation executive program for the Stanford Alumni Association. He has received honors including the award for the best paper published in the *Academy of Management Journal*, the Eugene L. Grant Award for Excellence in Teaching, and the McCullough Faculty Scholar Chair from the Stanford Engineering School. He has served as an editor and editorial board member of numerous scholarly publications and currently serves as Co-Editor of *Research in Organizational Behavior*. He has published more than 60 articles and chapters in scholarly and applied publications.